THE OLD EAST INDIAMEN

First published 1890
This edition published by Lector House in 2023

ISBN: 978-93-5800-761-9

Lector House LLP
Registered Office: H. No. 96, Block C, Tomar Colony,
Burari, Delhi – 110084, India
info@lectorhouse.com
www.lectorhouse.com

THE OLD EAST INDIAMEN

EDWARD KEBLE CHATTERTON

2023

LECTOR HOUSE LLP

The East Indiaman "Thomas Coutts," as she appeared in the year 1826.

(By courtesy of Messrs. T. H. Parker Brothers)

THE OLD EAST INDIAMEN

BY

E. KEBLE CHATTERTON

Lieutenant R.N.V.R.

Author of "Sailing-Ships and their Story,"
"Down Channel in the 'Vivette,'"
"Through Holland in the 'Vivette,'"
"Ships and Ways of Other Days," etc.

ILLUSTRATED

PREFACE

The author desires to acknowledge the courtesy of Messrs T. H. Parker Brothers of Whitcomb Street, W.C., for allowing him to reproduce the illustrations mentioned on many of the pages of this book; as also the P. & O. Steam Navigation Company for permission to reproduce the old painting of the *Swallow*.

Owing to the fact that the author is now away at sea serving under the White Ensign, it is hoped that this may be deemed a sufficient apology for any errata which may have been allowed to creep into the text.

CONTENTS

LIST OF ILLUSTRATIONS

THE OLD EAST INDIAMEN

CHAPTER I

INTRODUCTION

In this volume I have to invite the reader to consider a special epoch of the world's progress, in which the sailing ship not only revolutionised British trade but laid the foundations of, and almost completed, that imposing structure which is to-day represented by the Indian Empire. It is a period brimful of romance, of adventures, travel and the exciting pursuit after wealth. It is a theme which, for all its deeply human aspect, is one for ever dominated by a grandeur and irresistible destiny.

With all its failings, the East India Company still remains in history as the most amazingly powerful trading concern which the world has ever seen. Like many other big propositions it began in a small way: but it acquired for us that vast continent which is the envy of all the great powers of the world to-day. And it is important and necessary to remember always that we owe this in the first place to the consummate courage, patience, skill and long-suffering of that race of beings, the intrepid seamen, who have never yet received their due from the landsmen whom they have made rich and comfortable.

Among the Harleian MSS. there is a delightful phrase written by a seventeenth-century writer, in which, treating of matters that are not immediately concerned with the present subject, he remarks very quaintly that "the first article of an Englishman's Politicall Creed must be that he believeth in ye Sea etc. Without that there needeth no general Council to pronounce him uncapable of Salvation." This somewhat sweeping statement none the less aptly sums up the whole matter of our colonisation and overseas development. The entire glamour of the Elizabethan period, marked as it unfortunately is with many deplorable errors, is derived from the sea. With the appreciation of what could be attained by a combination of stout ships, sturdy seamen, navigation, seamanship, gunnery and high hopes that refused persistently to be daunted, the most farsighted began to see that success was for them. Honours, wealth, the founding of families that should treasure their names in future generations, the acquisition of fine estates and the building of large houses with luxuries that exceeded the Tudor pattern—these were the pictures which were conjured up in the imaginations of those who vested their fortunes and often their lives in these ocean voyages. The call of the sea had in England fallen mostly on deaf ears until the late sixteenth century. It is only because there were some who listened to it, obeyed, and presently led others to do as they had done, that the British Empire has been built up at all.

Our task, however, is to treat of one particular way in which that call has influenced the minds and activities of men. We are to see how that, if it summoned some across the Atlantic to the Spanish Main, it sent others out to the Orient, yet always with the same object of acquiring wealth, establishing trade with strange peoples, and incidentally affording a fine opportunity for those of an adventurous spirit who were unable any longer to endure the cramped and confined limitations of the neighbourhood in which they had been born and bred. And though, as we proceed with our story, we shall be compelled to watch the gradual growth and the vicissitudes of the East Indian companies, yet our object is to obtain a clear knowledge not so much of the latter as of the ships which they employed, the manner in which they were built, sailed, navigated and fought. When we speak of the "Old East Indiamen" we mean of course the ships which used to carry the trade between India and Europe. And inasmuch as this trade was, till well on into the nineteenth century, the valuable and exclusive monopoly of the East India Company, carefully guarded against any interlopers, our consideration is practically that of the Company's ships. After the Company lost their monopoly to India, their ships still possessed the monopoly of trading with China until the year 1833. After that date the Company sold the last of their fleet which had made them famous as a great commercial and political concern. In their place a number of new private firms sprang up, who bought the old ships from the East India Company, and even built new ones for the trade. These were very fine craft and acted as links between England and the East for a few years longer, reaching their greatest success between the years 1850 and 1870. But the opening of the Suez Canal and the enterprise of steamships sealed their fate, so that instead of the wealth which was obtained during those few years by carrying cargoes of rich merchandise between the East and the West, and transporting army officers, troops and private passengers, there was little or no money to be made by going round the Cape. Thus the last of the Indiamen sailing ships passed away—became coal-hulks, were broken up; or, changing their name and nationality, sailed under a Scandinavian flag.

The East India Company rose from being a private venture of a few enterprising merchants to become a gigantic corporation of immense political power, with its own governors, its own cavalry, artillery and infantry, its own navy, and yet with its trade-monopoly and its unsurpassed "regular service" of merchantmen. The latter were the largest, the best built, and the most powerfully armed vessels in the world, with the exception only of some warships. They were, so to speak, the crack liners of the day, but they were a great deal more besides. Their officers were the finest navigators afloat, their seamen were at times as able as any of the crews in the Royal Navy, and in time of war the Government showed how much it coveted them by impressing them into its service, to the great chagrin and inconvenience of the East India Company, as we shall see later on in our story.

The East India House.

(By courtesy of Messrs. T. H. Parker Brothers)

From being at first a small trading concern with a handful of factors and an occasional factory planted in the East in solitary places, the Company progressed till it had its own civil service with its training college in England for the cadets aspiring to be sent out to the East. It is due to the Company not only that India is now under the British flag, but that the wealth of our country has been largely increased and a new outlet was found for our manufactures. The factors who went out in the first Indiamen sailing ships sowed the seed which to-day we now reap. The commanders of these vessels made their "plots" (charts) and obtained by bitter experience the details which provided the first sailing directions. They were at once explorers, traders, fighters, surveyors. The conditions under which they voyaged were hard enough, as we shall see: and the loss of human life was a high price at which all this material trade-success was obtained. Notwithstanding all the quarrels, the jealousies, the murders, the deceits, the misrule and corruption, the bribery and extortion which stain the activities of the East India Company, yet during its existence it raised the condition of the natives from the lowest disorder and degradation: and if the Company found it not easy to separate its commercial from its political aspirations, yet the British Government in turn found it very convenient on occasions when this corporation's funds could be squeezed, its men impressed; or even its ships employed for guarding the coasts of England or transporting troops out to India.

It is difficult to realise all that the East India Company stood for. It comprised under its head a large shipping line with many of the essential attributes of a ruling nation, and its merchant ships not only opened up to our traders India, but Japan and China as well. And bear in mind that the old East Indiamen set forth on their voyages not with the same light hearts that their modern successors, the steamships of the P. & O. line, begin their journey. Before the East India Company's ships got to their destination, they had to sail right away round the Cape of Good Hope and then across the Indian Ocean, having no telegraphic communication with the world, and with none of the comforts of a modern liner—no preserved foods, no iced drinks or anything of that sort. Any moment they were liable to be plunged into an engagement: if not with the French or Dutch men-of-war, then with roving privateers or well-armed pirate ships manned by some of the most redoubtable rascals of the time, who stopped at no slaughter or brutality. There were the perils, too, of storms, and of other forms of shipwreck, and the almost monotonous safety of the modern liner was a thing that did not exist. Later on we shall see in what difficulties some of these ships became involved. It was because they were ever expectant of a fight that they were run practically naval fashion. They were heavily armed with guns, they had their special code of signals for day and night, they carried their gunners, who were well drilled and always prepared to fight: and we shall see more than one instance where these merchant ships were far too much for a French admiral and his squadron.

These East Indiamen sailing ships were really wonderful for what they did, the millions of miles over which they sailed, the millions of pounds' worth of goods which they carried out and home: and this not merely for one generation, but for two and a half centuries. It is really surprising that such a unique monopoly should have been enjoyed for all this time, and that other ships should have been (with the exceptions we shall presently note) kept out of this benefit. The result was that an East Indiaman was spoken of with just as much respect as a man-of-war. She was built regardless of cost and kept in the best of conditions; and all the other merchantmen in the seven seas could not rival her for strength, beauty and equipment. It was a golden age, a glorious age: an epoch in which British seamanhood, British shipbuilding in wood, were capable of being improved upon only by the clipper ships that followed for a brief interval. They earned handsome dividends for the Company, they were always full of passengers, troops and valuable freight; and, although they were not as fine-lined as the clipper ships, yet they made some astounding passages. They carried crews that in number and quality would make the heart of a modern Scandinavian skipper break with envy. The result was that they were excellently handled and could carry on in a breeze till the last minute, when sail could be taken in smartly with the minimum of warning.

The country fully appreciated how invaluable was this East India service, and certainly no merchantmen were ever so regulated and controlled by Acts of Parliament. To-day you never hear of any merchant skipper buying or selling his command, nor retiring after a very few voyages with a nice little fortune for the rest of his life. But these things occurred in the old East Indiamen, when commanders received even knighthoods and a good income settled on them, for life, as a reward of their gallantry. Those were indeed the palmy days of the merchant service, and many an ill-paid mercantile officer to-day, wearied of receiving owners' complaints and no thanks, must regret that his lot was not to be serving with the East India Company.

When we consider the two important centuries and a half, during which the East Indiamen ships were making history and trade for our country, helping in the most important manner to build up our Indian Empire, fighting the Portuguese, the Dutch and the French, privateers and pirates, and generally opening up the countries of the East, it is to me perfectly extraordinary that the history of these ships has never yet been written. I have searched in vain in our great national libraries—in the British Museum, the India Office, the Admiralty and elsewhere—but I have not been able to find one volume dealing exclusively with these craft. In an age that sees no end to the making of books there is therefore need for a volume that should long since have been written. Many of the story-books of our boyhood begin with the hero leaving England in an East Indiaman: but they say little or nothing as to how she was rigged, how she was manned, and what uniforms her officers wore.

I feel, then, that I may with confidence ask the reader who loves ships for themselves, or is fascinated by history, or is specially interested in the rise of our Indian Empire, to follow me in the following pages while the story of these old East Indiamen is narrated. In a little while we shall have passed entirely from the last of all surviving ocean-going sailing ships, but during the whole of their period none have left their mark so significantly on past and present affairs as the old East Indiamen. I can guarantee that while pursuing this story the reader will find much that will interest and even surprise him: but above all will be seen triumphant the true grit and pluck which have ever been the attributes of our national sailormen—the determination to carry out, in spite of all costs and hardships, the serious task imposed on them of getting the ship safely to port with all her valuable lives, and her rich cargoes, regardless of weather, pirates, privateers and the enemies of the nation whose flag they flew. And this fine spirit will be found to be confined to no special century nor to any particular ship: but rather to pervade the whole of the East India Company's merchant service. The days of such a monopoly as this corporation's trade and shipping are much more distant even than they seem in actual years: but happily it is our proud boast, as year after year demonstrates, that those qualities, which composed the magnificent seamanhood of the crews of these vessels, are no less existent and flourishing to-day in the other ships under the British flag that venture north, south, east and west. The only main difference is this:—Yesterday the sailor had a hundred chances, for every one opportunity which is afforded to-day to the sons of the sea, of showing that the grand, undying desire to do the right thing in the time of crisis is one of the greatest assets of our nation.

CHAPTER II

THE MAGNETIC EAST

WITHIN human experience it is a safe maxim, that if you keep on continuously thinking and longing for a certain object you are almost sure, eventually, to obtain that which you desire.

There is scarcely any better instance of this on a large scale than the longing to find a route to India by sea, and the attainment of this only after long years and years. As a study of perseverance it is remarkable: but the inspiration of the whole project was to get at the world's great treasure-house, to find the way thereto and then unlock its doors. For centuries there had been trade routes between Europe and India overland. But the establishment of the Ottoman Empire in the fifteenth century placed a barrier across these routes. This suggested that there might possibly be—there was most probably—a route via the sea, and this would have the advantage of an easier method of transportation. It is very curious how throughout the ages a vague tradition survives and lingers on from century to century, finally to decide men's minds on some momentous matter. It is not quite a literal inspiration, for often enough these ancient traditions had a modicum of truth therein contained.

In my last book, "Ships and Ways of Other Days," I gave an instance of this which was remarkable enough to bear repeating. A reproduction was given of a fourteenth-century portolano, or chart, in which the shape of Southern Africa was seen to be extraordinarily accurate: and this, notwithstanding that it was sketched one hundred and thirty-five years before the Cape of Good Hope had been doubled. Some might suppose this knowledge to have been the result of second-sight, but my suggestion is that it was the result of an ancient tradition that the lower part of the African continent was shaped as depicted. For there is a well-founded belief that about the beginning of the sixth century B.C. the Phœnicians were sent by Neco, an Egyptian king, down the Red Sea; and that after circumnavigating the African continent they entered the Mediterranean from the westward.

The dim recollection of this voyage over a portion of the Indian Ocean, coupled with other knowledge derived from the Arabian seamen, doubtless left little hesitation in the minds of the seafaring peoples of the Mediterranean that the sea route to India existed if indeed it could be found. The various fruitless attempts, beginning with Vivaldi's voyage from Genoa in 1281, are all evidence that this belief never died. For years nothing more successful was obtained than to get to Madeira or a little lower down the west coast of Africa, yet almost every effort was pushing on nearer the goal; even though that goal was still a very long way distant. The East was exercising a magnetic influence on the minds of men: India was bound to be discovered sooner or later, if they did not weary of the attempt.

Then comes on to the scene the famous Prince Henry the Navigator, who built the first observatory of Portugal, established a naval arsenal, gathered together at his Sagres headquarters the greatest pilots and navigators which could be collected, founded a school of navigation and chart-making, and then sent his trained, picked men forth to sail the seas, explore the unknown south with the hope ultimately of reaching the rich land of India. I have discussed this matter with such detail in the volume already alluded to that it will be enough if I here remark briefly that though Prince Henry died in the year 1460 without any of his ships or men attaining India, yet less than forty years were to elapse ere this was attained, and his was the influence which really brought this about. We must never forget that on the historical road to India through the long ages from the earliest times down to the fifteenth century the name of Prince Henry the Navigator represents one of the most important milestones.

You know so well how that thereafter, in the year 1486, the King of Portugal sent forth two expeditions with the desire to find an eastern route to India, and that one of these proceeded through Egypt, then down the Red Sea, across the Arabian Sea, and finally after some hardships reached Calicut, in the south-west of India. The other expedition consisted of a little squadron under Bartholomew Diaz, and although it did not get as far as India, yet it passed the Cape of Torments without knowing it—far out to sea—and even sighted Algoa Bay. The Cape of Torments he had called that promontory on his way back, remembering the bad weather which he here found: but the Cape of Good Hope his master, King John II., renamed it when Diaz reached home in safety. And then, finally, the last of these efforts was fraught with success when Vasco da Gama, in the year 1497, not only doubled the Cape of Good Hope, but discovered Mozambique, Melinda (a little north of Mombasa), and thence with the help of an Indian pilot crossed the ocean and reached Calicut by sea in twenty-three days—an absolutely unprecedented achievement for one who had sailed all the way from the Tagus.

This was the beginning of an entirely new era in the progress of the world, and till the crack of doom it will remain a memorable voyage, not merely for the fact that da Gama was able to succeed where so many others had failed, but because it unlocked the door of the East, first to the Portuguese, and subsequently to other nations of Europe. The twin arts of seamanship and navigation had made this possible, and it was only because the Portuguese, most especially Prince Henry, had believed "in ye sea" that the key had been found. As Columbus, by believing in the sea, was enabled in looking for India to open up the Western world, so was da Gama privileged to unlock the East. And since the sea connotes the ship we arrive at the standpoint that it is this long-suffering creature, fashioned by the hand of man, which has done more for the civilisation of the world than any other of those wonderful creations which the human mind has evolved from the things of the earth.

The Honourable East India Company's Ship "General Goddard," commanded by WM. Taylor Money, with His Majesty's Ship "Sceptre" and "Swallow," Packet, capturing Seven Dutch East Indiamen off St. Helena, on 14th June, 1795.

(By courtesy of Messrs. T. H. Parker Brothers)

The first cargo which da Gama brought home was, so to speak, merely a small sample of those goods which were to be obtained by the ships that came after for generation after generation till the present day. It showed how great and priceless were the riches of the East—spices and perfumes, pearls and rubies, diamonds and cinnamon. The safe arrival of these, when da Gama got back home, made a profound impression. But it was no mere sentimental wonder, for the receipt of all these goods repaid the cost of the entire expedition sixty-fold. From this time forth the Portuguese were busily engaged in extracting wealth as men get it out from a gold mine. Their ships went backwards and forwards in their long voyages, sometimes narrowly escaping the attentions of the Moslem pirates anxious to relieve them of their valuable cargoes. Some Portuguese settled in India, and gradually there came into existence a fringe of Portuguese nationality extending from the Malabar coast right away to the Persian Gulf. Even as far as Japan was the East explored, and the vast fortunes which were brought back ever astonished the merchants of Europe. The first Portuguese factory was established at Calicut in the year 1500. For about a hundred years they were able to benefit, unrivalled, by their newly found treasure-house and to use their best endeavours, unfettered, to empty it.

In 1503 they erected their first fortress and strengthened their position. In their hands was the monopoly: theirs were the great and invaluable secrets of this amazing trade. And considering everything—the enterprise and training of Prince Henry, the far-sighted prudence in believing in the sea, the years and years of distressful voyages, the final attainment of the treasure-land only after many vicissitudes and the loss of ships and men—we cannot marvel that the Portuguese preserved these secrets, and held on to their monopoly, to the annoyance of the rest of civilised Europe. The fact was that Portugal was then the sovereign of the seas: she was far too strong afloat for any other country to think of wresting from her by force what she had obtained only by much study, skill and perseverance. What she had obtained she was going to hold. Those who wanted these Eastern goods must come to Lisbon, where the mart was held: and come they did, but they went back home envious that Portugal should enjoy this secret monopoly, and wondering all the time how India could be reached by a new route.

Curiosity and envy combined have been the means of the unravelling of many a secret. It was so now. Let us not fail to realise how greatly these human feelings influenced many of the voyages during the next hundred years. We justly admire the great daring of the Elizabethan seamen, but though the spirit of adventure and the hatred of Spain had a great deal to do with the cause of their setting forth to cross the ocean, yet there was another reason: and this explains much that is not otherwise quite clear. It is always fair to assume that men do not act except at the instigation of some clear motive. They do not persuade merchants to expend the whole of their small wealth in buying or building ships, victualling them and providing all the necessary inventories, without some rational cause. In the Elizabethan times, when wealth was much rarer than it is to-day, the prime motive of these expeditions was the pursuit of greater wealth.

But as England was not yet as expert at sea as the Portuguese, she could not hope to obtain the treasures of distant lands. Before she was ready there was, however, still Spain: and the latter was determined to do her best to obtain on her own what Portugal was enjoying. In a word, then, many of the sixteenth-century voyages which we have attributed, rashly, solely to a hope for adventurous exploration were in fact animated by the desire to find some new route to India. To this inspiration must be attributed many of those long sea journeys to the north, the north-east and the north-west. Men did not endeavour to find north-east or north-west passages merely for fun, but in order to discover a road to India. No one knew that it was impossible: if the Portuguese had been able to go one way, why should not they themselves go by another route? Remembering this, you must think of Spain sending Magellan to the west; of England sending Davis to the north-west; and of Holland sending Barentsz to the north-east to find a passage to the treasure-land of India or China.

The Spaniards discovered a way to India through the straits which are called after Magellan, and henceforth did their utmost to keep the ships of other countries out of their newly found waters, until the increase of English sea-power and the daring of our more experienced seamen showed that this Spanish sovereignty on sea could not be maintained by force. But still the English seamen had not yet reached India. We must turn for a moment to the Dutch, who were destined to become a great naval power. In the year 1580 the Spanish and Portuguese dominions had become united under the Spanish crown, and the Dutch were excluded from trading with Lisbon, their ships confiscated and their owners thrown into prison. Now, one of these captains while undergoing his imprisonment obtained from some Portuguese sailors a good deal of information concerning the Indian Seas, so that when he reached the Netherlands again he told the most wonderful accounts to his countrymen. The latter were so impressed by what was related that they decided to send an expedition to find the Indies themselves.

Presently, then, we shall see the Dutch not merely casting longing eyes towards India, but actually getting a footing therein, building up a very lucrative trade and employing great, well-built craft: but before we come to that stage we must note the gradual and persistent way in which the countries outside the Iberian Peninsula felt their way to this land of spices and precious stones, and after groping some time in the dark found that which they had been searching for during generations.

CHAPTER III

THE LURE OF NATIONS

WHEN once it was realised how wonderful was Portugal's good fortune in the East, the nations of Europe one and all desired to enjoy some of these riches for themselves.

Even during the time of Henry VIII. one Master Robert Thorne, a London merchant, who had lived for a long time in Seville and had observed with envy the enterprise of the Portuguese, declared to his English sovereign a secret "which hitherto, as I suppose, hath beene hid"—viz. that "with a small number of ships there may bee discovered divers New lands and kingdoms ... to which places there is left one way to discover, which is into the North.... For out of Spaine they have discovered all the Indies and Seas Occidentall, and out of Portingall all the Indies and Seas Orientall." His idea, then, was to seek a way to India via the north. The same Robert Thorne, writing in the year 1527 to Dr Ley, "Lord ambassadour for king Henry the eight," concerning "the new trade of spicery" of the East, pointed out the wealth of the Moluccas (Malay Archipelago) abounding "with golde, Rubies, Diamondes, Balasses, Granates, Jacincts, and other stones and pearles, as all other lands, that are under and neere the Equinoctiall"; for just as "our mettalls be Lead, Tinne, and iron, so theirs be gold, silver and copper."

Now Master Thorne was a very shrewd investor. "In a fleete of three shippes and a caravel," he says, "that went from this citie armed by the marchants of it, which departed in Aprill last past, I and my partener have one thousand foure hundred duckets that we employed in the sayd fleete, principally for that two English men, friends of mine, which are somewhat learned in Cosmographie, should go in the same shippes, to bring me certaine relation of the situation of the countrey, and to be expert in the navigation of those seas, and there to have informations of many other things, and advise that I desire to know especially." His idea was that our seamen should obtain some of the Portuguese "cardes" (*i.e.* charts) "by which they saile," "learne how they understand them," and thus, in plain language, crib some of the Portuguese secrets.

Thorne shows that he was no mean student of geography himself. Already he possessed "a little Mappe or Carde of the world" and pointed out that from Cape Verde "the coast goeth Southward to a Cape called Capo de buona speransa" (the Portuguese name for the Cape of Good Hope). "And by this Cape go the Portingals to their Spicerie. For from this Cape toward the Orient, is the land of Calicut." "The coastes of the Sea throughout all the world I have coloured with yellow, for that it may appeare that all is within the line coloured yellow is to be imagined to be maine land or islands: and all without the line so coloured to bee Sea: whereby it is easie and light to know it." Now Thorne had obtained this "carde" somehow by stealth: by rights he should not have possessed it, for the Portuguese, as already mentioned, were most anxious that their Indian secrets should not be divulged. He therefore begs his friend not to show anyone this chart else "it may be a cause of paine to the maker: as well for that none may make these cardes, but certaine appointed and allowed for masters, as for that peradventure it would not sound well to them, that a stranger should know or discover their secretes: and would appeare worst of all, if they understand that I write touching the short way to the spicerie by our Seas."

We see, then, the determined desire to obtain the required information about a route to India obtained from the study of the very charts which the Portuguese made after some of their voyages, and by sending Englishmen out in their ships sufficiently expert in cosmography to learn all that could be known. It must not be forgotten, at the same time, that there were also land-travellers who journeyed to India and brought back alluring accounts of India. Cæsar Frederick, for instance, a Venetian merchant, set forth in the year 1563 with some merchandise bound for the East. From Venice he sailed in a vessel as far as Cyprus: from there he took passage in a smaller craft and landed in Syria, and then journeying to Aleppo got in touch with some Armenian and Moorish merchants whom he accompanied to Ormuz (on the Persian Gulf), where he found that the Portuguese had already established a factory and strengthened it, as the English East India Company's servants were afterwards wont, with a fort. From Ormuz he went on to Goa and other places in India. Already, he pointed out, the Portuguese had a fleet or "Armada" of warships to guard their merchant craft in these parts from attack by pirates. Proceeding thence to Cochin, at the south-west of India, he found that the natives called all Christians coming from the West Portuguese, whether they were Italians, Frenchmen or whatever else: so powerful a hold had the first settlers from the Iberian Peninsula gained on the Indians. We need not follow this traveller on his way to Sumatra, to the Ganges and elsewhere, but it is enough to state that the accounts which he gave to his fellow-Europeans naturally whetted still more the appetites of the merchant traders anxious to get in touch with India by sea. He told them how rich the East was in pepper and ginger, nutmegs and sandalwood, aloes, pearls, rubies, sapphires, diamonds. It was a magnificent opportunity for an honest merchant to find wealth. "Now to finish that which I have begunne to write, I say that those parts of the Indies are very good, because that a man that hath little shall make a very great deale thereof: alwayes they must governe themselves that they be taken for honest men."

When Magellan set forth from Seville to find a new route to India he had gone via the straits which now bear his name, and then striking north-west across the wide Pacific had arrived at the Philippine Islands, where he was killed. But his ships proceeded thence to the Moluccas, and one of his little squadron of five actually arrived back at Seville, having thus encircled the globe. Englishmen, however, were so determined that there was a nearer route than this that, in the year 1582, the Indian frenzy which enthralled our countrymen culminated in the voyage of Edward Fenton that set forth bound for Asia. This expedition consisted of four ships. It was customary in those days to speak of the Commodore or Admiral of the expedition as the "Generall," thus indicating, by the way, that not yet had the English navy got away from the influence of the land army. The flagship was spoken of as the "Admirall." These four ships, then, consisted, firstly, of the *Leicester*, the "Admirall" of the squadron. She was a vessel of 400 tons, her "generall" being Captain Edward Fenton, with William Hawkins (the younger) as "Lieutenant General," or second in command of the expedition, the master of the ship being Christopher Hall. The second ship was the *Edward Bonaventure*, a well-known sixteenth-century craft of 300 tons, which was commanded by Captain Luke Ward, and the master was Thomas Perrie. The third ship was the *Francis*, a little craft of only 40 tons, whose captain was John Drake and her master was William Markham. The fourth was the *Elizabeth*, of 50 tons; captain, Thomas Skevington, and master, Ralph Crane.

Before we proceed any further it may be as well to explain a point that might otherwise cause confusion. In the ships of that time the captain was in supreme command, but he was not necessarily a seaman or navigator. He was the leader of the ship or expedition, but he was not a specialist in the arts of the sea. As we know from Monson, Elizabethan captains "were gentlemen of worth and means, maintaining there diet at their own charge." "The Captaines charge," says the famous Elizabethan Captain John Smith, the first president of Virginia, "is to commaund all, and tell the Maister to what port he will go, or to what height" (*i.e.* latitude). In a fight he is "to giue direction for the managing thereof, and the Maister is to see to the cunning [of] the ship, and trimming the sailes." The master is also, with his mate, "to direct the course, commaund all the saylors, for steering, trimming, and sayling the ship": and the pilot is he who, "when they make land, doth take the charge of the ship till he bring her to harbour." And, finally, not to weary the reader too much, there is just one other word which is often used in these expeditions that we may explain. The "cape-merchant" was the man who had shipped on board to look after the cargo of merchandise carried in the hold.

On the 1st of April 1582 the *Edward Bonaventure* started from Blackwall in the Thames, and on the nineteenth of the same month arrived off Netley, in Southampton Water, where the *Leicester* was found waiting. On 1st May the four weighed anchor, but did not get clear of the land till the end of the month, "partly of businesse, and partly of contrary windes." The complement of these ships numbered a couple of hundred, including the gentlemen adventurers with their servants, the factors (who were to open up trade), and the chaplains. In selecting crews, as many seamen as possible were obtained, but by this time these were not at all numerous in England: and even then great care had to be taken to avoid shipping "any disordered or mutinous person."

The instructions given to Captain Fenton are so illustrative of these rules then so essential for the good government of overseas expeditions that it will not be out of place to notice them with some detail. As for the "Generall," "if it should please God to take him away," a number of names were "secretly set down to succeede in his place one after the other." These names were inscribed on parchment and then sealed up in balls of wax with the Queen's signet. They were then placed in two coffers, which were locked with three separate locks, one key being kept in the custody of the captain of the *Edward Bonaventure*, the second in the care of the *Leicester's* captain, and the third in the keeping of Master Maddox, the chaplain. If the general were to die, these coffers were to be opened and the party named therein to succeed him.

Fenton's instructions were to use all possible diligence to leave Southampton with his ships before the end of April, and then make for the Cape of Good Hope and so to the Moluccas. After leaving the English coast the general was to have special regard "so to order your course, as that your ships and vessels lose not one another, but keep companie together." But lest by tempest or other cause the squadron should get separated, the captains and masters were to be advised previously of rendezvous, "wherein you will stay certaine dayes." And every ship which reached her rendezvous and then passed on without knowing what had become of the other ships, was to "leave upon every promontorie or cape a token to stand in sight, with a writing lapped in leade to declare the day of their passage." They were not to take anything from the Queen's friends or allies, or any Christians, without paying therefor: and in all transactions they were to deal like good and honest merchants, "ware for ware."

With a view to inaugurating a future trade they were if possible to bring home one or two of the natives, leaving behind some Englishmen as pledges, and in order to learn the language of the country. No person was to keep for his private use any precious stone or metal: otherwise he was to lose "all the recompense he is to have for his service in this voyage by share or otherwise." A just account was to be kept of the merchandise taken out from England and what was brought home subsequently. And there is a strict order given which shows how slavishly the Portuguese example of secrecy was being copied. "You shall give straight order to restraine, that none shall make any charts or descriptions of the sayd voyage, but such as shall bee deputed by you the Generall, which sayd charts and descriptions, wee thinke meete that you the Generall shall take into your hands at your returne to this our coast of England, leaving with them no copie, and to present them unto us at your returne: the like to be done if they finde any charts or maps in those countreys."

At the conclusion of the expedition the ships were to make for the Thames, and no one was to land any goods until the Lords of the Council had been informed of the ships' arrival. As to the routine on board, Fenton was instructed to set down in writing the rules to be kept by the crew, so that in no case could ignorance be pleaded as excuse for delinquency. "And to the end God may blesse this voyage with happie and prosperous successe, you shall have an especiall care to see that reverence and respect bee had to the Ministers appointed to accompanie you in this voyage, as appertaineth to their place and calling, and to see such good order as by them shall be set downe for reformation of life and maners, duely obeyed and perfourmed, by causing the transgressours and contemners of the same to be severely punished, and the Ministers to remoove sometime from one vessell to another."

The "Essex," East Indiaman, as she appeared when refitted and at anchor in Bombay Harbour.

(By courtesy of Messrs. T. H. Parker Brothers)

But notwithstanding all these precautions this voyage was not the success which had been hoped for. After reaching the west coast of Africa and then stretching across to Brazil, where they watered ships, did some caulking, "scraped off the wormes" from the hulls, and learnt that the Spanish fleet were in the neighbourhood of the Magellan Straits, they determined to return to England. This they accordingly did. Before leaving England they had been instructed not to pass by these straits either going or returning, "except upon great occasion incident" with the consent of at least four of Fenton's assistants. But a conference had decided that it were best to make for Brazil. And then the news which they received there of the Spanish fleet convinced them that it were futile to attempt to get to India that way.

But as the Italian whom we mentioned just now got to India by the overland route, so an Englishman named Ralph Fitch, a London merchant, being desirous to see the Orient, reached Goa in India via Syria and Ormuz. He set sail from Gravesend on 13th February 1582, left Falmouth on 11th March, and then never put in anywhere till the ship landed him at Tripoli in Syria on the following 30th April. After being absent from home nine years, Fitch came back in an English ship to London in April 1591. The reports which he brought were similar to the Italian's verdict. India was rich in pepper, ginger, cloves, nutmegs, sandalwood, camphor, amber, sapphires, rubies, diamonds, pearls, and so on. There was not the slightest doubt that it was the country to trade with. But, as yet, no English ship had found the way thither.

During the years 1585-1587 John Davis tried to find a way thither by the North-West Passage. Davis had a fine reputation as "a man very well grounded in the principles of the Arte of Navigation," but none the less his efforts were unavailing. In 1588 the coming of the expected Armada turned the energies of the English seamen into another channel. But already, in the year 1586, Thomas Candish had set out from Plymouth with the *Desire*, 120 tons, the *Content* of 60 tons and the *Hugh Gallant* of 40 tons, victualled for two years and well found at his own expense. Journeying via Sierra Leone, Brazil and the Magellan Straits, he reached the Pacifice and China, and after touching at the Philippine Islands passed through the Straits of Java. From Java he crossed the ocean to the Cape of Good Hope, was able to correct the errors in the Portuguese sea "carts," and in September 1588 reached Plymouth once more, having learnt from a Flemish craft bound from Lisbon that the Spanish Armada had been defeated, "to the singular rejoycing and comfort of us all."[1]

The value of this voyage round the world was, from a navigator's point of view, of inestimable advantage. For the benefit of those English navigators who were, a few years later, to begin the ceaseless voyages backwards and forwards round the Cape of Good Hope, between England and India, Candish made the most elaborate notes and sailing directions, giving the latitudes (or, as the Elizabethans called them, "the heights") of most of the places passed or visited. Very

[1] Drake of course had previously encircled the globe in a voyage of twenty-six months, having set forth from Plymouth in 1577, though his was even more of a buccaneering expedition than that of Candish.

elaborate soundings were taken and recorded, giving the depth in fathoms and the nature of the sea-bed, wherever they went round the world, if the depth was not too great. In addition, he gave the courses from place to place, the distances, where to anchor, what dangers to avoid, providing warning of any difficult straits or channels, the variation of the compass at different places, the direction of the wind from certain dates to certain dates, and so on. But this, valuable as it undoubtedly was in many ways, did not exhaust the utility of the voyage. From China, whither the ships of the East India Company some years later were to trade, "I have brought such intelligence," he wrote on his return to the Lord Chamberlain, "as hath not bene heard of in these parts. The stateliness and riches of which countrey I feare to make report of, least I should not be credited: for if I had not knowen sufficiently the incomparable wealth of that countrey, I should have bene as incredulous thereof, as others will be that have not had the like experience."

And he showed in still further detail the fine opportunity which existed in the East and awaited only the coming of the English merchant. "I sailed along the Ilands of the Malucos, where among some of the heathen people I was well intreated, where our countrey men may have trade as freely as the Portugals if they will themselves."

It is not therefore surprising that in the following year the English merchants began to stir themselves afresh. The East was calling loudly: and with the information brought back by Candish and some other knowledge, gained in a totally different manner, the time was now ripe for an expedition to succeed. For in the year 1587 Drake had left Plymouth, sailed across the Bay of Biscay, arrived at Cadiz Roads, where he did considerable harm to Spanish shipping, spoiled Philip's plans for invading England that year, and then set a course for the Azores. It was not long before he sighted a big, tall ship, which was none other than the great carack, *San Felipe,* belonging to the King of Spain himself, whose name in fact she bore. This vessel was now homeward-bound from the East Indies and full of a rich cargo. Drake made it his duty to capture her in spite of her size, and very soon she was his and on her way to Plymouth.

Now the most wonderful feature of this incident was, historically, not the daring of Drake nor the value of the ship and cargo. The latter combined were found to be worth £114,000 in Elizabethan money, or in modern coinage about a million pounds sterling. But the most valuable of all were the ship's papers found aboard, which disclosed the long-kept secrets of the East Indian trade. Therefore, this fact, taken in conjunction with the arrival of Candish the year following, and the wonderful incentive to English sea-daring given by the victory over the Spanish Armada—the fleet of the very nation whose ships had kept the English out of India—will prepare the reader for the memorial which the English merchants made to Queen Elizabeth, setting forth the great benefits which would arise through a direct trade with India. They therefore prayed for a royal licence to send three ships thither. But Elizabeth was a procrastinating, uncertain woman. She had in that expedition of Drake in 1587 first given her permission and then had sent a messenger post haste all the way to Plymouth countermanding these orders. Luckily for the country, Drake had already got so far out to sea that it was impossible to deliver the message: and it was a good thing there was no such thing as wireless telegraphy in Elizabeth's time.

So, in regard to these petitioning merchants, first she would and then she wouldn't, and she kept the matter hanging indecisively until a few months before April 1591. By that time the necessary capital had been raised and the final preparations made, so that on the tenth of that month "three tall ships," named respectively the *Penelope* (which was the "Admirall"), the *Marchant Royall* (which was the "Vice-Admirall") and the *Edward Bonaventure* "Rear-Admirall") were able to let loose their canvas and sailed out of Plymouth Sound.

CHAPTER IV

THE ROUTE TO THE EAST

I WANT in this chapter to call your attention to a very gallant English captain named James Lancaster, whose grit and endurance in the time of hard things, whose self-effacing loyalty to duty, show that there were giants afloat in those days in the ships which were to voyage to the East.

The account of the first of these voyages I have taken from Hakluyt, who in turn had obtained it by word of mouth from a man named Edmund Barker, of Ipswich. Hakluyt was known for his love of associating with seamen and obtaining from them first-hand accounts of their experiences afloat. And inasmuch as Barker is described as Lancaster's lieutenant on the voyage, and the account was witnessed by James Lancaster's signature, we may rely on the facts being true. Hakluyt was of course very closely connected with the subject of our inquiry. When the East India Company was started he was appointed its first historiographer, a post for which he was eminently fitted. He lectured on the subject of voyaging to the Orient, he made the maps and journals which came back in these ships useful to subsequent navigators and of the greatest interest to merchants and others. And when he died his work was in part carried on by Samuel Purchas of *Pilgrimes* fame. The second of these voyages, in which Lancaster again triumphs over what many would call sheer bad luck, has been taken from a letter which was sent to the East India Company by one of its servants, and is preserved in the archives of the India Office and will be dealt with in the following chapter. But for the present we will confine our attention to the voyage of those three ships mentioned at the end of the last chapter.

After leaving Devonshire the *Penelope, Marchant Royall* and *Edward Bonaventure* arrived at the Canary Isles in a fortnight, having the advantage of a fair north-east wind. Before reaching the Equator they were able to capture a Portuguese caravel bound from Lisbon for Brazil with a cargo of Portuguese merchandise consisting of 60 tuns of wine, 1200 jars of oil, about 100 jars of olives and other produce. This came as a veritable good fortune to the English ships, for the latter's crews had already begun to be afflicted with bad health. "We had two men died before wee passed the line, and divers sicke, which tooke their sicknesse in those hote climates: for they be wonderful unholesome from 8 degrees of Northerly latitude unto the line, at that time of the yeere: for we had nothing but Ternados, with such thunder, lightning, and raine, that we could not keep our men drie 3 houres together, which was an occasion of the infection among them, and their eating of salt victuals, with lacke of clothes to shift them." After crossing the Equator they had for a long time an east-south-east wind, which carried them to within a hundred leagues of the coast of Brazil, and then getting a northerly wind they were able to make for the Cape of Good Hope, which they sighted on 28th July. For three days they stood off and on with a contrary wind, unable to weather it. They had had a long voyage, and the health of the crew in those leaky, stinking ships had become bad. They therefore made for Table Bay, or, as it was then called, Saldanha, where they anchored on 1st August.

The men were able to go ashore and obtain exercise after being cramped for so many weeks afloat, and found the land inhabited by black savages, "very brutish." They obtained fresh food by shooting fowl, though "there was no fish but muskles and other shel-fish, which we gathered on the rockes." Later on a number of seals and penguins were killed and taken on board, and eventually, thanks to negro assistance, cattle and sheep were obtained by bartering. But when the time came to start off for the rest of the voyage it was very clear that the squadron, owing to the loss by sickness, was deficient in able-bodied men. It was therefore "thought good rather to proceed with two ships wel manned, then with three evill manned: for here wee had of sound and whole men but 198." It was deemed best to send home the *Marchant Royall* with fifty men, many of whom were pretty well recovered from the devastating disease of scurvy. The extraordinary feature of the voyage was that the sailors suffered from this disease more than the soldiers. "Our souldiers which have not bene used to the Sea, have best held out, but our mariners dropt away, which (in my judgement) proceedeth of their evill diet at home."

So the other two ships proceeded on their way towards India: but not long after rounding the Cape of Good Hope they encountered "a mighty storme and extreeme gusts of wind" off Cape Corrientes, during which the *Edward Bonaventure* lost sight of the *Penelope*. The latter, in fact, was never seen again, and there is no doubt that she foundered with all hands. The *Edward*, however, pluckily kept on, though four days later "we had a terrible clap of thunder, which slew foure of our men outright, their necks being wrung in sonder without speaking any word, and of 94 men there was not one untouched, whereof some were stricken blind, others were bruised in their legs and armes, and others in their brests, so that they voided blood two days after, others were drawn out at length as though they had bene racked. But (God be thanked) they all recovered saving onely the foure which were slaine out right." The same electric storm had wrecked the mainmast "from the head to the decke" and "some of the spikes that were ten inches into the timber were melted with the extreme heate thereof." Truly Lancaster's command was a very trying one. What with a scurvy crew, an unhandy ship, now partially disabled, and both hurricanes and electric storms, there was all the trouble to break the spirit of many a man. Still, he held determinedly on his way whither he was bound.

But his troubles were now very nearly ended in one big disaster. After having proceeded along the south-east coast of Africa, and steering in a north-easterly direction, the ship was wallowing along her course over the sea when a dramatic incident occurred. It was night, and while some were below sleeping, one of the men on deck, peering through the moonlight, saw ahead what he took for breakers. He called the attention of his companions and inquired what it was, and they readily answered that it was the sea breaking on the shoals. It was the "Iland of S. Laurence." "Whereupon in very good time we cast about to avoyd the danger which we were like to have incurred." But it had been a close shave, and though Lancaster was to endure many other grievous hardships before his days were ended, yet but for the light of the kindly moon his ship, his crew and his own life would almost certainly have been lost that night.

But this was presently to be succeeded by the luck of falling in with three or four Arab craft, which were taken, their cargo of ducks and hens being very acceptable. They watered the ship at the Comoro Islands; a Portuguese boy, whom they had taken when the Arab craft were captured, being a useful acquisition as interpreter. But the master of the *Edward Bonaventure*, having gone ashore with thirty of his men to obtain a still further amount of fresh water, was treacherously taken and sixteen of his company slain. It was just one further source of discomfort for Lancaster now to have lost his ship's master and more of his crew. So thence, "with heavie hearts," the *Edward* sailed for Zanzibar, where they learnt that the Portuguese had already warned the natives of the character of Englishmen, in making out that the latter were "cruell people and men-eaters, and willed them if they loved safetie in no case to come neere us. Which they did onely to cut us off from all knowledge of the state and traffique of the countrey."

The jealousy of the Portuguese was certainly very great: they were annoyed, and only naturally, that another nation should presume to burst into the seas which they had been the first of Europeans to open. Off this coast, from Melinda to Mozambique, a Portuguese admiral was cruising in a small "frigate"—that is to say, a big galley-type of craft propelled by sails and oars. And had this "frigate" been strong enough she would certainly have assailed Lancaster's ship, for she came into Zanzibar to "view and to betray our boat if he could have taken at any time advantage."

It was whilst riding at anchor here that another electric storm sprung the *Edward's* foremast, which had to be repaired—"fished," as sailors call it—with timber from the shore. And, to add still more to Lancaster's bad luck, the ship's surgeon, whilst ashore with the newly appointed master of the ship, looking for oxen, got a sunstroke and died. But the sojourn in that anchorage came to an end on 15th February. The progress of this voyage had been slow, but it had been sure. Relying on what charts he possessed, and then, after rounding the Cape of Good Hope, practically coasting up the African shore until reaching Zanzibar, he had wisely remained here some time. For this was the port whence the dhows traded backwards and forwards across the Indian Ocean and the East, and it must be remembered that the Arabs were skilled navigators and very fine seamen, who had been making these ocean voyages for centuries, whilst Englishmen were doing little more than coasting passages. Zanzibar was clearly the place where Lancaster could pick up a good deal of valuable knowledge regarding the voyage to India, and, incidentally, he took away from here a certain negro who had come from the East Indies and was possessed of knowledge of the country.

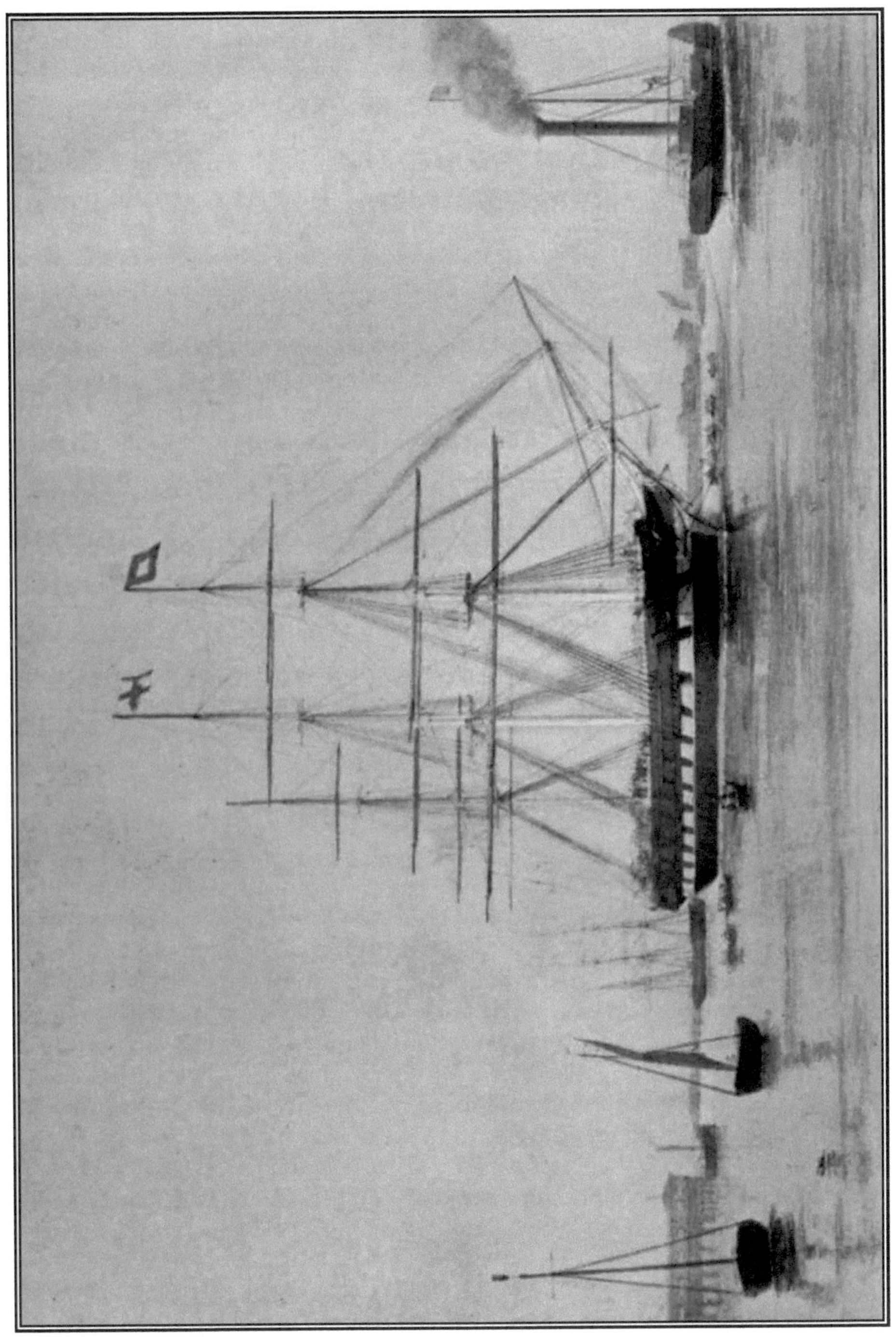

The East Indiaman "Kent," 1,000 tons.

(By courtesy of Messrs. T. H. Parker Brothers)

From Goa to Zanzibar the Arabian ships were wont to bring cargoes of pepper, and it was now Lancaster's intention to cut straight across the Indian Ocean and make Cape Comorin—the southernmost point of the Indian peninsula—as his land-fall. He then meant to hang about this promontory, because it was to the traffic of the East what such places as Ushant and Dungeness to-day are to the shipping of the West. He knew that there was plenty of shipping bound from Bengal, the Malay Straits, from China and from Japan which would come round this cape well laden with all sorts of Eastern riches. He would therefore lie in wait off this headland and, attacking a suitable craft, would relieve her of her wealth. But the intention did not have the opportunity of being fulfilled as he had wished it. "In our course," says Lancaster, "we were very much deceived by the currents that set into the Gulfe of the Red Sea along the coast of Melinde"—that is to say, from Zanzibar along the coast known to-day as British East Africa and Somaliland. "And the windes shortening upon us to the North-east and Easterly, kept us that we could not get off, and so with the putting in of the currents from the Westward, set us in further unto the Northward within fourescore leagues of" Socotra, which was "farre from our determined course and expectation."

Therefore, as they had been brought so far to the northward of their course, Lancaster decided that it were best to run into Socotra or some port in the Red Sea for fresh supplies; but, luckily for him, the wind then came north-west, which was of course a fair wind from his present position to the south-west coast of India. Being a wise leader he of course now availed himself of this good fortune and sped over the Indian Ocean towards Cape Comorin, when the wind came southerly: but presently the wind came again more westerly, and so in the month of May 1592 the Cape was doubled, but without having sighted it, and then a course was laid for the Nicobar Islands in the Bay of Bengal. But though they ran on for six days with a fair wind, and plenty of it, "these Ilands were missed through our masters default for want of due observation of the South starre." It would be easy enough to criticise the lack of skill in the Elizabethan navigators, but it is much fairer to wonder rather that they were able to find their way as well as they did over strange seas, considering that until comparatively recently it was to them practically a new art. Excellent seamen they certainly had been for centuries: but it was not till long after Prince Henry the Navigator had taught his own countrymen, that this new sea-learning of navigation had reached England and "pilots-major" instructed our seamen in the higher branch of their profession. They were keen, they were adventurous, and they knew no fear: but these mariners were rude, unscientific men, who could not always be relied upon to make observations accurately. They did the best they could with their astrolabes and cross-staffs, but they lacked the perfection of the modern sextant. The most they could hope for was to make a landfall not too distant from where they wanted to get, and then, having picked up the land, keep it aboard as far as possible. Thus they would approach their destined port, off which, by means of parleying with one of the native craft, they might persuade one of the crew to come aboard and so pilot them in.

As the *Edward Bonaventure* had missed the Nicobar Islands, it was decided to push on to the southward, which would bring them into the neighbourhood of

Sumatra. There they lay two or three days, hoping for a pilot from Sumatra, which was only about six miles off. And subsequently, as the winter was approaching, they made for the Islands of Pulo Pinaou, which they reached in June, and there remained till the end of August. Many of the crew had again fallen sick, and though they put them ashore at this place, twenty-six more of them died. Nor were there many sources of supplies, but only oysters, shell-fish and the fish "which we tooke with our hookes." But there was plenty of timber, and this came in very useful for repairing masts. When the winter passed and again they put to sea, the crew was now reduced to thirty-three men and one boy, but not more than twenty-two were fit for service, and of these not more than one-third were seamen: so the *Edward* was scarcely efficient.

But those which remained must have been of a resolute character, for in a little while they encountered a 60-ton ship, which they attacked and captured, and, shortly after, a second was also taken. Needless to say, the cargoes of pepper were discharged into the *Edward,* and even the sick men were soon reported as "being somewhat refreshed and lustie." Lancaster had not by any means forgotten the fact that richly laden ships from China and Japan would pass through the Malacca Straits, and having arrived here he lay-to and waited. At the end of five days a Portuguese sail was descried, laden with rice, "and that night we tooke her being of 250 tunnes." This was a big ship for those days, and so Lancaster determined to keep her as well as her cargo. He therefore put on board a prize crew of seven, under the command of Edmund Barker. The latter then came to anchor and hung out a riding-light so that the *Edward* could see her position. But the English ship was now so depleted of men that there were hardly enough men on board to handle her, and the prize had to send some of the men back to help her to make up the leeway. It was then decided to take out of the prize all that was worth having, and afterward, with the exception of the Portuguese pilot and four other men, she and her crew were allowed to go.

But it was not long before the *Edward* fell in with a much bigger ship, this time of 700 tons, which was on her way from India. She had left Goa with a most valuable cargo, and a smart engagement ended in her main-yard being shot through, whereupon she came to anchor and yielded, her people escaping ashore in the boats. Lancaster's men found aboard her some brass guns, three hundred butts of wine, "as also all kind of Haberdasher wares, as hats, red caps knit of Spanish wooll, worsted stockings knit, shooes, velvets, taffataes, chamlets, and silkes, abundance of suckets, rice, Venice glasses," playing-cards and much else. But trouble was brewing in the *Edward,* and a mutinous spirit was afoot. Lancaster's men refused to obey his orders and bring the "excellent wines" into the *Edward,* so, after taking out of her all that he fancied, he then let the prize drift out to sea.

From there the *Edward* sailed to the Nicobar Islands, and afterwards proceeded to Punta del Galle (Point de Galle, Ceylon), where she anchored. Lancaster's intention was again to lie in wait for shipping. He knew that more than one fleet of richly laden merchantmen would soon be due to pass that way. First of all he was expecting a fleet of seven or eight Bengal ships, and then two or three more from Pegu (to the north-west of Siam); and also there ought to be some Portuguese ships from Siam. These, he had learned, would pass that way in about a fortnight, bringing the produce of the country to Cochin (in the south-west of India), where the Portuguese caracks, or big merchantmen, would receive the goods and carry them home to Lisbon. It was a regular, yearly trade, the caracks being due to leave Cochin in the middle of January. A fine haul was certain, for these various fleets were bringing all sorts of commodities that were well worth having—cloth, rice, rubies, diamonds, wines and so on.

But Lancaster was again bound to bow to ill-luck. First of all, he had brought up where the bottom was foul, so he lost his anchor. He had on board two spare anchors, but they were unstocked and in the hold. This meant that a good deal of time was wasted, and meanwhile the ship was drifting about the whole night. In addition, to make matters worse, Lancaster himself fell ill. The current was carrying the ship to the southward, away from her required position, so in the morning the foresail was hoisted and preparations were being made to let loose the other sails, when the men mutinied and said they were determined they would remain there no longer but would take the ship to England direct. Lancaster, finding that persuasion was useless and that he could do nothing with them, had no other alternative but to give way to their demands: so on 8th December 1592 the *Edward* set sail for the Cape of Good Hope. On the way Lancaster recovered his health, and even amused himself fishing for bonitos. By February they had crossed the Indian Ocean and made the land by Algoa Bay, South Africa, where they had to remain a month owing to contrary winds. But in March they doubled the Cape of Good Hope once more, and on 3rd April reached St Helena. And here an extraordinary thing happened. When Edmund Barker went ashore he found an Englishman named Segar, like himself of Suffolk. He had been left here eighteen months before by the *Marchant Royall*, which you will remember had been sent home from Table Bay on the way out. On the way home he had fallen ill and would have died if he had remained on board, so it had been decided to put him ashore. When, however, the *Edward's* men saw him this time, he was "as fresh in colour and in as good plight of body to our seeming as might be, but crazed in minde and halfe out of his wits, as afterward wee perceived: for whether he were put in fright of us, not knowing at first what we were, whether friends or foes, or of sudden joy when he understood we were his olde consorts and countreymen, hee became idel-headed, and for eight dayes space neither night nor day tooke any naturall rest, and so at length died for lacke of sleepe."

On 12th April 1593 the *Edward* left St Helena, and the mutinous spirit was not yet dead on board. Lancaster's intention was to cross the Atlantic to Pernambuco, Brazil, but the sailors were infuriated and wished to go straight home. So, the next day, whilst they were being told by the captain to finish a foresail which they had in hand, some of them asserted determinedly that, unless the ship were taken straight home, they would do nothing: and to this Lancaster was compelled to agree. But when they were about eight degrees north of the Equator the ship made little progress for six weeks owing to calms and flukey winds. Meanwhile the men's victuals were running short, and the mutinous spirit reasserted itself strongly. They knew that the officers of the ship had their own provisions locked away in private chests—this had been done as a measure of precaution—and the men now threatened to break open these chests. Lancaster therefore determined, on the advice of one of the ship's company, to make for the Island of Trinidad in the West Indies, where he would be able to obtain supplies. But, being ignorant of the currents of the Gulf of Paria, he was carried out of his course and eventually anchored off the Isle of Mona after a few days more.

After refreshing the stores and stopping a big leak, the *Edward* next put to sea bound for Newfoundland, but a heavy gale sent them back to Porto Rico, the wind being so fierce that even the furled sails of the ship were carried away, and the ship was leaking badly, with six feet of water in the hold. The victuals had run out, so that they were compelled to eat hides. Small provisions were obtained at Porto Rico, and then five of the crew deserted. From there the ship went to Mona again, and whilst a party of nineteen were on shore, including Lancaster and Barker, to gather food, a gale of wind sprang up, which made such a heavy sea that the boat could not have taken them back to the *Edward*. It was therefore deemed wiser to wait till the next day: but during the night, about midnight, the carpenter cut the *Edward's* cable, so that she drifted away to sea with only five men and a boy on board. At the end of twenty-nine days a French ship, afterwards found to be from Dieppe, was espied. In answer to a fire made on shore she dowsed her topsails, approached the land, hoisted out her ensign and came to anchor. Some of the *Edward's* crew, including Barker and Lancaster, went aboard, but the rest of the party to the number of seven could not be found. Six more were taken on board another Dieppe ship and so reached San Domingo, where they traded with the people for hides. Here news reached them of their companions left in Mona. It was learnt that, of the seven men there left, two had broken their necks while chasing fowls on the cliffs, three were slain by Spaniards upon information given by the men who went away in the *Edward*, but the remaining two now joined Lancaster by a ship from another port.

Eventually Lancaster and his companions took passage aboard another Dieppe vessel, and arrived at the latter port after a voyage of forty-two days. They then crossed in a smaller craft to Rye, where they landed on 24th May 1594.

What good, then, had this expedition done? In spite of losing two out of the three ships, in spite of the losses of many men and the whole of the rich cargoes which had been obtained by capture, Lancaster and his companions had returned to England with something worth having. How had English trade with India been benefited? The answer is simple. If nothing tangible had been obtained, this expedition had been a great lesson. If it had brought back no spices or diamonds, it had brought much valuable information. Once again it showed to the English merchants that there was a fortune for all of them waiting in the Orient, and it showed by bitter experience the mistakes that must be avoided. The voyage had been begun at the wrong season of the year; it would have to be better thought out, and better provision would have to be taken to guard against scurvy. The route to India was now well understood, and it was no longer any Portuguese secret. England was just on the eve of sharing with the Portuguese their fortunate discovery, which eventually the latter were to lose utterly to the former.

CHAPTER V

THE FIRST EAST INDIA COMPANY

Although the expedition of those three tall ships related in the previous chapter had been commercially such a dismal failure, it had shown that James Lancaster was the kind of man to whom there should be entrusted the leadership, not only of a single ship, but of an entire expedition. With the greatest difficulty he had prevented his unruly crew from excesses, he had taken his ship most of the way round the world, he had shown that he could put up a good fight when needs be, and that he possessed a capacity for finding out information—a most valuable ability in these the first days of Indian voyaging. He had obtained information about winds, tides, currents, places, peoples and trade. He had got to know where the Portuguese ships were usually to be found, where they started from and at what times of the year. Clearly he was just the man for the big expedition which was shortly to start from England, after but a few years' interval.

We mentioned on an earlier page the travels of Ralph Fitch to India, though even prior to his setting forth another Englishman named Thomas Stevens had been to the East. This was in the year 1579, and although he was the first of our countrymen to reach India, yet he went out in a Portuguese ship, and is therefore entirely indebted to the Portuguese for having reached there at all. He had first proceeded from England to Italy, and then made his way from that country to Portugal. Having arrived in Lisbon, he went aboard and started eight days later when the Portuguese East Indian fleet sailed out. This was towards the beginning of April, which was very late for their sailing, but important business had detained them. Five ships proceeded together, bound for Goa, with many mariners, soldiers, women and children, the starting off being a solemn and impressive occasion, accompanied by the blowing of trumpets and the booming of artillery. Proceeding on their way via the Canaries and Cape Verde, they rounded the Cape of Good Hope, and afterwards steered to the north-east. And then occurred just that very incident which afterwards we have seen was to happen to Lancaster. Not knowing the set of the currents they got much too far to the northward and found themselves close to Socotra (at the entrance to the Gulf of Aden), whereas they imagined they were near to India. But eventually, having sailed many miles, and noticed birds in the sky which they knew came from their desired country, and then having seen floating branches of palm-trees they realised that they were now not far from their destination, and so on 24th October they arrived at Goa.

Stevens had watched the Portuguese navigators closely, and he had marvelled that these ships could find their way over the trackless ocean. "You know," he wrote to his father in England, telling him all about the voyage, "you know that it is hard to saile from East to West, or contrary, because there is no fixed point in all the skie, whereby they may direct their course, wherefore I shall tell you what helps God provide for these men. There is not a fowle that appereth or signe in the aire, or in the sea, which they have not written, which have made the voyages heretofore. Wherefore, partly by their owne experience, and pondering withall what space the ship was able to make with such a winde, and such direction, and partly by the experience of others, whose books and navigations they have, they gesse whereabouts they be, touching degrees of longitude, for of latitude they be alwayes sure."

It was a real difficulty in those early Indian ships to ascertain their longitude with any correctness. Longitude was reckoned from the meridian of St Michael, one of the Azores, on the grounds that there was no variation of the compass there. It was not, in fact, till the chronometer was invented in the latter half of the eighteenth century that the difficulty could be overcome. But these early East Indiamen were by no means devoid of the instruments of navigation, which included an astrolabe and cross-staff, as already mentioned, a celestial globe, a terrestrial globe, a calendar, a universal horologe for finding the hour of the day in every latitude, a nocturne labe for telling the hour of the night, one or more compasses, a navigation chart corrected according to the last voyagers who had used it: and, a little later on, printed charts, as well as a general map.

But whilst Lancaster had been away from England on his voyage to the East, Englishmen at sea had fallen in with two of the Portuguese East Indian caracks—the *Santa Cruz* and the *Madre de Dios*—homeward-bound from Goa. The former had been burnt and the latter taken into Dartmouth. When she arrived in that port her immense size and wealth made a great sensation. Even in Elizabethan money the value was assessed at £15,000. She was of no less than 1600 tons and chock-full of Oriental treasures, with about six or seven hundred souls aboard, and armed with thirty-two brass guns. This wonderful East Indiaman had, besides a number of precious stones, a cargo consisting of spices, drugs, silks, calicoes, quilts, carpets, canopies, pearls, ivory, Chinese ware and hides. In fact when all this cargo was taken out of her in Dartmouth and sent by sea to London, it freighted ten coasters. As you can well imagine, these west-country seamen were careful to note all her details when once they had her in port. She was completely surveyed, and found to be 165 feet long, and 46 feet 10 inches wide, and drew 26 feet, though when she left India she was drawing 31 feet. She had seven decks at the stern, the length of the keel being 100 feet, the height of the mast 121 feet, and the length of the main-yard 106 feet.

The consternation caused by the sight of the wonderful goods which eventually arrived at Leadenhall, London, fired the imaginations of the London merchants afresh. When, in September 1592, they observed the vast quantities of pepper, nutmeg, cloves, cinnamon, ginger, incense, damasks, golden silks, and saw with their own eyes the very goods which had come all the way from that Eastern land of wealth, they marvelled greatly. One of the results of all this was that the Levant Company, which had been founded in 1581 to trade with Turkey and the eastern ports of the Mediterranean, now became expanded into a more ambitious venture. Realising full well the amazing riches of the East Indies, it succeeded in obtaining from Elizabeth, in 1593, a charter to trade now with India, but via the overland route.

In passing we may just say a word about the English trading companies, some of which were of great antiquity. The oldest was the Hamburg Company, which consisted of English merchants trading to Calais, Holland, Zealand, the Low Countries, the Baltic and the inhabitants of modern Prussia. It had been first incorporated by Edward I. in 1296, and enjoyed special privileges during successive reigns. There was also the Russian Company, which had been inaugurated at the end of the reign of Edward VI. and the beginning of the reign of Philip and Mary, though its charter was received from Queen Elizabeth. This company had arisen from the enterprise of a number of English merchants, who had sent three ships to find, if possible, a north-east passage into Asia and the East. So, also, the Turkey or Levant Company, mentioned just now, had been founded in 1581 with a view of trading to the part of the world designated. All these various companies were just so many societies of merchant-adventurers who were bound together with one common interest by the royal charter. But the greatest of all was to be the celebrated East India Company, founded in 1600, about which we shall speak presently, though we may sufficiently anticipate matters by asserting that it grew out of the Levant Company.

But England was by no means to have the whole field to herself. If the Portuguese power was in the descendant: if her precious secrets of this East Indian trade had been ruthlessly revealed: if her ships and her rich cargoes had been repeatedly taken with the same determination that the Armada had been defeated; yet she was still active in India, and the only European nation there established. However, not merely England, but Holland, too, had been growing strong in maritime ability. The Dutch people had always been by nature seamen for centuries, and were able to rival any English ability in the maritime arts. They were intrepid mariners, they were excellent shipbuilders, and they were careful students of all the sea-knowledge which had come forth from Portugal. The influence of Prince Henry's cartographical school had spread northwards from Sagres, and Flemish printers had done much for map-making and thus made known this knowledge of the world far and wide. This was the final blow to the closely guarded Portuguese secrets of India. The first atlas ever printed was published by the Dutch at Leyden in the year 1585. The man to whom belongs the credit of this was named Wagenaer, and, according to the crude knowledge and the still more elementary buoyage, the Narrow Seas were well shown. The charts which Holland published were also brought out in English, together with little sketches of the various headlands, their latitude, distances, and so on, including sailing directions for entering various harbours. So also at Antwerp and at Bruges excellent schools of cartography grew up just as they had in Portugal and Spain: and fired with the amazing stories of the East, Holland was not merely anxious but well prepared for asserting herself in India and coming back with a series of rich cargoes for those prepared to venture.

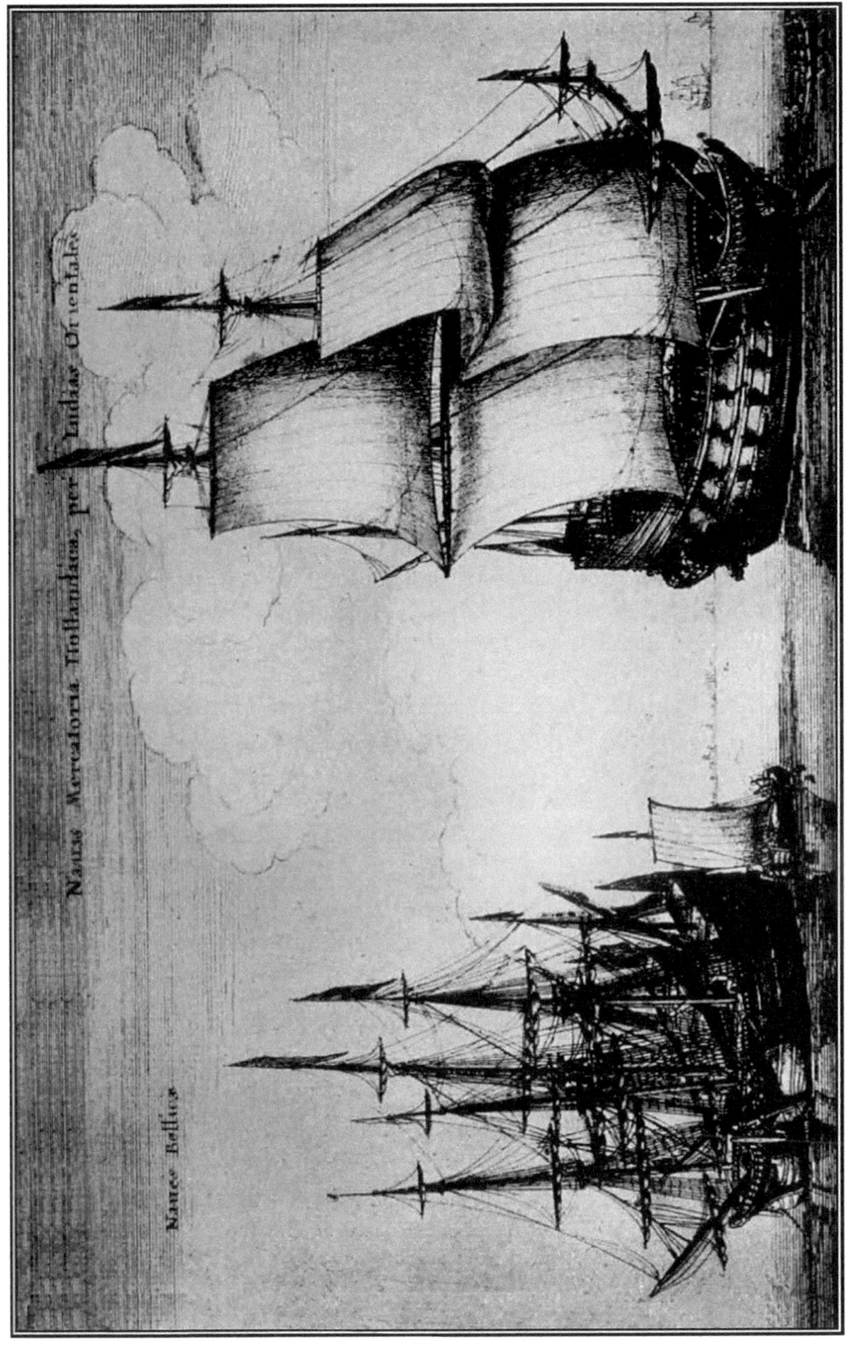

Dutch East Indiaman.

The vessel on the right shows the type of craft in the employment of the Dutch East India Company of about 1647.

Briefly, this was brought about as follows. We mentioned on an earlier page that though the Portuguese jealously guarded the secret of the India route, they were quite willing to dispose of these Indian goods. One of these marts, to which merchants came from other countries in order to purchase, was Lisbon. The second was Antwerp, which was convenient for the merchants of Northern Europe. England, by the way, had done a good deal of overseas trade between London and Antwerp for centuries, so this additional East Indian trade made the visits of our merchantmen even more important, and thus many first realised what India meant commercially, and could mean to them. And similarly the people of the Low Countries became equally impressed with what they learned. Thus very naturally we see in 1593—the actual year in which the Levant Company had obtained their extended charter—the first of a series of efforts made by Dutchmen to reach Asia by a north-east passage. And we must not omit to mention the very great influence which Jan Huygen von Linschoten, a native of Haarlem, had. The latter was a great student of geography, at a time when all knowledge of this kind was rare. For a while he was resident in Lisbon, where he amassed a large amount of invaluable data concerning the East—its harbours, configuration, trade-winds, and so on. Lisbon, in fact, was just the place in which all the East Indian information naturally collected itself. Later on Linschoten himself proceeded to India and dwelt at Goa, in the train of the Portuguese Archbishop, but in the year 1592 he returned to Europe, and the tales which this traveller told concerning India astonished the slow-reasoning minds of his fellow-countrymen. In the year 1596 he published a most valuable book dealing with the East, affording charts and maps and no end of information which would be priceless to any who might venture on a voyage to India. An English translation appeared two years later, and it certainly had a great influence on the founding of our first East India Company. So important was the book, indeed, that it was also translated and published in French, in Latin and German.

As for Holland, the tangible result was that four ships were fitted out, and under Cornelis Houtman were sent in 1595 to the countries situate the other side of the Cape of Good Hope, beyond the Indian Ocean. Houtman's voyage had been a success, for in the year 1597 he returned, bringing with him a treaty made with the King of Bantam, which was the means of opening up to Holland the Indian Archipelago. This voyage convinced even the most sceptical, and a new era had begun, in which Holland was to grow rich and powerful, a great commercial country and of considerable strength at sea. The handsome seventeenth-century buildings which you still find standing in Holland to-day, and the brilliant seventeenth-century Dutch painters of portraits and shipping scenes, are surviving evidences of a wonderful prosperity derived for the most part from the East India trade of that time.

It came about, then, that England was to find a keen rival for the possessions of the East. There was going to be a very hard struggle as to which would win the race. One voyage succeeded another, so that actually the Dutch were wanting in big craft and had to come over to England to buy up some of our shipping. But this was the final straw which broke the back of Englishmen's patience. They had looked on for some time with restraint at the progressive enterprise of the Dutch, and had become very jealous of their commercial prosperity. It was a condition to which the present Anglo-German rivalry is very similar in kind. But it was clear something must be done now. The London merchants who were interested in the Levant Company had found that their charter of extension granted in 1593 for overland trading with India availed them but little. Therefore, arising out of this company it happened that a number of merchants met together in London in the year 1599 and agreed to petition Elizabeth for permission to send a number of well-found ships to the East Indies, for which they prayed a monopoly, subscribing the sum of £30,133 for an East Indian voyage. It was certainly high time to be moving, for the Dutch were gaining all the foreign freight—they were nicknamed the "waggoners of the sea"—whilst English ships were rotting away in port, or doing little more than mere coasting.

This petition was not approved by the Privy Council, but in the year 1609, and on the last day in that year, it received the Queen's assent. More capital had been obtained, the exclusive privilege of this Indian trade had been granted for fifteen years, so there was nothing to do but obtain the necessary ships and men and hurry on the fitting-out. The Company was managed by twenty-four directors, under the governorship of Alderman James Smith, who was subsequently knighted, but altogether there were two hundred and eighteen of these merchants, aldermen, knights and esquires, who were made up by the title of "The Governors and Company of the Merchants trading unto the East Indies." The countries prescribed by this charter showed a rather extended area, embracing all ports, islands and places in Asia, Africa, America, between the Cape of Good Hope and the Straits of Magellan. The Company were promised that neither the Queen nor her heirs would grant trading-licences within these limits to any person without the consent of the Company: and the Company was furthermore granted the privilege of making the first four voyages without export duty, and the permission was further granted to export annually the sum of £30,000 in bullion or coin.

This "privilege for fifteen yeeres" "to certaine Adventurers for the discoverie of the Trade for the East-Indies" was to be a spirited reply to the action of the Dutch, and marks the beginning of that series of English East India companies which were in effect the means of acquiring India for the British crown after the Indian Mutiny in the nineteenth century. From now onwards the East Indiamen ships have a standing and importance which were not previously possessed, and we shall find this culminating in the amazingly dignified manner of the Indian merchantmen in the early part of the nineteenth century.

Among those who had agreed together for this expedition "at their owne adventures, costs and charges as well for the honour of this Our Realme of England, as for the increase of Our Navigation, and advancement of trade," was the Earl of Cumberland. He was one of those Elizabethan gentlemen who were wont to fit out a small squadron of ships for roving the seas and attacking the well-laden ships of the Spanish and Portuguese. It was a fine, adventurous game and there was a good chance of coming home with a fortune. Of those ships which the noble earl owned for this purpose one was a craft named the *Red Dragon*, and as she was built for fighting and ocean cruising she was just the ship for the first voyage of the East India Company, being of 600 tons. She was therefore purchased from her owner by this Company for the sum of £3700. Her name at one time had been the *Mare Scourge* (perhaps to suggest the terror of the sea which was thus exhibited), but at any rate in the year 1586 she was known as the *Red Dragon*.

Under their charter the Company were allowed to send "sixe good ships and sixe good pynnaces" and "five hundred Mariners, English-men, to guide and sayle." But not more than four ships were sent actually, for it was a costly venture. These London merchants had "joyned together and made a stocke of seventie two thousand pounds, to bee employed in ships and merchandizes"; but the purchase of four ships, the expense of fitting them out, furnishing them with men, victuals and munitions for a period of twenty months had eaten up the sum of £45,000. This left £27,000, which amount was taken out in the ships, partly in merchandise (with which to trade in Asia) and partly in Spanish money, with which the natives would be familiar. Advance wages were paid to the crew before setting forth.

The "Generall of the Fleet" was that same James Lancaster whom we considered just now, and his flagship was to be the *Red Dragon*. There was no better leader for the job, and the reader will shortly see how well he conducted himself in conditions that were not less trying than in his previous voyage to the East. To him Elizabeth entrusted letters of commendation addressed to "divers Princes of India," the vice-admiral being John Middleton; and the celebrated John Davis, of Arctic fame, was to go as pilot-major, or navigating expert—another excellent man for the undertaking. After a busy winter the four ships were ready and fitted out, so that on 13th February 1601 they were able to leave Woolwich, their crews amounting to 480. In addition to the *Red Dragon* there were the *Hector*, of 300 tons and 108 men; the *Ascension*, 260 tons and 82 men; the *Susan* (which had been bought from a London alderman for £1600), 240 tons and 88 men; and in addition they took a victualling ship called variously the *Guift* or *Guest*. The latter was a ship of 130 tons, but had cost only £300.

In their holds these ships carried such English products as were likely to be appreciated in the East. Such commodities were taken as iron, lead, tin, cloth; while the presents to be given to the Indian princes comprised a girdle, a case of pistols, plumes, looking-glasses, platters, spoons, glass toys, spectacles, drinking-glasses and a plain silver ewer. But the progress of this squadron was distinctly slow. From the Thames they had dropped down to the mouth and anchored in the Downs. Here they waited so long for a fair wind that already it was Easter Day before they reached Dartmouth, where they "spent five or sixe dayes in taking in their bread and certaine other provisions," as one of the letters received by the East India Company has it. Leaving Dartmouth they "hoysed their anchors" and sped across the Bay of Biscay, and continued to the south. Off the coast of Guinea they fell in with a Portuguese vessel, which they captured, and from her they took much wine, oil and meal for the good of the squadron.

During the month of June they crossed the Equator, and in the following month discharged the *Guest* victualler—that is to say, they took out of her the masts, sails and yards and whatever else was worth keeping, and then broke down her "higher buildings for firewood, and so left her floting in the sea." And now scurvy attacked many of the squadron's crew, so that there were hardly men enough to handle the sails. Even the "merchants tooke their turnes at the Helme: and went into the top to take in the top-sayles, as the common Mariners did." However, on the 9th of September 1601 they arrived at Saldanha (Table Bay), where they anchored and "hoysed out their boats." (There were of course no such things as boat davits in those days, the boats being lifted out from the waist of the ship by blocks and ropes.) But so weak were the crews of three of the ships that Lancaster's crew had to go aboard the other craft and do the work of getting these boats into the sea.

How was it, then, that the flagship's crew had kept so free from scurvy and were in better health than the other men? The answer is that Lancaster had learnt a lesson from the terrible death-roll which this disease had caused in his previous voyage already noted. "The reason," runs the document, "why the Generals men stood better in health then the men of other Ships was this: he brought to sea with him certaine Bottles of the Juice of Limons, which hee gave to each one, as long as it would last, three spoonfuls every morning fasting: not suffering them to eate any thing after it till noone. This Juice worketh much better, if the partie keepe a short Dyet, and wholly refrains salt meate, which salt meate, and long being at the sea is the only cause of the breeding of this Disease. By this meanes the Generall cured many of his men, and preserved the rest." Considering this practical proof of the value of lime juice as an anti-scorbutic, it is surprising that it was not till many years later lime juice was, as it is to-day, always carried in English ships and given out to the men, especially in wind-jammers.

After allowing the men shore leave and laying in very necessary provisions, the squadron got under way and left again on 29th October, doubling the Cape of Good Hope on the 1st of November, "having the wind West North-west a great gale." Madagascar was reached on 17th December, and they remained there until 6th March. Actually they did not even sight India, but held on across the Indian Ocean until they reached those Nicobar Islands visited in the previous voyage. A short stay was made and then they pushed on to the southward till they came to Acheen, which is at the north-west extremity of Sumatra, arriving there on the 5th of June 1602. Here Lancaster was entertained hospitably by some of the Dutch factors who had already established themselves, and also obtained a concession from the King of Acheen granting freedom of trade and immunity from paying customs. Thus a beginning was made, if not actually with India, at any rate with a part of the East Indies. Trade between England and the Orient was established, only to be developed in the years that were to follow.

In order to proceed with their trade, Lancaster put ashore two of the factors who had come out with him from England, these employing their time now in getting together a cargo of pepper against the date of Lancaster's return. Meanwhile the squadron sailed from Acheen on 11th September 1602, and then engaged in that favourite occupation of roving about till some well-filled merchantman fell into his hands, relieving her then of her valuable cargo. Strictly speaking, as the reader is aware, this expedition to the East Indies had been fitted out for the purpose of opening up trade. But no Elizabethan sailor could content himself with such lawful limits. Privateering was in his blood: he was always spoiling for a fight at sea, especially against any Spanish or Portuguese ship. It was a much quicker way of winning wealth and, incidentally, of paying back old scores to the people who had tried to keep Englishmen out of the strange seas of the world. And Lancaster was a sufficiently good strategist to know that if he selected some pivot of a busy trade-route, such as some narrow straits, all that he had to do was to hang about there long enough and it was only a question of time as to whether a big haul would be made. He could rely implicitly on his own men and their gunnery, even against superior strength. It only wanted the opportunity, and that, again, demanded merely a little patience.

So whilst his factors were busy at Acheen buying a cargo, he betook himself to the Straits of Malacca, the gateway for the shipping which voyaged between the Pacific and the Indian Ocean; and before long he had descried a fine Portuguese craft of 900 tons called the *St Thomé*. It was a little unfortunate that the day was nearly spent, as that meant that the enemy might possibly escape under cover of darkness. "And being toward night," wrote one who was there at the time, "a present direction was given that we should all spread our selves a mile and a halfe one from another, that she might not passe us in the night." So the four English ships did as the admiral wished them. The *Hector* shot two or three "peeces of ordnance," and this warned the other three ships, who now closed in and surrounded the Portuguese carack on all sides. Then the *Red Dragon* began to fire at her from the bow guns, with the satisfactory result that the carack's main-yard came tumbling down.

That was deemed enough for the present: it would be better to wait till the night had passed, thought Lancaster, for he feared "least some unfortunate shot might light betweene wind and water, and so sinke her," which would mean that her valuable cargo would be for ever lost. He therefore stayed his hand for a little while: but next morning at daybreak he again attacked and this time took the prize. Only four of Lancaster's men were placed on board, "for feare of rifling and pillaging the good things that were within her ... and their charge was, if any thing should be missing, to answer the same out of their wages and shares." For he knew full well that when once a band of these rough seamen were aboard they would stop at nothing, and no threats could prevent them from helping themselves to the rare cargo in the holds.

So full was this *St Thomé* of Eastern goods that it took six days to unload her of her 950 packs of calicoes, etc. And then, as a storm came up, she had to be left behind, so Lancaster returned to Acheen, and took in his cargo of pepper, cinnamon and spices, together with a letter and presents from the King of Acheen to Elizabeth. He then set sail for Bantam, in the Island of Java, on the 9th of November, and soon after sent home to England the *Ascension* and the *Susan*, which had completed their cargoes. In the meantime Lancaster continued his cruise with the *Dragon* and *Hector*, and arrived at Bantam, "in the island of Java major," which he reached on the 16th of December. Here, as was the routine of the venture, he put his merchants ashore with their goods and began trade with the natives. And although the English reckoned the Javanese "among the greatest pickers and theeves of the world," yet our merchants were able to do some very good business; and so again the ships were laden with cargoes of pepper, and a regular factory was here established for further trade between England and the East. Lancaster had as fine an ability for trading enterprise as he had for capturing a Portuguese ship, and he obtained a 40-ton pinnace laden with merchandise, which was sent to the Moluccas to trade and establish a factory there, in charge of Master William Starkey. When the next English ships should come out they would thus find immediate opportunity for getting rid of their lead, iron, tin, cloth, and another cargo waiting to be taken on board.

Such, then, was the completion of the business in the Orient. The first voyage under the East India Company had done its work in the East Indies. It had got there in safety, it had established factories, it had disposed of its freights and obtained very valuable goods to take home. It had certainly been fortunate, the only real calamity being the sickness and death of Captain John Middleton of the *Hector*. It was a long period since they had set out from the Thames, and the time had now arrived when they must weigh their anchors and start back to England: so early in the new year they took on board stores and made their final preparations for the long voyage back over lonely seas.

CHAPTER VI

CAPTAIN LANCASTER DISTINGUISHES HIMSELF

On the 20th of February the two ships were ready for sea. "We went all aboord our ships, shot off our ordnance, and set sayle to the sea toward England, with thankes to God, and glad hearts, for his blessings towards us." On the 13th of March they crossed the Tropic of Capricorn, steering south-west "with a stiff gale of wind at south-east," and this was sending them over the Indian Ocean towards the African coast in fine style. But "the eight and twentieth day we had a very great and a furious storme, so that we were forced to take in all our sayles. This storme continued a day and a night, with an exceeding great and raging sea, so that in the reason of man no shippe was able to live in them: but God (in his mercie) ceased the violence thereof, and gave us time to breath: and to repaire all the distresses and harmes we had received, but our ships were so shaken, that they were leakie all the voyage after."

This was, in fact, to be a return full of excitement and those serious incidents which bring out all the seamanship and resource of the real sons of the sea. If it be true that a man's real character is exhibited only in big crises, then we see Lancaster standing out magnificently as a cool, resourceful, self-sacrificing leader of men, for whom we cannot help having the highest admiration. These Elizabethans were very far from perfect. They were guilty of some abominable and atrocious acts of sacrilege on occasions: their hatred of the Portuguese and Spaniards knew few bounds. They imagined that might on the sea was right, and honesty was deemed not always the best policy. But among their virtues they were the very opposite of cowards. They knew how to bear all kinds of pain with a courage and resignation that are to be extolled. And if things went against them they knew how to die as bravely as they had fought and striven. There was no panic, no kicking against the inevitable: they did their best, and according to their own rough morality left the rest to God.

Another "very sore storme" overcame them on the 3rd of May, "and the seas did so beate upon the ships quarter, that it shooke all the iron worke of her rother [*i.e.* rudder]: and the next day in the morning, our rother brake cleane from the sterne of our shippe [*i.e.* the *Red Dragon*], and presently sunke into the sea." Here was a terrible predicament, for of all the casualties which can befall a ship at sea not one is more awkward than this. And to-day only the steamship with more than one propeller can continue on her way without worrying much about such an occurrence. If, however, the vessel is a sailing ship, or has only one propeller, the only recourse is to tow a spar or sea-anchor (cone foremost) with a rope from each quarter. Then, if an equal strain is kept on both ropes, the spar will be thus in line with the ship's keel, but as soon as one rope is slacked up and another tightened, the vessel's quarter will be pulled to one side and her head pay off to the opposite.

Let us now see what they attempted in the *Dragon*. You will of course understand that the rudder was attached to the stern-post by means of irons on either side of the former, these working on their respective pins attached to the stern-post. Consequently, if these irons carried away, either through rust or the violence of the waves, there was nothing to hold the rudder in place and the ship was not under command. This is exactly what had happened in the present instance, and the means of steering was vanished. Naturally, therefore, the *Dragon* "drave up and downe in the sea like a wracke," but all the while the *Hector* stood by, though unable to do anything. At length the commander of the *Dragon* decided to do exactly what the master of a modern sailing vessel would set about. Her mizen-mast was unstepped, and they then "put it forth at the sterne port to prove if wee could steere our shippe into some place where we might make another rother to hang it, to serve our turnes home." The spar was placed over the side and lashed to the stern, but it was found to put such a heavy strain on the latter that the mast had to be brought on board again.

Lancaster then ordered the ship's carpenter to make the mast into a rudder, for in those days the shape of the latter was very long and narrow: but when they wanted to fix it in position it was noticed that the rudder irons "wherewith to fasten the rother" had also gone. However they were not to be dismayed by this very inconvenient discovery, and were determined to do what they could. One of the crew accordingly went overboard to make an examination, and found that two of the rudder irons were still remaining and that there was one other broken. This was a slice of luck, so, when the weather eased down a little later, the new rudder was able to be fixed into position and once more the *Dragon* got on to her course. However, this good fortune was but short-lived, and after three or four hours "the sea tooke it off againe, and wee had much adoe to save it. Wee lost another of our irons, so that now we had but two to hang it by."

Matters began to look pretty desperate by now, the men wanted to abandon the ship and be picked up by the *Hector*, and the position of Lancaster was no easy one. On the one hand, he knew that they could not continue like this, making no headway and with provisions running out and a dissatisfied crew against him. On the other hand, he was responsible to the East India Company for the safety of the ship and all that valuable cargo that was in her hold. It was sheer hard luck that for the second time in his life he should be returning from the Orient well laden with riches, only to be brought up short by an unexpected event that boded ill. Still, he was not the type of man to give way in such a critical time, and he for his part was going to stand by his ship, whatever else might happen. He appreciated quite fully the seriousness of the case, and yet for all that he was prepared to go through with it. There must be no sort of flinching.

He went below into the privacy of his cabin, and unknown to the crew sat down and wrote the following letter, having resolved to give it to the captain of the *Hector*, sending her home at once, and on her arriving back to have this letter handed over to the directors of the Company. This epistle read thus:

> "Right Worshipfull,—What hath passed in this voyage, and what trades I have settled for this companie, and what other events have befallen us, you shall understand by the bearers hereof, to whom (as occasion hath fallen) I must referre you. I will strive with all diligence to save my ship, and her goods, as you may perceive by the course I take in venturing mine own life, and those that are with mee. I cannot tell where you should looke for mee, if you send out any pinnace to seeke mee: because I live at the devotion of the wind and seas. And thus fare you well, desiring God to send us a merrie meeting in this world, if it be his good will and pleasure.
>
> "The passage to the East India lieth in 62½ degrees, by the North West on the America side. Your very loving friend,
>
> "James Lancaster."

Such was the brief, matter-of-fact, intensely practical letter which he indited—the very letter which we should have expected from a leader of this type. He succeeded presently in getting it put aboard the *Hector*, with the order to her captain to proceed. Night came on and when the morning broke Lancaster little expected to find his "chummy ship" still by his side. But he had forgotten that the *Hector's* commander was a man like himself, and being a real good fellow he declined to leave a friend in distress, even though it was disobeying the orders of his admiral. So with excellent seamanship the *Hector* was kept at a reasonable distance from the *Dragon*, determined to stand by. Meanwhile the *Dragon's* carpenter had got to work again and the rudder had been repaired. As if to encourage them, the weather after two or three days began to get better, and the sea to go down. The admiral therefore made a signal ordering the *Hector* to come nearer. This she did, and then her master, Sander Cole by name, was able to come aboard the flagship, bringing with him the best swimmer in the ship, and the best divers. These men were of the greatest assistance, and did their work round the stern of the ship to such good effect that the rudder was eventually hung again on the two remaining hooks. It was a triumph of patience, persistence and pluck, that the *Dragon* was able once again to go ahead and let her sheets draw.

But all this time things on board had been very trying. The ship had been buffeted about ceaselessly by many storms for week after week. Men had fallen sick and the ship could not be worked as she ought. However, the Cape of Good Hope was rounded, and then there had to be endured the weary, agonising experience of being becalmed. Still they knew "by the height wee were in to the Northward" that they had long since passed the dreaded Cape of storms. Just one more casualty convinced them that they were not yet out of danger, and this occurred when the main-yard fell down and knocked a man into the sea, drowning him.

But on the 5th of June they passed the Tropic of Capricorn, and on the sixteenth of that month sighted St Helena, where they let go in twelve fathoms. Here they took on board fresh water, shot some wild goats and hogs, refitted the ships and inspected the *Dragon's* rudder, "which wee hoped would last us home." During the sojourn here all the sick recovered their health, and on the 5th of July they set out again to the north-west. Five days more they were becalmed, but before that they had succeeded in passing Ascension, on 11th July, and then fell in with a favourable south-east wind. Thus they proceeded until the 7th of September, when they imagined themselves near to home. "Wee tooke sounding, judging the Lands end of England to be fortie leagues from us. The eleventh day we came to the Downes, well and safe to an anchor: for the which, thanked be almightie God, who hath delivered us from the infinite perils and dangers, in this long and tedious Navigation." Thus the voyage which had been begun on 13th February 1601 was now brought to a finish on 11th September 1603. It had been a most successful voyage, and 1,030,000 lb. of pepper had been brought to England by these four ships. But, important as that was to the merchants, still more admirable was the achievement of Lancaster in getting his ship home at all. However, he was not to go without his reward. He had had the responsibility of bringing this first voyage of the English East India Company to a conclusion that was as happy as financially it was successful, and he was granted a knighthood by James I. Those who had invested their money in this concern could scarcely regret their decision, for they eventually received 95 per cent. on their capital, and it was now established beyond doubt that henceforth the East Indian trade was the thing for enterprising London merchants. For a hundred years the Portuguese had kept the secret to themselves and succeeded in preventing other countries from coming as interlopers. But that was now all past and done with. The future rested not with the Portuguese, whose Indian colonial system proved to be an utter failure, but with the English or the Dutch, between whom the contest would soon become keen. For already the latter had formed so many associations for trade that by the year 1602 they were amalgamated by the States-General into one corporation entitled the Dutch East India Company.

As this first voyage had been so fortunate, it was not long before a second was inaugurated by the English East India Company. During that winter preparations went ahead, and on the following Lady Day 1604 another expedition left Gravesend, this time under the leadership of Henry Middleton, a kinsman of the Middleton who had died during Lancaster's voyage. This project consisted of the same ships as before, and these duly arrived at Bantam on the 20th of December. From here two of the ships were sent home—namely, the *Hector* and the *Susan*, eight months ahead of the other couple, which proceeded first to the Moluccas before leaving Bantam finally for England. Middleton found that trading was not quite as easy as it might be, for the Dutch gave him a great deal of opposition in the East. However, you will realise that this second voyage was far from being a failure when it is stated that the profits were just under 100 per cent. to those who had raised the capital. And this in spite of the fact that the *Susan* was lost on her way home. It is a singular coincidence that when this ship had been purchased, as already noted in the preceding chapter, from a London alderman at the price of £1600, the condition was that he should buy her back from the Company at the end of the voyage, for half the purchase price. Middleton had reached the Downs on 6th May 1606, and it was not long before preparations began to be made for next year's voyage. The second expedition had necessitated a capital of £60,000, of which only £1142 had been spent in goods, so you will understand to what extent privateering was responsible for swelling the profits.

On 12th March 1607 an expedition was off again, for the third voyage. This time the sum of £53,000 had been subscribed, £7280 being expended in merchandise to take out. There were only three ships on the present occasion, consisting of those two veterans, *Red Dragon* and *Hector*, and a vessel named the *Consent*, of 105 tons. The "Generall" in this case was Captain Keeling. The latter left England on 12th March, alone, and reached the Moluccas. Although he was unable to obtain a cargo from there, yet he purchased from a Java junk a cargo of cloves for £2948, 15s., which on their arrival in England fetched the considerable sum of £36,287. The reason why spices of the East were so readily bought up by the West is explained at once by the fact that a great demand existed throughout civilised Europe at that time for their employment in cookery and in certain expensive drinks.

The *Dragon* and *Hector* had left the Downs on the 1st of April, and, like those previous voyages which we have noted, they again went round the Cape of Good Hope and then as far north-east as Socotra, where the two ships separated, the *Dragon* proceeding to Sumatra and Bantam, while the *Hector* went on to Surat, just north of Bombay. Thus, at last and for the first time, one of the Company's ships had brought up in a port of the Indian continent, as distinct from those East Indian islands which had been previously visited. The captain of the *Hector* was Hawkins, whilst the *Dragon* was under the command of Captain Keeling. Some historians assert that Captain Keeling himself went to Surat, where he landed a Mr Finch to form a factory, and then sent Captain Hawkins to persuade the Great Mogul at Agra to order his officers to deal justly with the English: but at any rate Hawkins remained ashore, as there was a fine opportunity for inaugurating a big business, and sent the *Hector* on to Bantam to join Captain Keeling. Hawkins had come out from England with a letter from King James I. to the Great Mogul, and the latter promised to grant the Company all the privileges asked for. This Indian potentate further suggested that Hawkins should remain at his Court as English representative at a commencing salary of £3200 a year. This offer Hawkins accepted, but not unnaturally the appointment aroused a good deal of jealousy both among the Portuguese and the officials of the Court. In a little time the Great Mogul had regretted his decisions both as to Hawkins and the East India Company. The Englishman therefore was compelled to leave Agra (minus his promised salary), and then went down to the coast again at Surat. As to the privileges which had been promised to the Company, these also vanished. Trouble was obviously brewing. But this third voyage, yielding a profit of 234 per cent., had not by any means been a failure, but a great financial success. The *Dragon* had been sent home with a good cargo, and then Captain Keeling (this time in the *Hector*) had visited the Moluccas and Bantam, where the factory had been more firmly established, subsequently reaching England on 9th May 1610.

It will be remembered that the original charter granted to the Company by Elizabeth was for a period of fifteen years. But in the year 1609 the Company were compelled to petition James I. for a renewal, or rather for much greater powers, notwithstanding that the original charter had still six years to run. The reason for this application is not hard to appreciate. The Portuguese now began to realise that the Englishmen were very serious rivals, and they must be met by force. The East India Company, on the other hand, were equally determined that they would not give up such a valuable trade that had paid them so handsomely during these few years. Therefore opposition must be met by other force: in other words, a greater number of ships would be required. King James also recognised this, so the application was granted, the number of merchant-adventurers was increased from 218 to 276, the Crown to have the power of repealing the Company's charter after three years' notice.

So three new ships were fitted out for the sixth voyage. (There had in the meanwhile been two "separate" voyages, about which we shall speak presently.) The cost of these three new ships, together with the merchandise which they carried out, was £82,000, this large sum being rendered possible only by the increased members of the Company. The leader of this voyage was that same Henry Middleton whom we saw taking out the second voyage: but since that time he had received a knighthood. This time his flagship was to be the *Trade's Increase*. And as this was one of the most famous of all the seventeenth-century ships, and certainly the largest East Indiaman built up till then, we must say something about her.

At the time of her launch she was the biggest merchantman of any kind that had been built in England. She created, in fact, to the Jacobeans something of the sensation which the launch of the *Mauretania* in our own time created. James I. attended the ceremony, together with other members of the royal family, and attended by his nobles. This was on the 13th of December 1609, her first voyage being due to commence on the following 1st of April. In consequence of the high position which the East India Company had now begun to occupy, and not less owing to the phenomenal size of this ship, the incident was made the most of. After the ship was afloat in the water, the King and his retinue were entertained on board with a magnificent dinner provided at the Company's expense and served on some of those dishes and plates of China ware which had been brought home from the East by the Company's ships and were then looked upon as something rare and wonderful, nothing of the kind having yet been seen in the country. But the *Trade's Increase*, with her 1100 tons, was a clumsy, unwieldy ship and somewhat top-heavy. She was anything but a lucky craft, and we shall see presently that her end was to be tragic. For English shipbuilding was in a transition stage, which lasted about another two hundred years or more. It was trying hard to get away from the unscientific, rule-of-thumb method which had come down from the Middle Ages and had not yet come under the influence of science and the principles of true naval architecture.

CHAPTER VII

THE BUILDING OF THE COMPANY'S SHIPS

Now, before we proceed with the further voyages and trading of these Indiamen, we shall find it very interesting if we attempt to paint the picture of the building of these ships. Happily the data handed down are of such a nature that we can learn practically all that we should like to know on the subject.

The reader will remember that the ships which went on the first and second voyages had been obtained by purchase. But, then, since it was obvious that more ships would be required as the trade increased and losses occurred by wrecks, the Company had to look out for additions to their small fleet. It was then that they were confronted with a big problem. First of all, England was still a comparatively new-comer into the position of an ocean-going shipowner, as distinct from Portugal, Spain, Venice and Genoa. Practically all her shipping consisted either of fishing or coasting craft. Therefore she possessed only a very small supply of what could be called in those days large vessels. This supply had been still further depleted by the purchases which the Dutch East India companies had made from English owners at the beginning of the East Indian boom. The result was that those very few big ships which remained in England were at a premium. To voyage round the Cape of Good Hope and across the Indian Ocean, able to fight stalwart Portuguese craft and to carry well a heavy cargo, in addition to provisions for many months, demanded a big-bellied ship of exceptional strength; and that was why the *Mare Scourge* (which had been built for privateering) was just the thing.

But now the owners of the small amount of big shipping that still survived, in consequence of the big financial success which the East India Company had made from their first two voyages, were determined not to let them have any more ships except at very high prices. The rates which these sellers now asked were preposterous—as much as £45 a ton being demanded. The East India Company, being therefore in the position of needing ships and yet unable to purchase such at a reasonable figure, were compelled to decide on building for themselves. This dates from the year 1607, and a yard was leased at Deptford, the first two craft thus built being the *Trade's Increase*, mentioned in the last chapter, and the *Peppercorn*, both of which went out under Sir Henry Middleton in the spring of 1610. From the first this change of policy was found to be justified, for the Company was able to build their ships at £10 a ton instead of £45, which meant the very handsome saving of £38,500 in the case of a ship the size of the *Trade's Increase*—or two ships equal to her tonnage.

The launch of the Honourable East India Company's ship "Edinburgh" (Captain Henry Bax).

(By courtesy of Messrs. T. H. Parker Brothers)

In this yard before very long the Company were employing no fewer than five hundred ships' carpenters, caulkers, joiners and other workmen. The result was that by the year 1615 the Company had built more ships in those short eight years than any other trade had done. Altogether they had owned during that period twenty-one able ships, and by the year 1621 the Company owned not less than 10,000 tons of shipping, employing as many as 2500 seamen. When we consider that even as late as the year 1690 the whole population of England was less than 5,500,000, and that of this number the seafaring people were a very small figure, it is obvious what this great East India Company meant to the country, with its wealth, enabling large sums of money to be spent in wages to seamen, workmen and factors. After the Company had been trading only twenty years there were about 120 of these factors alone. But, in addition, the Company was paying out large sums of money for the relief of seamen's widows and their children. I will not burden the reader with statistics, but I may be allowed to state that up to November 1621 the Company had exported woollen goods, lead, iron, tin and other commodities from England to the value of £319,211. From the East these ships had brought back cargoes which had been purchased in the East for the sum of £375,288. But you will appreciate the profit when it is stated further that these cargoes were sold in England for £2,044,600. As against this there was always the possibility of losing the ships and the cargoes in their holds either outward or homeward bound. There was the cost of building and upkeep of ships and dockyard. There was the heavy expense, too, of victualling the ships for many months, the purchasing of English merchandise, the various stores, the wages of captains, officers and crews, and factors, as well as the payment of customs. And though it is perfectly true that the average profit made by the first twelve voyages was not less than 138 per cent., yet we must remember that the voyages were never made in less than twenty months and often extended to three and four years.

So also we must remember that after the arrival in this country of the goods from India they were sold at long credits—even as much as eighteen months and two years. Owing to the irregularity of the factors in keeping and transmitting their accounts, the concerns of the voyage could not be finally adjusted under six or eight years. "Taking the duration of the concern at a medium of seven years," says Macpherson in his "History of European Commerce with India," "the profit appears to be somewhat under twenty per cent. per annum." The current rate of interest in those days was about 8 per cent., so that 20 per cent. could not be deemed for that time a very abnormal rate of remuneration when we consider the amount of enterprise required at the outset, and the vast risks which necessarily had to be run. Included in these profits were also the results of privateering and bartering. Between the years 1601 and 1612 the profits ranged from 95 to 234 per cent., with the exception of the year 1608, when both ships were wrecked.

Nowhere was the Company's system of thoroughness better shown than in the completeness and organisation of her shipyard. The East India Company took itself very seriously and arrogated to itself all the dignity and self-importance which its unique prerogatives permitted. The Court was presided over by the Governor and it had its own rules of procedure. "Every man," for instance, "speaking in the Court shall stand up and be bareheaded, and shall addresse his speach to the Gouernour or Deputy in his absence." So runs one of the Company's rules. Now the connecting link, so to speak, between the Company and its ships was the man who was known as the ship's husband, one of its salaried servants. When the Court were met to discuss the plans for the yearly voyages to India, the husband had to attend in order to learn what shipping would be required. He then had to draw out a table of the proportion of victuals and other necessaries for each ship and to see that such were provided. After being got together these stores were then placed in the Company's warehouses. In addition to being the victualler of the ships he was responsible also for providing the amount of iron likely to be required—"yron both English and Spanish"—and had to deliver it to the smiths at Deptford yard for the rudder irons and other purposes, and also to the coopers for making the hoops of the casks. The husband was also responsible for the supervision of the clerks and for keeping the account-books, the stores in the London warehouses being under the care of a "Clerke of the Stores."

In the Deptford yard large stocks of "timber, planckes, sheathing-boards, and treenayles" had to be maintained by officials called "purveyers," or, as we should name them nowadays, "buyers." These men had to see to the purchasing of all kinds of wood used. It was kept in the Company's private timber-yards at Reading, whence it was put into barges and so brought down the Thames to Deptford. The trenails were the old-fashioned means of fastening a ship's timbers and planking and had existed from the times even of the Romans and the Vikings. They were small wooden pegs—"tree-nails"—driven in something after the appearance of the modern rivet, but minus the head. The sheathing-boards were a very necessary protection for the ship's hull in hot climates against the insidious attacks of the worm. (In another chapter will be found an instance of this.) There was also employed a "measurer of timber and plancke," whose job was to go down to the waterside and mark the timber.

But it was the "Clarke of the Yard" who had the supervision of the shipwrights, the "cawlkers," carpenters and labourers, and one portion of his duties was to see that the men "doe not loyter in the Taphouse." For the Company certainly allowed such a tap-house in their yard, which was "lycensed by the Companie from yeare to yeare" to certain persons on condition that they retailed the beer at not more than six shillings the barrel and not less than "three full pynts of Ale measure for a penny." The tap-house also sold to the workmen of the yard such victuals as bread, "pease," milk, porridge, eggs, butter, cheese, but they were not allowed to sell anything else, nor were they allowed to sell to any person other than one of the Company's workmen in the yard.

The whole of the work at the yard was subdivided under so many responsible heads of departments, just as it is to-day in any shipyard. The Master Shipwright's duties were to build and repair the Company's ships and to design the "plots and models compleat, of all the new ships." And he was forbidden to build ships for anyone else except this Company. It is significant of our modern system of extreme division of labour that the duties of ship-designer and ship-builder have become quite separate and distinct.

Then there was another important official attached to the Company, known as the "Master-pilot." "The Mr Pylot his office is to commaund and order the workes which concerne the setting up and taking downe of Masts, Yards, Rigging, unrigging and proportioning the quantities, sorts and sizes of Cordage to the Companies ships ... and to use care and diligence ... that the Company may not be ouercharged with idle, unskilfull, or a needlesse number of workmen, or in the rate of their wages." This same master-pilot had to survey the Company's ships at Deptford and Blackwall and to see that, after being launched, they were safely moored. He had also to see that the canvas given out was duly made into sails, and was further responsible that the Company's ships set forth up to time from Deptford, Blackwall and Erith. In addition he took charge of them whilst in the Thames to "pylot downe the Companies ships to Eirth and Grauesend, attending them there untill they shall be dispatched into the Downes." So also when they came back from India he would pilot them up from Gravesend "untill they be safely moored at an Anchor, or indocked at Blackwall." This official was assisted in the supervision of cordage by a man called the "Boatswaine Generall."

The treasurers looked after the Company's accounts, and once a week they handed to the "Purcer-Generall" the sums of money for paying the wages of the sailors and labourers: also the "harbour wages" to "officers and Maryners, who goe the Voyage." Every ship of course also carried its own "purcer," who with their mates had to look after the lading, the ship's accounts and the conditions of the victuals on board, etc.

After the end of the day's work the Clerk of the Works would go round the yard to see that there was no risk of fire breaking out owing to negligence in respect of the pitch cauldrons or other instances. The yard boasted of a "porter of the lodge," and as soon as the workmen had done for the day watchmen came on duty in the yard, where they remained until the bell rang next morning summoning the labourers back to their work. The Company insisted on these watchmen doing their supervision thoroughly, "often calling one to another to prevent sleepe, and euery houre when the clocke strikes" they were bidden to "walke round" and ring a bell in the yard.

The "Clarke of the Cordage" looked after the ropes, marlin, "twyne," ordnance, "great shot," pulleys, blocks and the like. The "Clarke of the Iron Works" was similarly responsible for all the anchors, nails, bolts, chain-plates, and so on, and had to look to these when the ships came home from the East. He was further responsible for the lead and copper. If an anchor or anything had to be made or repaired in this metal it was done by the Company's smith on the yard.

The "Chirurgion Generall" and his deputy had their lodgings in the yard, and one or the other was bound to be in attendance daily from morning till night "to cure any person or persons who may be hurt in the Service of this Company, and the like in all their ships riding at an anchor at Deptford and Blackwall, and at Erith, where hee shall also keepe a Deputy with his Chest furnished, to remaine there continually, until all the said ships be sayled downe from thence to Grauesend." And it is amusing to read that the duties of the "chirurgion" included that of cutting the "hayre of the carpenters, saylors, caulkers, labourers" and other workmen once every forty days "in a seemely manner, performing their works at Breakfast and Dinner times, or in raynie weather, and in an open place where no man may loyter or lye hidden, under pretence to attend his turne of trimming." In addition this same surgeon had to report all persons who seemed to be decrepit or unfit: and every carpenter, sailor, labourer or workman in the yards or ships had to pay twopence every month out of his wages to the said "Chirurgion Generall"; so you may take it as certain that he was not the most popular of beings. He was also compelled to find "skilfull and honest chirurgions and their Mates" for the ships. The Company took special precautions to see that these vessels set out with all the medical comforts and supplies of those days, having regard to the changing climates and the heavy losses of life through scurvy and dysentery (or flux). Thus these medicine-chests had to be brought into the Company's house fourteen days before the ships sailed, so that the doctors and apothecaries and other people appointed by the Committee dealing with this subject might make a full inspection.

In addition to the officials on the Thames there was also a "Keeper of Anchors and Stores in the Downes," at Deal, who looked after the cables, hawsers, anchors and ships' boats sent to the Downs, so that whenever any of the Company's ships arrived there lacking any of these articles they could always be supplied. At Deptford yard there was every single trade represented that was employed in the construction and fitting out of a seventeenth-century ship. There were coopers and boatmakers and the carvers who deftly gave those fantastic decorations to the ships' hulls. There were smiths and painters and riggers, but in addition to the large staff which were concerned with the ships themselves, there was another staff who had to look after the providing of the salt meat for the voyages. For the Company was determined to keep the profit of victuals to itself. This department was under the management of the "Clerk of the Slaughter-house," his duties being to look after the killing, salting, pickling and packing of the "beefes and hogges." This salt beef and pork comprised the main food of these sailormen to the Far East and back. They had no vegetables except dried peas and beans, no bread other than mouldy ship's biscuit, and no fruit.

The Company included a "Committee for Entertaining of Marriners," and they were on the look-out for "able men, unmarryed and approved saylors." Many of these fellows were of the reckless, dare-devil type, coarse of morals and frequently drunk when ashore: yet heroic in a crisis, imprudent, contemptuous of danger, brutal and unruly. Many a young man—sailor and factor alike—was sent in these ships in order that he might be got out of the way after disgracing his family: and numbers of them never again set foot in England. If the seamen who were shipped happened to be married, the "Clarke of the Imprest" paid the wages allowed to their wives whilst the men were at sea. This official was also bound to pay the wages to the "marriners which shall returne home in the Companies ships, or to their Assignes."

India House—the Sale room.

(By courtesy of Messrs. T. H. Parker Brothers)

After the masters and their mates of the respective ships had been hired for a voyage, their names were entered under the list of harbour-wages, and they took their oaths openly in the Court of the Committees of the Company. After this they sought able and good mariners "whom they shall preferre for entertainment unto the Committees appointed to that businesse." These masters were bound to sleep on board the ships to which they had just been appointed, every night, and there keep good order. They were also to appoint quartermasters and boatswains, who were to see that the victuals, provisions, stores and merchandise were properly stowed. The boatswain, gunner, cook, steward, carpenter and other officers were each responsible for their own special stores.

Within ten days after the arrival of their ship in the Thames from India the master was bound to deliver to the Governor of the Company four copies of his journal and other "worthy observations" of his voyage. When the ship was bound out the master was always to be on board and to assist the master-pilot. When the ship returned home, a Committee of the Company for the Discharge of the Ships was always present on board in order to see the hold opened. This was to prevent theft. The goods were then placed in lighters and one of the Company's "trusty servants" then went in the latter to watch that no embezzlement occurred. The goods were then taken to Leadenhall, where they were sold. "The custome hath been used heretofore [*i.e.* prior to 1621] in selling the wares of this Company at a Generall Court, and the Remnants of small value in the Warehouses by the light of a candle," and this custom was continued. Selling by the "light of a candle" was as follows:—The article was put up for auction, a small piece of candle burning the while. So long as that piece of candle was there the bids could go on, but as soon as it burned out the last bid was completed and no more could be made for that commodity.

Before the crew put to sea, two months' wages were allowed ahead, and "gratifications" were also paid "unto worthy and well deserving persons." In these ships there went out also the merchants, factors and supercargoes. Some, as we have already seen, founded factories where they landed and circumstances permitted: but later on there were factors resident in every port, just as each steamship company to-day has its own agents wherever the ships touch.

The Deptford yard, which the Company leased from the year 1607 and used for the next twenty years, was of the greatest assistance to the Company. The best merchant ships in the country there came into being, were fitted out, repaired on their return, resheathed and then sent to sea in excellent condition. It was true that the saving in building for themselves was to the Company's great benefit; but, on the other hand, the yard with all this staff and detail was found in the long run to be so costly that it swallowed up too much of the capital, which could more profitably have been employed in hiring ships. It was seen also that even with the carefulness expended in the construction of the Company's ships, the latter became worn out after four voyages: so at the end of twenty years it was decided to give up this expensive yard and to revert to the original custom of hiring vessels as required. Later on we shall see that this system developed in a curious manner, but for the present we must go back to see the progress which the voyages of these early East Indiamen brought about in the Eastern trade. It took four months to fit out these ships for sailing again to the East, and the refit was very thorough. A large magazine of warlike stores to the value of £30,000 was kept always ready, and this was really a very useful asset in the country, since in the time of necessity the material could be used by the English navy. Even in the year 1626, within a few months of the closing down of the shipyard, the Company were so enterprising as to erect mills and houses for the manufacture of their own gunpowder, obtaining the saltpetre from the East, which of course came home in their own ships. If ever monopoly was allowed to have its own way, surely it never had such good opportunity as was vouchsafed to the East India Company, with its own shipyards, victualling, and its own particular trade with full cargoes each way and a high percentage almost assured. We are accustomed in this twentieth century to bewail the existence of "corners" and trusts: yet these are as nothing compared with the privileges which the East India Company enjoyed and so jealously guarded through generation after generation, through two centuries and well into a third. And that meant more than was really apparent. The whole world had not been developed and opened out as it is to-day. Rather this exclusive privilege meant the granting of about half the world to a select few, and the democratic spirit of the twentieth century would instantly revolt against any such condition of affairs. It must not be thought that there were not those who protested even in the seventeenth century. Some did certainly protest—in a very forcible manner—by cutting in as interlopers. But it was a short-lived victory and had no lasting effect.

CHAPTER VIII

PERILS AND ADVENTURES

It is only by examining the official correspondence which passed between the Company's servants and themselves that we are able to get a correct insight into the lesser, though usually more human, details connected with these ships. In the last chapter but one we saw that the third voyage had been financially satisfactory. But there are a few sidelights which show that these voyages were not mere pleasure cruises. If this particular one earned 234 per cent. it was by sheer hard work on the part of the men and of the ships. Captain Keeling writes that he had, whilst in the East, to buy "of the Dutch a maine top-sayle (whereof we had extreame want) and delivered them a note to the Company, to receive twelve pounds twelve shillings for the same." So also it was with men as with sails. Anthony Marlowe writes home to the Governor of the Company, under date of 22nd June 1608, from on board the *Hector*, that during the voyage "there hath died in our ship two foremast men—Wallis and Palline: and two lost overboard, Goodman and Jones: also there hath died Dryhurst, steward's mate, John Newcome, John Asshenhurst, purser's mate, Mr Quaytmore, purser, and Mr Clarke, merchant."

If there was ill-feeling ashore between the English and the Portuguese, and the English and Dutch, so all was not ever as happy as wedding bells in the English ships. One June day in 1608, during this third voyage, a violent enmity had broken out between Anthony Hippon, master of the *Dragon*, and his mate, William Tavernour. Someone endeavoured to get them to make up their quarrel, but Hippon was obdurate, and "was heartened forward in his malice against the said Tavernour by Matthew Mullynex the master of the *Hector*."

And there is a further letter, dated 4th December 1608, which was sent by another of the Company's servants named James Hearne, which again calls attention to the *Dragon's* want of sails, the ship then being at Bantam. There was no canvas procurable out there, "therefore," he suggests, "one hundred pound more or less, would not be lost in laying it out in spare canvas in such a voyage as this." And then he concludes his letter with a postscript, which shows that the life of a factor in the Company's service ashore out in the East was not a lucrative occupation. "That it may please your worships," he petitions, "to consider me somewhat in my wages, for I have served 2 years already at £4 a month, and in this place I am in, my charge will be greater than otherwise."

We have already alluded to the setting forth of the sixth expedition under Sir Henry Middleton in 1607. Middleton was instructed to proceed to the west coast of

India with the intention of obtaining from Surat Indian calicoes which would find a ready sale at Bantam and the Moluccas. Having set forth from England in the year 1610, he arrived at Aden, where he left the *Peppercorn,* and then with his flag in the *Trade's Increase* sailed for Mocha, which is at the southern end of the Red Sea. No English vessel had yet thrust her bows into this sea, though the Portuguese had been there even during the previous century. And here the *Trade's Increase,* which had received such an ovation when she was first launched at the Deptford yard, was to begin the first of her serious mishaps. Like many another ship that came after her, famous for unprecedented size, she was destined to be unlucky.

She was making for Mocha with the assistance of native pilots when she had the misfortune to get badly aground. She was a clumsy, unhandy ship, and it was natural enough that the natives who had been accustomed only to their smaller craft might get her into trouble. The incident occurred in November 1610, and the following account sent home by one who was on board her at the time may be taken as representative of the facts. "About five a clocke," runs the account, "in luffing in beeing much wind, we split our maine toppe sayle, and putting abroad our mizen, it split likewise: our Pilots brought our shippe a ground upon a banke of sand, the wind blowing hard, and the Sea somewhat high, which made us all doubt her coming off ... we did what we could to lighten our ship, sending some goods a-land and some aboard the *Darling* ... we land as well our Wheat-meale, Vinegar, Sea-coles, Pitch and Tarre, with our unbuilt Pinnasse, and other provisions which came next hand, or in the way, as well as Tinne, Lead, Iron, and other merchandise to be sould, and staved neare all our water." The reference to the "unbuilt pinnasse" is explained by the fact that it was the custom of the Elizabethan and later voyagers to take out from home the necessary timber and planks and to build the little craft on board as they proceeded. This kept the men occupied and was a saving in wages, besides not involving the risk of losing such a craft before the end of the voyage was being approached. Such a top-heavy, cumbrous vessel as the *Trade's Increase* would need very careful "nursing" in a squall to prevent her from capsizing, and it is perfectly clear that the sudden luffing up into the wind to ease her was too much for the canvas that had already been considerably worn and chafed during the voyage across the Equator and round the Cape of Good Hope up to the Gulf of Aden.

After some anxious hours the ship was eventually got afloat again, but Middleton was taken prisoner by the Arabs. For a long while he was compelled to endure his captivity, but was eventually released and sailed for Surat, where he arrived with his ships on 26th September 1611, a great deal of valuable time having been lost. Here again he was unlucky, for a Portuguese squadron of seven ships was waiting outside. The Portuguese were now so indignant and jealous of the English interlopers that they were resolved to resist them to the utmost: otherwise it was obvious that the hard-won wealth of the East would before long slip right away. All the inspiration and enthusiasm of Prince Henry the Navigator, all the heroic voyages of the first Portuguese navigators to the East, all the capital which had been expended in building and fitting out their expensive caracks would assuredly be thrown into the sea unless the aggressive Englishmen, who had penetrated their secrets, were to be thwarted now with determination. The Portuguese were expecting Middleton's arrival, for they had already heard of his being in the Red Sea, and now they were in sufficient and overwhelming strength to oppose him: for besides the big ships outside, there were nearly twice as many smaller craft waiting inside the bar. The Portuguese contention was that they alone had the right to trade with Surat: the English were not wanted and had no justification to be there at all.

Middleton's position was that he had come out from the King of England bearing a letter and presents to the Great Mogul to put on a firm footing that trade which Englishmen had already inaugurated, and that India was open to all nations who wished to trade with her. But, of course, Middleton did not know at the time the incident which has already been mentioned in connection with Hawkins and the Great Mogul. When, however, the news presently reached him, it was to modify his plans entirely: there could be no good object attained in endeavouring to establish trade against the opposition of the Mogul and the Portuguese. The natives were clearly under the thumb of the Portuguese, and, however willing they might have been, no trade with them was possible.

So, after taking Hawkins on board, together with the Englishmen who had been left at Surat, a council was held and ultimately it was decided to return to the Red Sea so that he could there trade with the ships from India, since to deal with them in their own country was not practicable. This decision was carried out, and whether the traders liked it or not they were compelled to barter the goods which Middleton required to take farther eastwards to the Indian Archipelago as previously indicated. But meanwhile there had set out from England another expedition, consisting of the three ships *Clove*, *Thomas* and *Hector*, under the command of Captain Saris, bound for the Red Sea, having previously obtained a firman, or decree, from Constantinople which would grant him and his merchants kindly treatment in the neighbourhood of Mocha and Aden. But on arriving at Socotra, Saris found a letter from Middleton giving warning of the treacherous treatment to expect. In spite of this, however, Saris found that the firman was respected, but eventually deemed it prudent to make for the Straits of Bab-el-Mandeb, where he met Middleton and agreed with him to engage in privateering the ships of India. If you had questioned these English seamen they would have replied unhesitatingly that they were merely engaged in trade by barter, and that as they had been prevented by circumstances from carrying on this direct with the Indian continent they had no other opportunity than to do it at sea. They had been sent out by the English Company to get the cloths and calicoes to exchange farther east and they were merely fulfilling their instructions. But in plain language there was little difference between this and robbery, or, at the best, compulsory sale at the buyer's own price.

The Honourable East India Company's ship "Bridgewater" entering Madras roads under Jury-Rig after encountering Gales of Wind.

(By courtesy of Messrs. T. H. Parker Brothers)

But when all this "trading" was finished and the *Trade's Increase* went to Malay Archipelago, she was to bring to a tragic end her short and adventurous career. Middleton had gone ahead in the *Peppercorn,* and the *Trade's Increase* had been ordered to follow after. Unfortunately she needed some repairs to her hull. It was customary before an East Indiaman left the East on her homeward voyage for the sheathing outside to be attended to, in order that she might make as fast a passage home as possible. But there were no dry docks out there, and very few anywhere, even in England or Holland. The practice, which lasted well into the nineteenth century, was to careen a ship if she required any attention below the water-line—her seams caulked, or her bottom tarred. This was done in the case of the *Trade's Increase* whilst she was at Bantam, where her sheathing was being seen to. But she fell over on to her side and became a total loss. One contemporary account states that whilst the repairs were being done "all her men died in the careening of her," and that then some Javanese were hired to do the job, but five hundred of these "died in the worke before they could sheath one side: so that they could hire no more men, and therefore were inforced to leave her imperfect, where shee was sunke in the Sea, and after set on fire by the Javans." This was towards the end of the year 1613. Another contemporary account states that she was laid up in the ooze, and was set on fire from stem to stern, having been previously fired twice, at the supposed instigation of a renegade Spaniard, "which is turned Moor." She blazed away during the whole of one night, and her wreck was eventually sold for 1050 reales. When Sir Henry Middleton heard the news of the loss of his famous flagship, the pride of all the seas, he was so heart-broken that he died. Thus both admiral and flagship had perished: it had been a calamitous voyage.

As for Captain Saris, he had sailed to Japan in order to establish a factory. Notwithstanding the opposition of the Dutch, who were as jealous of his arrival in the Far East as the Portuguese had been in India, the Emperor received him favourably and the seeds were sown for future trade with England which, to change the metaphor, were to prepare the way for the adoption of Western ideas by the Japanese during the nineteenth and the twentieth centuries. Strictly speaking, Japan and China have nothing to do with India. But historically, so far as our present subject is concerned, they are to an extent bound together. Not merely did these first captains of the English East India Company sail thither, but, as the reader will see further on in this volume, a great deal of trade was done with those parts by the Company's servants: and at least one interesting engagement took place on sea near by, in which the Company's merchant ships distinguished themselves.

Notwithstanding the sad loss of the costly *Trade's Increase,* Middleton's voyage had yielded to the Company a profit of 121 per cent. Captain Saris's voyage had done even better still, earning 218 per cent.; but, as we have shown, this was not all earned by legitimate trade.

The journal of Captain Nicholas Downton of the homeward voyage of the *Peppercorn* (which you will remember had been built at the Deptford yard and went out in company with the *Trade's Increase*) shows the kind of hardships which our sailors had to endure whilst earning such handsome profits for their owners. With thankful hearts this craft started back from Bantam, though it was to be no pleasant voyage. On getting under way Downton saluted the admiral by way of farewell. "I gave him 5 shot," he writes, "having no more pieces out nor ports uncaulked"—that is to say, he had prepared his ship for sea, having run inboard most of his guns and caulked up the ports. The ship had previously had her sheathing attended to, and all the stores were aboard. The meat was kept in casks, while the bread and corn were kept in a "tight room" in order to avoid the ravages of the cacara—"a most devouring worm," as Downton quaintly calls it, "with which this ship doth abound to our great disturbance." The drinking-water to the extent of twenty-six tons had also been brought aboard, where it was kept in casks. But as these were decayed, weak, rotten and leaky the crew were bound to suffer before they reached home. He did his best to make her what he calls "a pridie ship"—that is, a trim ship—but though this was her first homeward voyage she leaked like a basket through the trenail holes in the stern, owing to the negligence of the wicked Deptford carpenters, who had scamped their work. The result was that there were soon twenty inches of water "on our lower orlop." Certainly the Company's yard had not earned much real credit for the way they had designed and built the *Peppercorn* and the *Trade's Increase*.

And so this leaky, crank, badly built ship came fighting her way along over the trackless ocean, a continuous source of anxiety to her commander. Troubles often enough come not singly, and the *Peppercorn* was another unlucky ship. By sheer carelessness she and all hands barely escaped ending all things by fire at sea. "At noon," says Downton, "our ship came afire by the cook his negligence, o'erguzzled with drink, digged a hole through the brick back of the furnace and gave the fire passage to the ship's side, which led to much trouble besides spoil to our ship." The punctuation of this sentence needs no modification to show the short, sharp impressions jotted down by a choleric captain. The name of this "o'erguzzled" cook was Richard Hancock, and no doubt he had so undermined his health with drink, or had been so severely punished by his commander that he could not long survive, for he died shortly after one day at noon and was buried at sea.

But he was not the only careless member of the ship's company. At least one of the watch-keeping officers was just as bad in his own sphere. "The 27th at 2 after noon we were suddenly taken short with a gust from the SE, which by neglect of the principal of the watch not setting in time, not only put us to much present trouble but also split us two topsails at once, and blew a third clean away." The following month on the eleventh the *Peppercorn* was at midnight overwhelmed by heavy squalls which "split our main bonnet and fore course, whereby we were forced to lie a try with mainsail, the sea very violent, we mending our sail."

The meaning of this may not be quite apparent to those unfamiliar with the ships of those days. The "bonnet" was an additional piece of canvas laced on to the foot of these square-sails. It had been long in use by the ships of the Vikings and the English craft of the Middle Ages, and continued to be used during the Tudor period and the seventeenth century. Even in the twentieth century it is not quite obsolete, and is still used on the Norfolk wherries and on some of the North Sea fishing vessels. It was such a canvas as certainly ought to have been taken in quickly if the *Peppercorn* was likely to be struck by a heavy squall, being essentially a fine-weather addition. And whenever it was unlaced the equivalent was obtained of putting a reef in the sail. To "lie a try" was a well-known expression used by the Elizabethan seamen and their successors: it meant simply what we mean to-day when we speak of heaving-to. The ship would just forge ahead very slowly under her mainsail only, being under command but making good weather of the violent sea of which Downton speaks, and allowing most of the hands to get busy with the sails, which had to be sent down and repaired.

They had barely begun to resume their voyage when, on the thirteenth of the month, the *Peppercorn* broke her main truss—that is to say, the rope which kept the yard of the mainsail at its centre to the mast. The main halyards also carried away and again the main bonnet was split, but this time the mainsail as well. The "main course," says Downton, "rent out of the bolt rope"—that is to say, blew right away from the rope to which it is sewn—and so they were, owing to "want of fit sail to carry, forced to lie a hull," which means that they had to heave-to again. Meanwhile the *Peppercorn* was still leaking away merrily. "This day again," reads an entry in the journal a little later on, "by the labouring of the ship and beating of her bows in a head sea, whereby we found in the powder room in the fore part on the lower orlop, 20 or 24 inches water, which have so spoiled, wet and stained divers barrels, so that of 20 barrels of powder I do not now expect to find serviceable 2 barrels, besides all our match and divers other things." It would therefore have gone ill with the *Peppercorn* if she had fallen in with a big, powerful Spanish ship on the high seas ready to blaze away at her.

It took thirty-six hours to get these sails repaired and new ropes spliced. This mending became in fact the rule rather than the exception. "Our daily employment either mending of our poor old sails daily broken, or making new with such poor stuff as we have." There can be no doubt whatever that these ships were sent to sea with all too few stores to allow of accident. We have already seen that additional canvas could not be obtained in the East, except with the indulgence of some Dutch captain, who would naturally charge the English the full value of a new sail, and a bit more. One wonders, indeed, how often those London merchants realised how dearly these big percentages had been bought—how only the dogged determination of the captains and masters, the sufferings of the crews in the leaky, ill-found ships could provide fortunes and luxuries for those who stayed at home in ease. However, little though they knew it at the time, it was these ill-faring mariners who were really building up the foundations of England's Eastern wealth and her Eastern Empire. Human lives in those harsh days were rated low enough, and a poor, common sailor was not slobbered over. He was merely one of the meshes of the big net cast into the sea to bring in large spoil to the financiers of that time. But it has always been thus, and the more long-suffering the seaman has shown himself, the more courageous and patient he has been, the more he has been treated with contumely by those very persons who have obtained all that they possess through his achievements.

The "Halsewell," East Indiaman.

(By courtesy of Messrs. T. H. Parker Brothers)

It cannot be supposed that these seventeenth-century Indiamen were on the whole happy ships. The captains feared mutiny all the time, and the men were compelled to live and work under trying conditions which were enough to break the spirit of any landsman. Downton's journal shows this all too well. Take the following entries, which are sufficiently expressive:—

"July 2. Mr Abraham Lawes conceives he is poisoned for that his stomach falls away, and he hath often inclination to vomit, for he saith he was so at Venice, when he was formerly poisoned."

Three days later Thomas Browning died, and on 27th July comes this entry:

"This day Mr Lawes died and is opened by the surgeon who took good note of his inward parts which was set down by the surgeon and divers witnesses to that note." Similarly on 21st August: "Men daily fall down into great weakness"; and, again, four days later: "Edw. Watts, carpenter, died at midnight." Under the twenty-ninth of the same month we find the following entry:—"Stormy weather, dry, the night past Thomas Dickorie died. Most of my people in a weak estate." The last day of the month we read that "John Ashbe died by an imposthume at 7 o'clock after noon," and other members of the ship's company continued to die almost daily. An "imposthume," by the way, is an abscess.

But the *Peppercorn*, though she had long since crossed the line, and was even now beyond the Bay of Biscay, was destined to suffer ill luck right to the end of her voyage. She ought, of course, to have rounded Ushant and then squared away up the English Channel. But as a fact Downton got right out of his reckoning. He rather imagined that his reckoning was wrong and suspected "all the instruments by which we observed the variation by." The result was that he got farther to the north than he expected. He therefore ran right across the western mouth of the English Channel without sighting anything, so that eventually he found himself between Wales and Ireland—miles and miles out of his course. All too late he realised the mistake, so determined to put in to the nearest port. He thought of Milford, but as the *Peppercorn* would not fetch thither, he decided to run for Waterford in Ireland. He ran down to the coast, but when off the entrance a thick fog enshrouded the land, so he had to put out to sea once more, being able eventually to run into Waterford river when a more favourable opportunity presented itself. He had got his ship safe back into the Narrow Seas, but he had arrived a long way short of the River Thames and the port of London, and it would mean the wasting of further delay before the *Peppercorn's* rich cargo could be sold in the metropolis. But with what success this voyage concluded to the stock-holders we have already seen.

Apropos of this voyage there is still preserved a letter written by Downton "aboard the *Peppercorn* to the Right Worshipful the Indian Company in Philpot Lane, September 15, 1613," in which this captain asks for "3 cables and other cordage of divers sizes, a set of sails, sail needles and twine, and some Hamburrough lines for sounding lines." With regard to the bad land-fall which Downton made coming home, there can be no doubt that he had reason to suspect those crude, inaccurate navigation instruments to which we have already called attention. In addition, of course, the early seventeenth-century charts bristled with errors. As for Eastern waters, the English skippers were much indebted to the charts which the Dutchmen had made for themselves, the Dutch at this time being the best cartographers in the world. There is at least one instance of a navigator of one of the English East India Company's ships "finding it to be truely laid down in Plat or Draught made by Jan Janson Mole, a Hollander, which he gave to Master Hippon, and he to the Companie." To this knowledge received by the Company were added the "plots" (*i.e.* charts) which their own masters of ships brought home at the end of every voyage, amended and added to as their experience dictated. We have already seen that it was compulsory for the master of every East Indiaman to deliver to the Governor of the English East India Company four copies of his journal and other "worthy" observations of his voyage within ten days of his arrival back in the Thames. The information thus derived was systematised, and as time went on and the voyages became more numerous still there was thus accumulated a number of invaluable sailing directions which were to be condensed into "Rules for our East India Navigations" by the famous John Davis of Limehouse, who had himself made no less than five voyages. The East India Company thus not only built its own ships at its own dockyard, victualled them from its own stores, but conducted its own hydrography department. It was therefore positively unique in its monopolies and self-dependence. England has never had any corporation like it: and it is pretty certain it never will.

CHAPTER IX

SHIPS AND TRADE

We alluded on an earlier page to what were known as "separate" voyages. In the year 1612 the owners of the different stocks joined together and made one common capital of £740,000. Until that year the custom had been for a number of men to subscribe together for one particular voyage out and home. This was found by no means satisfactory, for it meant there was too much rivalry and no co-operation. Before one voyage was completed another would be sent out, and it happened that out in the East several agents in their zeal to obtain cargoes for their ships would be found bidding against each other, to the great advantage of the natives and the loss of the English stock-holders. Then, again, it would also happen that the ship of one particular voyage might be lying empty at some Indian port waiting till her factor had obtained the spices and other goods destined for England. Meanwhile the factor of a second voyage had *his* goods ready but no ship in which to send them home. Each "voyage" was thus a separate and distinct concern, declining to have anything to do with any other "voyage," or group of adventurers. When, therefore, this practice came to an end, the union made for strength and did away with the ill feeling and waste of energy till then so noticeable. The first joint stock began in the year 1613 and ended in 1617.

During this period twenty-nine ships of the Company were employed, and by the end of the year 1617 eight had returned with cargoes, four had been either lost or broken up, two had fallen into the hands of the Dutch, and fifteen were still in the East Indies. When the new stock was undertaken, most of these ships still in India were taken over at valuation. The biggest East Indiaman craft at this time were the *Royal James*, of 1000 tons; the *Anne Royal*, of 900 tons; and *The New Year's Gift*, of 800 tons.

The Master Hippon, of whom we made mention in the last chapter, had command of the *Globe*, which set forth from England alone and made direct for the Coromandel coast (the south-east portion of India). He called neither at the Red Sea, the Nicobars, nor the East Indian Archipelago. His mission was to inaugurate a new sphere of trade, and in so doing he was laying the foundations of those rich commercial centres of Madras and Calcutta. His work was not easy, for the Dutch would not allow him to operate in their neighbourhood, but he left a little band of men near Masulipatam to found a factory, and then went on to establish other factories in the Malay Peninsula and Siam. In the year 1612 Captain Best had obtained from the Court of Delhi considerable privileges, including that of establishing a factory at Surat. This was to become the chief English station in India until the acquisition of Bombay. In establishing these factories, the English were but copying the example of the Portuguese and Dutch. They were essential as depots for the goods brought from home and the commodities which had been obtained from the natives, and were awaiting the arrival of the Company's ships. In charge of these factories were the Company's agents and their clerks. But it is well to bear in mind that these factories and factors were destined to undergo development. As a measure of precaution the former were in the course of time strengthened, and at a still later stage they became even forts, so that the agents and clerks developed into a garrison. And from a strictly defensive policy a more aggressive influence occurred which resulted in acquisition of territory as well as trading rights.

Captain Best had sailed from Gravesend on 1st February 1612, with the *Red Dragon* and the *Hoseander,* and arrived in the Swally, the roadstead for Surat, on 5th September. Here also were the Portuguese fleet a few weeks later ready to thwart the English, but Best was ready for them, and eventually hostilities were inevitable. But Best had the true English spirit in him, and besides being an excellent leader of a trading expedition, he was also no mean tactician, taking advantage of tide and the proximity of sandy shoals. The result was that the English were victorious and the Portuguese admiral defeated. But this meant something more than was immediately apparent. In a word it was to have a considerable influence on the future Anglo-Indian trade, and so give a still greater demand for the Indian merchant ships. In order properly to realise the position, you have to think of a weak man over-awed by a giant. Another giant comes along and asks the weak man for certain favours. The latter replies that he would be willing to make the concessions if the second giant could conquer the first, for whom the weak man has no real love. In the present instance the first giant is represented by the Portuguese, the weak man is the Great Mogul, and the second giant the English. The latter had been thwarted from trading with Surat by the Portuguese. What the Mogul had said amounted to this: "Defeat the Portuguese and I will give you and yours every opportunity to trade in my dominions: your merchants shall not be molested, the customs imposed shall be as light as possible, and if there is any delinquency by which my people shall in any way injure your men, I will see that the matter is soon set right and redress given. Your country shall be allowed to send its ambassador and reside at my Court—but you must first exhibit your strength by conquering the hated Portuguese."

So Best's victory succeeded as only success can. The mighty power of the Portuguese was now broken like a reed. They had been defeated on sea who prided themselves on sea-power. They had lost their prestige with the natives, who had had the first Europeans in awe. The whole of the Portuguese Indian system, which had amounted to piracy, oppression and native ruin, had been, in the words of India's great modern historian, Sir Wm. Wilson Hunter, "rotten to the core." It was now to receive its death-blow, and a new order of things was to follow. Instead of the previous opposition, the English were now allowed to open their trade and to start factories both at Surat and elsewhere, and the English East India Company obtained a most firm footing—not as interlopers doing the best they could against Portuguese vigilance, but recognised by the Great Mogul as an important and powerful trading corporation. It was after these concessions had been made and various factories set up that the latter needed obvious protection both from the Portuguese and the pirates who were greatly harassing the trading ships. Thus on land the nucleus was formed of an Indian army: thus afloat the nucleus also was formed of the Bombay Marine, afterwards to be known as the Indian navy.

For the latter the Company's Surat agent was compelled to do the best with local material, collecting native craft called grabs and gallivats and commanded by officers who volunteered from the Company's merchant ships. As these craft, like all other local craft, were the most suitable for the conditions of the place, the Company was well able to patrol the Gulf of Cambay and protect the vessels loaded with merchandise. This Indian marine had come into being during the year 1613, and two years later consisted of ten local craft. In the same year arrived from England four of the Company's ships, under Captain Keeling, with Sir Thomas Roe, who had been sent by James I. as ambassador to the Great Mogul, and the treaty with the latter was ratified.

So the voyages continued to be made between England and the East. There was still opposition on the part of the Dutch, who would occasionally seize the Company's ships, and in the year 1623 this opposition reached its crisis in the notorious Massacre of Amboyna, when the English Company's agent and nine more Englishmen were executed on a trivial charge. Nor were the Portuguese ships swept from the Eastern seas. The sea-power was broken, but it still existed in its weakly condition, and nothing gave the English seamen greater pleasure than to meet any of their big caracks in the Indian Ocean or elsewhere and attack them. But the factors who had been installed at Surat were in no way deficient in enterprise. They were doing an excellent trade, not merely between England and India, but between India and Bantam. This was not enough: they were determined to open up commerce with the Persian Gulf.

Now this meant that trouble was inevitable. If the Portuguese had lost their hold on India, they were certainly just as strong as formerly at Ormuz and other parts of the Persian Gulf. To traffic, or to attempt to traffic, with this part of the Orient was certain to mean further conflict with the nation which had received so much injury from Captain Best. For most of a hundred years the Portuguese had been enjoying their monopoly up the Gulf. However, neither this nor the certainty of conflict could turn aside the ambition of the English East India Company. Their ships were sent from Surat with Indian goods, the Portuguese vessels opposed them, the victory went to the English, and thus once more, as it had been in the territory of the Great Mogul, so the result was to be in regard to the Persian trade. The natives realised that the English were worth listening to, and their prestige was raised to the height from which the Portuguese simultaneously dropped. Henceforth the English factors could bring from Surat their calicoes and take back silks. A little later Ormuz was destroyed—Ormuz which had been the seat of Portuguese supremacy in the Persian Gulf and the centre of its wealthy trade in that region—and thus once more the nation which had been the first of European countries to unlock the secrets of the East was told to quit. By the year 1622—a short enough period since the inauguration of the East India Company in

London—the Portuguese had thus been driven out from those very places in the East which had been so dear to them and the means of so much wealth. By the year 1654 they had been compelled to agree that the English should have the right to reside and trade in all these Eastern possessions. It was a terrible blow to Portuguese pride, a grievous disappointment to a nation which had done so much for the discovery of the world, and enough to make Prince Henry the Navigator turn in his grave. But it was inevitable, for the reason that as the Portuguese had declined in sea-power, so the English had been rising ever since the mid-sixteenth century, though more especially during the latter half of Elizabeth's reign. The call of the sea to English ears was being listened to more attentively than ever, and when that call summoned men to such profitable trade it continued to be heard through the centuries. Each success added zest and gave an increased enthusiasm. Men who wanted to see the world, or to increase their meagre incomes, or to get away from the narrow confines of their own town or village were eager to take their oath to the Company and go East, where a more adventurous life awaited them. But with the Portuguese it was not so. Most of their Latin enthusiasm had run out: they had begun well, but they had been unable to sustain. And the series of blows—the capture of their finest caracks, the revelation of their East Indian secrets, the colossal defeat of the Armada, the persistent and successful impertinence of English interlopers in India, the glaring proof that English seamanship, navigation, naval strategy, tactics and gunnery were as good as their own—this succession of hard facts tended to break their spirit, made them compelled to bow to the inevitable. *Sic transit gloria mundi.*

Between the years 1617 and 1629 the English East India Company had sent out no fewer than 57 ships, containing 26,690 tons of merchandise. In addition they employed eighteen pinnaces which spent their time trading from port to port in the East Indies. We have already alluded to the inception of the Indian navy by the Surat factory. As time went on this flotilla of local craft was strengthened by big ships sent out from England. But as this volume is not a history of either the East India Company or of the development of the Indian navy, we must confine our attention to the story of the Company's merchant ships during the many years in which they existed with such marvellous and unprecedented benefit to India and the English nation. Those who are interested merely in the rise of the Indian navy will find the account in Captain Low's volumes.

Now covetousness is a sin which is peculiar not merely to individuals, but to corporations and even nations. You may be sure that all this success on the part of the East India Company's ships and of their trading ashore led to no small amount of jealousy and longing at home. It is true that the State had assisted and encouraged the Company in every way: for it was obvious that it was for the nation's welfare generally, and in particular a fine support for the navy in respect of ships, men and stores. But the time arrived when the Company began to be pinched and squeezed by the power that hitherto had given only assistance. Covetousness was at the bottom of it all, but the actual opportunity had arisen over the capture of Ormuz, from which, it had been reported, a large amount of spoil had been taken. It was easy enough to invent some excuse, and this came in the year 1624 when the Company, understanding that the Portuguese were preparing a fleet against them in Indian waters, began to get ready a squadron of seven ships to leave England. When these ships were ready to sail, the Lord High Admiral of England, who happened to be the Duke of Buckingham, obtained from Parliament an order to lay an embargo on these ships, lying at Tilbury. A claim was made for a portion of the spoil supposed to have been taken at Ormuz and elsewhere. And in spite of protests the sum of £10,000 had to be paid before the ships were released. About this time, also, the Company were attacked in Parliament on three grounds: (1) For exporting the treasure of the kingdom, it being alleged that £80,000 had been sent out yearly in money: (2) For destroying the invaluable timber of the country by building exceedingly great ships, the timber being wanted for the navy: (3) For causing the supply of mariners to become injured by these voyages. The last item was certainly unreasonable: for, as a fact, about one-third, or sometimes one-half, of every ship's complement consisted of landsmen, who went on board "green" to sea life. But as happens over and over again, even in our luxurious times, many a green-horn discovers after a while that the life of a seaman is just what really suits him: and it was so with these landsmen to a large extent. The service opened up a new career for them, and these fellows were to add to rather than diminish the country's supply of sailors.

The ships were getting slightly more habitable and better built, though no very great change was taking place. How unseaworthy were some of the Company's best vessels may be seen from a letter sent on 10th June 1614 by Robert Larkin, who murmurs bitterly of his craft, the *Darling*. "The *Darling*," he writes, "complaineth sore, but I hope to God she will carry us well to Puttam, and further tediousness I omit. But I wish to God I were well rid of my captainship, or the *Darling* a sounder vessel to carry me in." So also that big East Indiaman, the *Royal James*, during the year 1617 sprang a serious leak, and the way in which this was stopped makes most interesting reading to all lovers of ships. Her commander at that time, Captain Martin Pring, wrote to the Company on the 12th of November of the year mentioned that about a fortnight before the *Royal James* had reached Swally—the port of Surat—"we had a great leak broke upon us in the *James*, which in four hours increased six foot water in hold, and after we had freed it and made the pumps suck, it would rise thirteen inches in half-an-hour. It was a great blessing of God that it fell out in such weather, by which means we had the help of all the fleet, otherwise all our company had been tired in a very short time. The 9th, we made many trials with a bonnet stitched with oakum under the bulge of the ship, but it did no good. The 11th, we basted our spritsail with oakum and let it down before the stem of the ship and so brought it aft by degrees: in which action it pleased God so to direct us that we brought the sail right under the place where the oakum was presently sucked into the leak: which stopped it in such sort that the ship made less water the day following than she had done any day before from the time of our departure out of England."

The device here employed was well known to the old-fashioned sailor, and designated "fothering." Briefly the idea was as follows. In order to stop the leak a sail was fastened at the four corners and then let down under the ship's bottom, a quantity of chopped rope-yarns, oakum, cotton, wool—anything in the least serviceable for the job—being also put in. If you were lucky you would find that after the first few attempts the leak would have sucked up some of the oakum or whatever was put into the sail, and so the water would not pour in as badly. This device certainly saved Captain Cook during one of his voyages after his ship had struck a rock and the sea poured in so quickly that the pumps were unable to cope with it. In the description given above by Captain Pring you will notice that he used his spritsail for this purpose. This was a quadrilateral sail set at the end of the bowsprit, but was abolished from East Indiamen and other ships in the early part of the nineteenth century. At first, you will observe, the bonnet—doubtless the bonnet of the mainsail—the use of which we described on an earlier page, was tried and lowered under the "bulge" (or, as we now say, the "bilge") of the ship. "Stitched with oakum" means that the little tufts of oakum were lightly stitched to the canvas just to keep them in position until the suction of the leak drew them up the hole away from the canvas. When he says he "basted" the spritsail with oakum he means again that the latter was sewn with light stitches. This spritsail was lowered down at the bows till it got below the ship's forefoot and then brought gradually aft till the position of the leak was reached, and then the oakum was sucked up with the happy result noted. This all reads much simpler than it was in actuality: and you can imagine that it was no easy matter getting this sail into its exact position while the ship was plunging and rolling in a seaway.

Eventually the *Royal James* got over the bar at Swally, and a consultation was then held aboard her by Captain Pring and a number of other captains as to what had now best be done. One opinion was to careen her so as to get at the leak and caulk it. Another opinion was to "bring her aground for the speedy stopping of her dangerous leak." But these captains had before their minds the recollection that the *Trade's Increase* had been lost whilst being careened, and another ship named the *Hector* likewise: so they unanimously agreed that the best thing would be to put the *Royal James* ashore, first taking out of her the merchandise. They were more than a little nervous as to how this big ship would take the ground, so "for a trial" they brought ashore the *Francis*, an interloping vessel which they had captured. When it was seen that the *Francis* seemed to take the ground all right and that she lay there three tides without apparent injury "and never complained in any part," they put the *Royal James* ashore also. Unluckily this was not with the same amount of success, "for she strained very much about the midship and made her bends to droop: which caused us to haul her off again so soon that we had not time to find the leak. Yet (God be praised) since we came afloat her bends are much righted and she hath remained very tight: God grant she may so long continue."

When Sir Thomas Roe went out from England in the year 1615 to Surat as English Ambassador to the Great Mogul, he was accompanied by Edward Terry, his chaplain. The latter has left behind an account of his voyage to India, and though we cannot do much more than call attention thereto, we may in passing note that this setting forth shows how much valuable time was wasted in those days waiting for a fair wind. For these seventeenth-century ships had neither the fine lines nor the superiority of rig which was afterwards to make the East Indiamen famous throughout the world. The Company's seventeenth-century ships were clumsy as to their proportions, they were built according to rule-of-thumb, the stern was unnecessarily high, the bows unnecessarily low. Triangular headsails had not yet been adopted, except by comparatively small fore-and-aft-rigged craft, such as yachts and coasters. The mizen was still of the lateen shape, but all the other sails were quadrilateral, even to the spritsail, which was suspended at the outer end of the bowsprit and below that spar. Above the latter on a small mast was hoisted another small squaresail, and then at the after end of the bowsprit (which was very long and practically a mast) came the foremast, stepped as far forward as it could go.

With this unhandy rig, the bluff-bowed hulls with their clumsy design and heavy tophamper could make little or no progress in a head wind. They were all right for running before the wind, or with the wind on the quarter: but not only could they not point close to the wind, but even when they tried they made a terrible lot of leeway. It was therefore hopeless to try and beat down the English Channel. Most seamen are aware that the prevailing winds over the British Isles are from the south-west, but that often between about February and the end of June, more especially in the earlier part of the year, one can expect north-east or easterly spells. The old East Indiamen therefore availed themselves of this. For a fair wind down Channel was a thing much to be desired, and a long time would be spent in waiting for it. As these awkward ships had to work their tides down the River Thames, then drop anchor for a tide, and take the next ebb down, their progress till they got round the North Foreland was anything but fast.

Of all this Edward Terry's account gives ample illustration. He was a cleric and no seaman, but he had the sense of observation and recorded what he observed. It was on the 3rd of February 1615 that the squadron, including the flagship *Charles*—a "New-built goodly ship of a thousand Tuns (in which I sayled) ... fell down from Graves-send into Tilbury Hope." Here they remained until 8th February, when they weighed anchor, and not till 12th February had they weathered the North Foreland and brought up in the Downs, where they remained for weeks waiting till a fair wind should oblige them. On the 9th of March the longed-for north-easter came, when they immediately got under way and two days later passed the meridian of the Lizard during the night. With the wind in such a quarter these Indiamen would bowl along just as fast as their ill-designed hulls could be forced through the water, making a lot of fuss and beating the waves instead of cutting through them as in the case of the last of the East Indiamen which ever sailed.

By the 19th of May they had passed the Tropic of Capricorn and Terry marvelled at the sight of whales, which were "of an exceeding greatnesse" and "appear like unto great Rocks." Sharks were seen, and even in those days the inherent delight of the seaman for capturing and killing his deadly enemy was very much in existence. As these cruel fish swam about the *Charles* the sailors would cast overboard "an iron hook ... fastened to a roap strong like it, bayted with a piece of beefe of five pounds weight."

The "Seringapatam," East Indiaman, 1,000 tons.

The squadron duly arrived in Swally Roads on the 18th of September. Sir Thomas Roe performed his mission to the Great Mogul, and eventually reached England again. So also Edward Terry, after having been for some time in the East India Company's service, was made rector of Great Greenford, Middlesex, and in the year 1649 we find him one day in September preaching a "sermon of thanksgiving" in the Church of St Andrew's, Undershaft, before the Committee of these East India Company merchants. The occasion was the return of seven of the Company's ships which had arrived from the Orient together—"a great and an unexpected mercy" after a "long, and tedious, and hazardous voyage." Terry's discourse is typical of the pompous, obsequious period. We can almost see these worthy East India merchants strolling into the church and taking their places by no means unconscious of their self-importance, yet not ashamed to do their duty and give thanks for the safe arrival of ships and their rich cargoes. Many of them, if not all, had never been out of England. Terry had been to India and back: he was therefore no ordinary rector, and he rose to the occasion. He hurls tags of Latin quotations at his hearers and then, after referring to the great riches which they were obtaining from the East, reminds these merchants that there are richer places to be found than both the East Indies and the West, better ports than Surat or even Bantam, and so went on to speak of the land where "nor rust, nor moth, nor fire, nor time can consume," where the pavement is gold and the walls are of precious stones. And then, after this simple, direct homily, the Committee came out from their pews and went back to their daily pursuits.

If these seventeenth-century men were crude and had lost some of the religious zeal of the pre-Reformation sailors, they still retained as a relic of the Puritan influence a narrow but sincere personal piety. And this comes out in the following prayer which was wont to be used aboard the East Indiaman ships of the late seventeenth century. It is called "A prayer for the Honourable English Company trading to the East Indies, to be used on board their ships," and bears the imprimatur of the Archbishop of Canterbury and the Bishop of London, who append their signatures to the statement that "we do conceive that this prayer may be very proper to be used, for the purpose express'd in the tittle of it." It has none of the beautiful English of the Middle Ages, for liturgical ability, like stained-glass window painting, was at this time a lost art. But for its simple sincerity, its suggestive deep realisation of the terrors of the sea, its true pathos and its plain religious confidence, it is characteristic of the period and the minds of the men who joined in this prayer:—

"O Almighty and most Merciful Lord God, Thou art the Soveraign Protector of all that Trust in Thee, and the Author of all Spiritual and Temporal Blessings. Let Thy Grace, we most humbly beseech thee, be always Present with thy Servants the English Company Trading to the East Indies. Compass them with thy Favour as with a shield. Prosper them in all their Publick Undertakings, and make them Successful in all their Affairs both by Sea and Land. Grant that they may prove a common Blessing, by the Increase of Honour, Wealth and Power ... by promoting the Holy Religion of our Lord Jesus Christ. Be more especially at this time favourable to us, who are separated from all the world, and have our sole dependance upon thee here in the great waters. Thou shewest they wonders in the Deep, by commanding the Winds and the Seas as thou pleasest, and thou alone canst bring us into the Haven where we would be. To they Power and Mercy therefore we humbly fly for Refuge and Protection from all Dangers of this long and Perilous voyage. Guard us continually with thy good Providence in every place. Preserve our Relations and Friends whom we have left, and at length bring us home to them again in safety and with the desired Success. Grant that every one of us, being always mindful of thy Fatherly Goodness, and Tender Compassion towards us, may glorifie thy Name by a constant Profession of the Christian Faith, and by a Sober, Just and Pious Conversation through the remaining part of our Lives. All this we beg for the sake of our Saviour Jesus Christ, to whom with thee and the Blessed Spirit be ascrib'd all Honour, Praise and Dominion both now and for evermore. Amen."

CHAPTER X

FREIGHTING THE EAST INDIAMEN

THE joint stock arrangement, as distinct from the separate voyages, which had been instituted in 1613 worked very well: and after the Restoration the practice of buying and selling shares became common, the system approximating to that of modern times. The Company's ships were continuing to bring back much wealth to the shareholders, but again covetous desires had to be appeased. In the year 1649 the Commissioners of the Navy constrained the East India Company to lend them £4000. It was in the year 1654 that Cromwell, by means of his treaty with the Portuguese, obtained the right of English ships to trade with any Portuguese possessions in the East Indies. Now this meant a very handsome additional benefit to the East India Company's ships. Cromwell was shrewd enough to know what he was about, and accordingly in the following year got his *quid pro quo* when he succeeded in borrowing £50,000 from the Company, seeing that the latter had gained so much from national successes; and a little later on in the same year obtained from the same source another £10,000 to pay Blake's seamen, whose wages were in arrears. And this was not the last instance of the Company being fleeced by the State.

In the year 1640 permission had been obtained from the native authorities to build the first of the Company's forts in India. This became known as Fort St George (Madras), and in the year 1658 the Madras settlement was raised to a presidency. In 1645 the Company had begun to establish factories in Bengal, so the ports for the East Indiamen were now becoming more numerous, and the area from which the cargoes could be obtained was being widely extended. The Portuguese, as we have seen, were now out of the running as regards the East. And as for the repeated collisions which the English had with the Dutch, the three Anglo-Dutch wars which had been long foreseen, as they were destined long to last, had given quite a new complexion to affairs in India, leaving the English East India Company in a position stronger than ever. One of the stipulations had been that the Dutch should indemnify the English merchants and factors in India with regard to the massacre at Amboyna, and the guilty parties therein concerned were to be punished. In 1664 the French East India Company had been formed, and ten years later the foundation of their settlement at Pondicherry was laid.

In the year 1681 the Company had developed their fleet to such an extent that they now owned about thirty-five ships, ranging in size from 775 to 100 tons. In customs alone the Company were paying £60,000 a year, and they were carrying out to India £60,000 or £70,000 worth of lead, tin, cloth and stuffs every year, bringing back raw silk, pepper and other goods of the East. By the year 1683 so profitable were the annual results of the Company's trading that a £100 share would sell for £500. Before long the size of the ships just mentioned was to increase to 900 and even to 1300 tons, such was the demand for Indian products; and between the years 1682 and 1689 no fewer than sixteen East Indiamen varying in size from 900 to 1300 tons were constructed. All the East Indiamen were well armed, for even in the year 1677, when the Company owned from thirty to thirty-five ships of from 300 to 600 tons apiece, these vessels each mounted from forty to seventy guns.

It will be recollected that Bantam had been the first headquarters or chief factory whither the Company's ships went for their trade. This continued until 1638, when Surat had developed so much, thanks to the concessions by the Great Mogul, that it replaced Bantam in pre-eminence. The last-mentioned factory, together with Fort St George in Madras, Hooghly in Bengal, and those establishments in Persia were all made subservient to Surat. A far-sighted person could have foreseen that all these scattered strongholds of trade might not improbably develop eventually into something very much more important politically. But it was Sir Josiah Child, the principal manager of the Company's affairs at home, who was one of the first to project the forming of a territorial Empire in India.

We had reason to mention just now a ship which we described as being an interloper. The reader is well aware that in the first instance the charter granted to the English East India Company by Queen Elizabeth conveyed to them the exclusive privilege of trading to the East. This charter was renewed in the years 1609, 1657, 1661 and subsequently in other years. But such was the jealousy, such the covetousness which were aroused by the Company's successful voyages that a number of interlopers, quite contrary to the terms of the charter, fitted out expeditions of their own. These were evidently successful, too, especially during the latter part of the reign of Charles II., for the number of these private adventurers increased considerably. The result, of course, was that the Company became exceedingly indignant and had to exert themselves to put an end to the trouble. But this, again, opened up the whole of the question as to whether the Company should continue to enjoy such a fine monopoly. There was a good deal of resentment against India being restricted to a favoured few. However the Government favoured the Company, for it had been found more than useful to the country in times of crisis, so again in the year 1693 it received its fresh charter.

But between the years 1694 and 1698 this Eastern trade practically was thrown open. And then the State happened to require a loan of £2,000,000. This was found by a newly formed company of associated merchants who had been very vigorous in opposing the East India Company's privilege. And since this new company wanted only eight per cent. (not a high rate for those days) for their loan, they also received a charter. The result was that there were two companies trading to India and each with its own charter. The title of this fresh association was the New East India Company, and presently a kind of third company arose as an offshoot from this second one. All this competition had a most disastrous effect and brought both the old and new companies almost to ruin. Each company hated the other, while the public detested both most heartily. There were only two possibilities open. Either both companies must be wrecked or they must amalgamate. It was wisely decided to choose the latter. They therefore adjusted their differences, and in the year 1708 were amalgamated into one corporation, calling themselves "The United Company of Merchants of England Trading to the East Indies." The capital was increased to £3,200,000. They were the means of aiding the Government by advancing to the latter £1,200,000 without interest, and the Government in turn agreed to extend the Company's charter till the year 1726, with three years' notice of termination. And it was subsequently extended till 1766.

During the last decade of the seventeenth century when hostilities existed between England and France the East India Company laid before the House of Lords an account of the great losses which the former had incurred at sea, owing to the lack of English cruisers. Those were no easy times for the ships bound either to or from the Orient, for, besides possible attacks from French men-of-war, the English Channel and approaches thereto were alive with privateers, to the great detriment of the Anglo-Indian trade. Some idea of the size and strength of the East India Company's ships about this time may be gathered from the following list of craft which the French captured from them during the year 1694 alone:—

Name of Ship	Tonnage	Men	Guns
Princess of Denmark	670	133	40
Seymour	500	—	—
Success	400	80	32
Defence	750	150	50
Resolution	650	130	40

In later years one of the most valuable commodities which India was to produce and send to England in these ships was tea. The first importation by us was in the year 1667. Only a small amount, consisting of 100 lb., was sent, but it was not long before this was greatly exceeded. However, the early years of the eighteenth century were marked by a disappointment in the trade which the Company was doing. Although the latter's ships were now trading also with China, yet the value of our exports to the East were less than £160,000 a year: and this, let it be remembered, included also military stores for the Company's settlements in the East and at St Helena. The reason for this slump is easily explained. Every authority will admit that the finest tonic for trade is competition. Monopoly is death to enterprise, while a spirit of rivalry encourages progress. The East India Company was suffering from the decaying, deadening influence of its exclusive privilege and this went on till about the middle of the eighteenth century. The first half of that century is decadent, not merely with regard to India, but most things English. Art was at its lowest, manners were never less sincere, morals were corrupt, politics were little better. It almost seems as if England had lost the fair wind which had carried her through the Tudor times and then become gradually becalmed in the Stuart era till she rolled about with no progress, making only stern-way. And then, after a period of profitless existence, she seems to have picked up another breeze which has sent her along through the successful industrial age, the great wars, the Victorian and Edwardian years of prosperity up till to-day. The end of the eighteenth century is a period quite different from its first portion. And if it was so generally it could scarcely be different in regard to a corporation directed and managed by men of this period.

A Barque Free-trader in the London Docks.

Just for a moment let us go back to that time when the East India Company decided it were best to close the Deptford yard and obtain their ships ready built. Now as time went on the hiring of ships to the Company for this Eastern trade led to great abuses. Officially the Company did no longer build their ships. But the Company's directors used to build them privately and then hire them out to the Company, to the great personal gain of the directors. There were few other ships big enough or strong enough. The directors would know how many to build and to what extent prices could be demanded from the Company: and altogether they feathered their nests very nicely. This went on till the year 1708, when the old and new East India companies had become amalgamated. After this year the directors were prohibited by Act of Parliament from supplying ships to the Company.

Instead of the former corrupt arrangement, ships for the East India Company were to be hired in the future by open tender from the commander and two owners. But here again was a difficulty. Inasmuch as a special type of stalwart ship was required for this trade, the supply was small and in the hands of a ring called the Marine Interest. Therefore the Company was just about as badly off as before. And throughout the eighteenth century there was one continued contest between the East India Company and the shipbuilders, who did their level best to fleece the former as it had been fleeced by the State at different dates.

For the East India Company did not literally own their ships, even though they were called East Indiamen, flew the Company's flag and made their regular voyages. A shipping company to-day buys and owns its own ships, but the East India Company had quite a different method. Up to the time when the old and new companies were amalgamated, in the year 1708, the owners and the Company were unfettered by any legislative provision. They could settle and adjust the points between themselves, and since the directors were part owners you may be sure there was little cause for dispute! But the by-law which came into force after the union of the two companies, prohibiting directors from being concerned in hiring ships to the Company, brought about a rather curious order of things. They were hired for so many voyages at so much a ton, the Company binding itself to freight a stipulated number of tons. These, by the way, were generally less than the official measurement. About the year 1700 the largest East Indiamen were under 500 tons, though their burthen was one-third greater.

Under the new arrangement the ships were to be taken up by the Company and their respective voyages agreed to in a Court of Directors by ballot. No tenders were to be accepted except such as had been made by the commander and two owners of each ship. Furthermore, the sale of the post as captain or any other office was forbidden in the Company's ships. This latter was an important modification. The actual owner of the ship from whom the vessel was hired was termed the ship's husband, and the practice had been for him to sell the command of the ship to a captain whom he would select. The expression in this case was to "sell the ship," and a captain would sometimes pay as much as £8000 or £10,000 for the privilege of the appointment, because this position afforded him unique opportunities of making some handsome profits by the goods he brought home from the East in his ship as his own perquisites. To such an extent did this practice become established that the sale of a command became transferable property of the captain who had bought it. Whenever he died or resigned his heirs or he himself had the undoubted right to dispose of the billet to the highest bidder.

The reason for the abolition of this custom was that it was largely responsible for the high rates of freight which the Company was forced to pay. A compensation was paid to the captains in the service at the time of the abolition, but henceforth money could not buy the command of a ship for a man that was not adequately qualified for the post. Previously commands of ships had been held in some cases by men who possessed no right to such responsible tasks. Captain Eastwick, a master mariner of the eighteenth century, who has happily left behind his autobiography, relates among a number of interesting personal reminiscences that he married the niece of a man who was sole owner of one East Indiaman and part owner of two more of these ships. It was therefore suggested that Eastwick should enter the Honourable Company's service, and a command was promised as soon as he was qualified. "This was a very tempting offer," writes the old sailor, "as there was no service equal to it, or more difficult to get into, requiring great interest."

"It was the practice of the Company in those days to charter ships from their owners; these vessels were especially built for the service, and were generally run for about four voyages, when they were held to be worn out, and their places taken by others built for the purpose. About thirty ships were required for the Company every year," he states, and then goes on to say that "there was never any written engagement on the part of either the owners or the Company as to the continuance of these charters, but the custom of contract was so well established that both parties mutually relied upon it, and considered themselves bound by ties of honour to observe their implied customary engagements. When, therefore, a ship's turn arrived to be employed, the owner, as a matter of form, submitted a tender in writing to be engaged, and proposed a particular person as captain, and this tender and proposal were always accepted. Thus the owners of these East Indiamen had everything in their own hands, and the favour of one of them was a fine thing to obtain, leading to appointments of great emolument."

Some idea of the value of the East Indiaman captain's appointment may be gathered from what Eastwick remarks under this head. "The captain of an East Indiaman, in addition to his pay and allowances, had the right of free outward freight to the extent of fifty tons, being only debarred from exporting certain articles, such as woollens, metals, and warlike stores. On the homeward voyage he was allotted twenty tons of free freight, each of thirty-two feet; but this tonnage was bound to consist of certain scheduled goods, and duties were payable thereon to the Company. As the rate of freight in those days was about £25 a ton, this privilege was a very valuable one. Of course much depended upon the skill and good management of the individual commander, the risk of the market, his knowledge of its requirements, and his own connections and interest to procure him a good profit. In addition to the free tonnage, he further enjoyed certain advantages in the carrying of passengers, for although the allowance of passage money outward and homeward was arbitrarily fixed by the Company, there being a certain number of passengers assigned to each vessel, and their fares duly determined, ranging from £95 for a subaltern and assistant-surgeon to £235 for a general officer, with from one and a half to three and a half tons of free baggage, exclusive of bedding and furniture for their cabins, yet it was possible for captains, by giving up their own apartments and accommodation, to make very considerable sums for themselves. In short, the gains to a prudent commander averaged from £4000 to £5000 a voyage, sometimes perhaps falling as low as £2000, but at others rising to £10,000 and £12,000. The time occupied from the period of a ship commencing receipt of her outward cargo to her being finally cleared of her homeward one was generally from fourteen to eighteen months, and three or four voyages assured any man a very handsome fortune."

But though these commands were very expensive to purchase and highly remunerative when obtained, yet like the professional man to-day this high remuneration was preceded by years of bad pay. Before a man could obtain the command of an East Indiaman he must necessarily have made a voyage as fifth or sixth mate, then another voyage as third or fourth mate, and finally a third voyage as first or second mate. Now these junior officers in the Company's service were quite unable to live on their pay "and it required a private capital of at least five hundred pounds to enable a man to arrive at the position of second mate, which was the lowest station wherein the pay and allowances afforded a maintenance."

Whenever an Indiaman became worn out, or condemned, another ship was hired to replace her, and was said to be "built upon the bottom" of the first. The member or members of the Marine Interest who had built the first ship claimed the right of building the second, and so it went on. The result was that there arose what were known as "hereditary bottoms." This went on till the year 1796, when some of the more public-spirited of the directors and shareholders of the East India Company put their heads together and determined to have this system entirely altered. It is indeed most extraordinary that the principle of monopoly seemed to pervade every feature of the Company's transactions, from the broad, important principle of exclusive trade with the East down to the building of ships and the exclusive privileges of their commanders. In any other line of commerce the rate of freight found its own level, but in the East India Company there was but one bidder, and that also a monopoly. As the voyage was long and difficult and full of dangers, it was natural enough that good commanders should be desired. If an owner had a good captain, the Company were only too pleased to have him.

The passing of a by-law in the year 1773 prevented a ship from being engaged for the Company's service for more than four voyages at a certain freight, this being calculated on an estimate of the building and the cost of fitting out a vessel with provisions and stores for a certain number of months. In the years 1780 and 1781 differences of opinion arose between the owners of the ships and the Court of Directors of the East India Company as to the rate of freight demanded. Owing to the hostilities with the Dutch, the rates of insurance and fitting out were stated to have caused an additional charge of £10, 14s. a ton. The contest between these two opposing sets of monopolists was always amusing to an outsider. The Company wanted the ships badly, for their very existence depended on their ability to carry cargoes between England and India. On the other hand the owners had built these ships especially for the Company's service. They represented a great outlay of capital, and they were so big and efficient that there was practically no other trade in which they could be profitably employed. So, after a certain amount of mutual indignation had cooled off, and the usual haggling had proceeded, both parties were wont to come to a compromise and matters went on as before till the next dispute occurred.

Thus, for instance, in the year 1783 the Court of the East India Company's directors fixed the rate of freight at £32 per ton for a ship of 750 tons. To this the owners replied that it was quite impossible to provide the ships under £35 a ton. The Court then showed their independence. They were resolved not to suffer the intolerable humiliation of being dictated to by these owners, so the Company advertised for tenders. Eventually twenty-eight ships were offered the Company by various private owners in respect of this advertisement. But after the Company's inspecting officer had carefully examined these vessels he had to report that they were either foreign-built, or weak of structure, or else almost worn out: in any case quite unfitted for the long voyage to India and back. This placed the Company in rather a dilemma, and gave something of a shock to their independent spirit. Meanwhile the owners who had hitherto provided the Company with ships had taken alarm at thus throwing open the tender for competition. They were in serious danger of losing their own monopoly: so they began to climb down and offered the Company the rate of £33 a ton. And inasmuch as the latter required as much as 10,000 tons the two parties agreed on this last-mentioned price, more especially as the ships were known to be sound in every respect, having actually been built under the direction of the Company's officials.

CHAPTER XI

EAST INDIAMEN AND THE ROYAL NAVY

THE East India Company's progress was anything but a straight, easy path. We must never forget that if it made big profits—and when examined these figures, taken on an average, are not so colossal as they seem at first sight—the risks and responsibilities were very far from insignificant. Quite apart from the difficulties out in India, and the absence of the invention of telegraphy thus making it difficult to keep a complete control over the factors and trade; quite apart, too, from the pressure which was harassing the Company from all sides—public opinion which grudged this monopoly: shipowners who wanted to raise the cost of hire: and Parliament which kept controlling the Company by legislation—there were two other sources of worry which existed.

The first of these was the continued insults by the press-gangs, and the consequent inconvenience to the East India Company and the great danger to their ships and cargoes. The second worry was the ever-present possibility during the long-drawn-out wars of losing also ships and goods by attack from the enemy's men-of-war. In both respects the position was not easy of solution. On the one hand, it was obvious that the Company's trade was likely to be crippled; but, on the other, the Government must come first in both matters. The navy was in dire need of men. All that it had were not enough. Men who had been convicted and sentenced for smuggling—some of the finest sailors in the country—were shipped on board to fight for the land that gave them birth. All sorts of rough characters were rounded up ashore and sent afloat by the press-gangs, but even then the warships needed more.

Now the crews of these eighteenth-century East Indiamen were such skilled seamen, so hardened to the work of a full-rigged ship, so accustomed to fighting pirates, privateers and even the enemy's men-of-war, that it was no wonder the Admiralty in their dilemma overstepped the bounds and shipped them whenever they could be got. A favourite custom was to lie in wait for the homeward-bound East Indiamen, and when these fine ships had dropped anchor off Portsmouth, in the Downs, or even on their way up the Thames, they would be boarded and relieved of some of their crew: to such an extent, sometimes, that the ship could not be properly worked. I have carefully examined a large number of original manuscripts which passed between the Admiralty and the East India Company of the eighteenth century, and there runs through the period a continuous vein of complaint from the latter to the former, but there was very little remedy and the Company had to put up with the nuisance.

On the 21st of December 1710, for instance, the Company's secretary, Thomas Woolley, sends a letter from the directors complaining to the Admiralty of the press-gang actually invading East India House, Leadenhall Street, one day during the same month, "on a pretence of searching for seamen." As a matter of fact the press-gang had come to carry off the most capable of the Company's crews, who happened to be present at that time. Very strongly the Company wrote complaints to the Admiralty that the press-gangs would board the East Indiamen lying off Spithead (bound for London) and take out all the able-bodied seamen they could lay their hands on. These men had to go whether they liked it or not, and the Company's officers were indignant but powerless. But it added injury to insult that the press-gangs replaced the picked men taken out by "such as have been either unskilful in their duty or careless and refractory in the performance of it," as one of the letters remarks. The Company therefore begged that no man might be taken out until the East Indiamen should arrive at their moorings, or at least till they came into the London river: for, they pointed out, the ships had very valuable cargoes on board, and this seizing of men exposed them to very great danger, it being often impossible to replace the men taken out.

When the Company's ships at length reached the Thames, the directors would often send down hoys to meet them and to bring the goods up to London, where they could be placed on view in the warehouses to show the buyers before the sale opened. But the naval authorities had given the crews of these hoys such a fright that they refused to go even down towards the mouth of the river, fearing that the press-warrants, which were out, would be put into execution and they themselves would be sent to serve in the warships. These hoys were fore-and-aft-rigged vessels of about 40 or 50 tons, the crew consisting of a skipper and two men. Such craft were sloops—that is to say, practically cutters, the only difference being purely technical and legal—and were built for the purpose of carrying passengers and goods from one place to another along the coast or up estuaries, where ordinary lighters were not able to be taken with convenience or safety. The Margate hoy, for instance, was very well known to Londoners at this time.

But the need for naval seamen was so urgent, consequent on the wars, that the Admiralty had to go to even further extremities. They actually sent to sea a press smack with a naval officer on board, and this craft would cruise up and down the English Channel. On one occasion Captain Mawson of the Company's ship *Cardonell*, homeward bound, was followed all the way from Portsmouth to the Downs by such a smack. And when the bigger ship brought up off Deal, Lieutenant Hutchinson, R.N., came aboard and used his best endeavours to take away every one of the *Cardonell's* crew, with the exception only of the ship's officers. The skipper of the merchantman naturally resented this very strongly, but offered to let Mr Hutchinson have most of his men provided the naval officer would supply him with others to take their place so that the ship might be safely brought to her moorings in the Thames. But it was no good. Hutchinson absolutely declined to make a compromise, and according to Mawson's account behaved very rudely and, not content with the able seamen, carried off also the *Cardonell's* second mate.

The Press-Gang at Work.

(By courtesy of Messrs. T. H. Parker Brothers)

The only way in which this annoyance and danger could be overcome was for the Admiralty to issue what were known as "protections." The holder of a protection was thus made immune from arrest by a press-gang. It was a document which gave the name of the man, his age, stature, stated whether he wore a wig or his own hair, and other particulars of identification. No man with this authorisation could be forced into his Majesty's service, but it was valid only for three months or the period written thereon. There is preserved an original protection certificate in the archives of the Public Record Office, and it is a quaint document which must have been very keenly appreciated by its eighteenth-century owner. On the other hand, when the East India Company had lost some of their seamen by desertion, they would petition the Admiralty to allow naval men to be lent.

Every student of history is aware of the unfortunate friction which existed at this time between the officers of the Royal Navy and the officers of the Mercantile Marine. Happily in the present century this slow-dying spirit is almost extinct. In my volume, "King's Cutters and Smugglers," I showed what altercations used to arise, what petty jealousies existed between the officers of the Revenue cutters and those of his Majesty's navy. The captains and officers of the East India Company were often indebted to the protection and assistance of naval officers, but the latter were often overbearing in the exercise of their duties, and despised any seaman who was not in the King's navy. On the other hand, the East Indiamen's officers most heartily disliked these gentlemen, and the insults from the press-gangs were too poignant to be forgotten easily.

As an instance, let us refer to the 14th of August 1734, when the East India Company complained to the Admiralty of what seems certainly a very high-handed action. It appears that the Company's ship, the *Duke of Lorrain*, had arrived in the Downs on the previous Sunday, and her master, Captain Christopher Wilson, sent in a very indignant report to the Court of Directors to the effect that "the men of war at the Nore treated him more like an enemy than a Merchant Ship coming into Port in such weather as he had, it being very bad, they firing near Twenty Shott at his Ship, some of which came among the Rigging, might have been of dangerous consequence to the Ship, and to the Company who had a Cargo on board to the Value of Two hundred thousand Pounds. This action being what the Company did not expect from any of the Men of War, as the Captain of the *Duke of Lorrain* has assured the Court that he lowered his sails, and did what was safe to be done, they have commanded me to signify the same to you," continued the Company's letter to the Admiralty, "that so the Right Honourable the Lords of the Admiralty may be inform'd thereof."

But if the East India Company thought it necessary sometimes to complain of the treatment at the hands of the Admiralty the former were none the less glad to have the assistance and protection of the navy in the time of war. There is a voluminous correspondence still preserved in which the Company write to the Admiralty asking for convoys of the East Indiamen both outward and inward bound. The French were very much on the *qui vive*, but unless the regular income of the East India Company were for the present to be stopped, and the entire Anglo-Indian trade suspended, the Company's ships must go on their way. This could be done only with the assistance of his Majesty's ships. In order to deal with this matter there was a special department of the Company designated the Secret Committee, which communicated with the Admiralty as to where the East Indian merchant fleet were to rendezvous and the convoy join them, the confidential signals to be employed, and so on. The following letter sent by the Company to the Admiralty on 12th December 1740 is typical:—

> "Secrett Committee of the United East India Company do humbly represent to your Lordships That they do expect a considerable fleet of ships richly laden will return from the East Indies the next summer and do therefore earnestly beseech your Lordships That three or four of His Majesty's ships of good force may be appointed to look out for and convoy them safe to England."

These convoys took the East Indiamen sometimes even from the Thames down Channel as far as Spithead. Sometimes they picked the latter up only at the Downs, escorting them for several hundred miles away from the English coast out into the Atlantic. These merchantmen were similarly met at St Helena and escorted home, the men-of-war being victualled for a period of two months. Even if an East Indiaman were able to arrive singly and run into the Hamoaze (Plymouth Sound) on her way home, having successfully eluded hostile ships roving off the mouth of the English Channel, it was deemed advisable for her to wait at Plymouth until she could be escorted by the next man-of-war bound eastward to the Thames. There were plenty of French privateersmen lurking about the Channel, and, at any rate about the year 1716, there were also Swedish privateers on the prowl in the same sea ready to fall upon any East Indiaman going in or out of the Downs.

One notorious Swede of this occupation was *La Providence*, of 26 guns. She was commanded by Captain North Cross. The latter was an Englishman who had been tried and sentenced to death for some crime, but he had succeeded in making his escape from Newgate, and had fled the country. He had crossed the North Sea and had obtained from Sweden letters of marque to rove about as a privateer. His crew were a rough crowd of desperate fellows of many nations, and this ship was very fond of lying in Calais roads ready to get under way and slip across the English Channel so soon as an outward-bound East Indiaman was known to be in the Downs. Now, in the month of November 1717, the skipper of *La Providence* was lying in his usual roadstead, and tidings came to him concerning one of the Company's ships then in the Downs.

The privateer was kept fully informed by means of those fine seamen, but doubtful characters, who lived at Deal. They were some of the toughest and most determined men, who stopped at nothing. For generations the men of Deal had been the most notorious smugglers of the south-east corner of England: and that was saying a great deal. They were a brave, fearless class of men, but brutal of nature and always ready to get to windward of the law, if ever a chance presented itself. They handled their open luggers with a wonderful dexterity, for which their successors are even yet famous. But they were lawless to their finger-tips. So on the present occasion when the East Indiaman was in the Downs, one of these Deal men sailed his little craft across the strong tides of Dover Straits and brought the information to the privateer. The messenger asserted that the East Indiaman had nearly £60,000 on board in cash, so Cross got under way, averring that he would get this amount or "Loose his Life in the Attempt." Whether he succeeded in his attempt I regret I am unable to say. As far as was practicable these East Indiamen were wont, in those strenuous times, to wait for a convoy, but there were times when they could not afford to wait till one of his Majesty's ships was at liberty. On those occasions the ships would wait till they numbered a small squadron, and then voyaging together would resolve to run all risks. There is on record the case of a French squadron consisting of a "64" and two frigates arriving off the island of St Helena, where the East Indiamen were wont to call. The Frenchmen had come here in order to fall upon the homeward-bound fleet who would soon be seen. But the longboat[2] of one of these merchantmen was fitted out, and under the command of a midshipman succeeded in getting to windward of the Frenchmen unperceived and was able to give the approaching English ships warning of the danger that awaited them. Six of the Company's fleet fell in with the enemy and kept up a running fight for several days, until they anchored in All Saints' Bay. Here the French blockaded them, but it was to no purpose, for these merchantmen succeeded in escaping and reaching England in safety.

The Royal Navy assisted the Company's ships in quite another manner as well. Often enough after enduring heavy weather in the Bay of Biscay or English Channel these East Indiamen would put into Plymouth and obtain permission from the Admiralty to obtain from the latter's stores a new bowsprit, a new mast, or other spar, the Company of course paying for the expense. The royal dockyard also on the Medway was similarly found of great service, as, for instance, early in the eighteenth century, when the Company's ship *Hannover* had the misfortune to run on to a sandbank whilst going down the Thames to the Downs. The ship thus suffered damage and was not in a fit condition to proceed to the East. Permission was asked and obtained for her to be taken into Sheerness, where the naval authorities could admit her into dry dock, warehouse her cargo, supply materials and repair the injuries that had been made.

So also on another occasion, in September 1720, the East Indiaman *Goodfellow* was lying at Gravesend outward bound. It was discovered at the last moment that unfortunately all the beer on board was spoilt, and since there was no time "to detain her till more can be brew'd," the Company's directors had to request the Admiralty victualling office to furnish the ship with 12 tons of beer at the Company's expense. But the naval officials were not always so obliging as this. Towards the end of the year 1721 the East Indiaman *Cæsar*, outward bound for Mocha, had the misfortune to damage by friction one of her cables[3] owing to the latter getting foul of the wreck of the *Carlisle*. Those were the days when cables were still made of hemp, and were always liable, except when special steps were taken, to injury when rubbing along foul ground. As she lay in the Downs, the *Cæsar's* master, Captain Mabbott, asked the naval storekeeper at Deal if he would spare him a new

[2] The longboat carried by these East Indiamen measured from twenty-seven to twenty-nine feet in length.

[3] The East Indiamen of about the middle of the eighteenth century rode to fifteen-inch cables.

cable in case another storm should spring up. Mabbott was by no means pleased when the storekeeper replied very properly that inasmuch as he had received no orders to oblige merchant ships in that manner, he was not able to comply with the request. However matters were eventually set right by the Company obtaining the Admiralty's permission.

A voyage in an East Indiaman of those days was often full of adventure. After proceeding from the Downs the ship cleared the western mouth of the English Channel and then steered "W and to WSW." It took three months to reach the Cape of Good Hope, and even then it was not too far south to fall in with French men-of-war. After calling at Spithead outward bound they were wont to sail through the Needles passage. The seamen were probably better situated in these East Indiamen than in any other merchant ship, but they were not allowed a soft time. They were kept at it with setting and stowing of canvas, spreading stuns'ls in fair weather or taking in upper canvas in heavy gales. There were plenty of guns on board to be served, so drill formed no small part of their duties. A seaman went on board with his sea-chest and his bedding, and in those rough, hard-swearing days, long before ever the sailor had his trade union, he was treated with no light hand. There is an instance of the way slackness was wont to be punished on board the East Indiaman *Greenwich*. This particular occurrence belongs to the year 1719 and happened when the watch had been called. As some of the men did not turn out as smartly as they ought, the boatswain took out his knife and cut down their hammocks, to their great discomfort and indignation. So infuriated in fact were the crew that they declined to go on the next voyage until the boatswain had been discharged.

Some idea of the kind of vessels which the Company were hiring for their service about the year 1730 may be gathered from the following list, which has been taken direct from the original official documents:—

Name of Ship	Commander	Tons	Men	Guns
Devonshire	Lawrence Prince	470	94	30
Prince Augustus	Francis Gostlin	495	99	36
Lyell	Charles Small	470	94	30
Princess of Wales	Thomas Gilbert	460	92	30
Middlesex	John Pelly	430	86	30
Mary	Thomas Holden	490	98	34
Derby	William Fitzhugh	480	96	32
London	Robert Bootle	490	98	34
Dawsonne	Francis Steward	480	96	32
Craggs	Caleb Grantham	380	76	26
Bridgwater	Edward Williamson	400	80	28
Prince William	William Beresford	480	96	30
Lethieullier	John Shepheard	470	94	30

Hartford	Francis Nelly	460	92	30
Macclesfield	Robert Hudson	450	90	30
Cæsar	William Mabbott	440	88	30
Harrison	Samuel Martin	460	92	30
Walpole	Charles Boddam	495	99	32
Frances	John Lawson	420	84	30
Duke of Cumberland	Benjamin Braund	480	96	30
George	George Pitt	480	96	30
Aislabie	William Birch	400	80	26
Stretham	George Westcott	470	94	30
Ockham	William Jobson	480	96	30

It will be noticed that not one of these is really a big ship and that while the average is somewhere between 400 and 500 tons, yet not one exceeds 495 tons. The directors settled the size of ship required and the owners saw that it was supplied. The size of the crews will be seen to be very large, but this is explained not only because wages were low in those days and safety was a dominating factor—allowing plenty of men in each watch for handling sail—but because each ship carried about thirty guns, and though both broadsides would not be fired at once, yet even half those guns would necessitate a good number of the crew. At various dates during the eighteenth century, when the country needed ships, the Admiralty commissioned a number of these East Indiamen and also gave commissions in the Royal Navy to their commanders.

Those were the days, too, when merchantmen frequently obtained letters of marque for acting against the ships of a nation with which our country was at war. During the year 1739 Britain declared war against Spain, and so one comes across a document of that year in which the directors of "The United Company of Merchants of England Trading to the East Indies"—for this was the official style of the East India Company at that time—petition for "Letters of Marque or General Reprizals against Spain." The request is made on behalf of their ship, *Royal Guardian*, 490 tons, 98 men and 30 guns; and for other vessels of their fleet. These were duly granted, and such stout, well-armed craft were able to render an excellent account of themselves against the foe. They were necessarily built of great strength, they carried so many guns, their crews were such seasoned men, and their commanders such determined fellows, that they formed really a most valuable reserve to the Royal Navy. They were not individually a match for the biggest of the enemy's battleships, but none the less they were equal to any frigate and of far greater utility to the King's service than any merchant liner would proportionately be to-day in the time of war.

CHAPTER XII

THE WAY THEY HAD IN THE COMPANY'S SERVICE

In order that the East Indiamen might be able to make themselves known on the high seas to the British men-of-war, a special code of signals was accustomed to be arranged by the Admiralty for the former. This was for use during war-time, so that the Company's vessels on meeting with other craft might know at a distance whether these were the friends who would convoy them or the enemy who would assail them. Some time during the autumn, during these eighteenth-century wars when England always seemed to be engaged in hostilities, the custom was for the Admiralty to appoint a fresh code so that the naval and the Company's ships might know each other. This code was then sent sealed to the Secret Committee of the East India Company, and handed over to the latter's commanding officers. Similarly special signals were arranged so that when calling at St Helena the Governor of that island might be able to recognise the homeward-bound East Indiamen.

The following document, dated 5th November 1733, from the Admiralty will give some idea of the nature of these signals:—

> "Signals to be observed by the East India Company's ships in their next homeward-bound passage upon their meeting with any ships near the Channell or else where which they may supose to be the King's Ships, the better to know.
>
> "The Company's ships whether to Windward or to Leeward, shall make a Signal by hailing up their Foresail, and lowering down the Main Top Sail, and spreading an English Ensign, the Cross down-ward, from the main Top Mast head down the Shrouds; and They shall be answered by the King's ships by lowering down their Fore top sail, and spreading an Ensign, in the same manner, from their Fore topmast head downward, hailing up their Main Sail, and hoysting their Mizen top sail, with the Clue lines hail'd up.
>
> "In the case of Blowing weather that the Top Sails are in, the other Signals will be sufficient.
>
> "Signals by Night.
>
> "The Company's Ships shall make a Signal by hoysting three

Lights one over another on the Ensign Staff, and One at the Bolt sprit end.

"The King's ships will answer by shewing three Lights of equal height, One of 'em in the Fore, One in the Main, and One in the Mizen shrouds."

And in order to know any of his Majesty's ships when encountered in the East Indian waters the signal was to be as follows:—The ship to windward was to hoist an English Jack at the fore t'gallant masthead, and the ship to leeward was to answer by furling the mizen topsail and hoisting a French Jack at the mizen topmasthead.

The Company had their own agent at Deal, and considering the number of days that were spent by the East Indiamen in the Downs, both outward and homeward bound, his presence was very necessary. The ships were taken down the Thames by the Company's own pilots, and this corporation owned its own pilot-cutter, which was a 60-ton craft with a master and six men, her cruising ground being between Gravesend and the Downs. However, even then, the Company's ships were by no means immune from getting ashore, although it ought to be mentioned that by the middle of the eighteenth century a really good chart of the Thames estuary did not exist, and the exact nature of some of the numerous shoals was unknown. It is not surprising, therefore, to find casualties occurring as these big ships went up and down the London river. For instance, in March 1734 the East Indiaman *Derby*, outward bound in charge of a "Pylot," ran aground "on the Mouse Sand below the Nore." (This shoal is a few miles to the east of Southend pier.) She sustained so much damage that she had to put into Sheerness for dry-docking and repairs.

So also, a few days before Christmas in the year 1736, the East Indiaman *Lyell* "by the Unskilfulness of the Pilote has been Onshore on the Spaniard Sand,[4] in going down for the Downs." So she also had to use Sheerness dock for repairs. Captain John Acton, the commander of the *Lyell*, in his report stated that the "Pylots" pretended not to have seen the "Buoy of the Spill," and "borrowing too near on the Kentish Shore, he run us aground on the Spaniard at High Water, the wind blowing fresh N.W." The "Spill," or, as it is now called, the "Spile" buoy, marks the western end of the Spile Sand. The pilots had clearly got out of their course, for these East Indiamen, drawing as they did 20 feet of water, would never have taken the inner passage along the Kentish shore known as the Four Fathoms Channel. They should have left the Spile buoy to starboard and not to port, as clearly was the case in the present instance among the shoals. The north-west was a fair wind from the Thames to the Downs all the way, so that no one except by accident would have chosen to take such a ship so far out of the main, deep-water channel.

The ship was hard and fast on the Spaniard, and the conditions could scarcely have been worse—a fresh onshore wind, and the accident occurring at top of high water. All night the ship lay on the shoal bumping and injuring herself so that there were soon seven feet of water in the hold, and the pumps could not cope

[4] The Spaniard is a treacherous patch off the north-east corner of the Isle of Sheppey.

with it. But on the morning of Christmas Eve by a great piece of luck the ship was got off, for the wind veered to the north and sent in a bigger tide, as of course it would, and a local fisherman—doubtless from Whitstable or the East Swale—came and assisted with his local knowledge so that "thank God the ship floated and we got her off here." Making a fair wind of it the *Lyell* then ran into the East Swale and anchored off Faversham. And a very handsome sight she must have looked lying to her hempen cable in that winding river.

One bleak day in January 1737 the East Indiaman *Nassau* had the misfortune to run on the south end of the Galloper in a "hard gale at SW," as her captain reported. The Galloper is a treacherous bank in the North Sea off Harwich, and many a ship used to get picked up here in the olden days. The *Nassau* was now in a critical position, and every moment those on board expected her to go to pieces: "but," wrote her skipper, "by the Providence of the Almighty in about an Hours time we forc'd her off again with her head sails, but had the misfortune at the same time of losing our Rudder, Main and Mizen Top Mast which obliged us soon after to come to an anchor." But here again, just as had been the case with the *Lyell*, local assistance came to them. For after a time the Harwich packet passed them bound for Holland, and her captain, seeing the *Nassau*, hailed her skipper and advised her to stand in for Orfordness, and even sent on board his mate, as he knew every inch of that coast. However, the wind now veered to the north-north-west, which made it fair for running down the North Sea, so the *Nassau* sailed down towards the North Foreland and anchored in Margate Roads, whence her captain was able to send information to the East India Company, where also he would wait for orders.

Another peril which these East Indiamen had to remember was the presence of pirates. These consisted not merely of local Eastern craft, but of such people as Captains Avery and Kidd, two of the most notorious men in the whole history of piracy. In the early part of the eighteenth century the latter were found in many parts of the Indian Ocean. Madagascar was a favourite base for these rovers, but they would be found off Mauritius, or at the mouth of the Red Sea awaiting the East Indiamen returning from Mocha and Jeddah. Not content with this, these European pirates would hang about off the Malabar coast, and the East India Company's ships suffered considerably, and feared a repetition of these attacks. And yet, when we consider the matter dispassionately, were Avery, Kidd and his fellow-pirates very much worse than some of those captains who first took the English ships out to the Orient, who thought it no wrong but a mere matter of business to stop a Portuguese ship and relieve her of her cargo just as these eighteenth-century pirates would assail the ships of the present monopolists of the Eastern trade? The only difference that seems obvious is that Lancaster and those other early captains were acting on behalf of a powerful corporation having a charter from the sovereign: whereas Avery, Kidd and the like were acting on their own and were outlaws. And even this cannot be pushed too far, seeing that at one time of his career Kidd received a commission from William III. to go forth and, as "a private man-of-war," capture other notorious "pirates, free-booters and sea-rovers," on the old principle of setting a thief to catch a thief.

Sometimes these East Indiamen were taken for the enemy even by English men-of-war. You will remember the famous voyage of Lord Anson round the world in the years 1740-1744. One day whilst they were in the South Atlantic they saw a sail to the north-west, and the squadron began to exchange signals with each other and to give chase "and half an hour after we let out our reefs and chased with the squadron ... but at seven in the evening, finding we did not near the chace ... we shortened sail, and made a signal for the cruisers to join the squadron. The next day but one we again discovered a sail, which on nearer approach we judged to be the same vessel. We chased her the whole day, and though we rather gained upon her, yet night came on before we could overtake her, which obliged us to give over the chace, to collect our scattered squadron. We were much chagrined at the escape of this vessel, as we then apprehended her to be an advice-boat sent from Old Spain to Buenos Ayres with notice of our expedition. But we have since learnt that we were deceived in this conjecture, and that it was our East India Company's packet bound to St Helena." This is certainly a fair proof of the sailing qualities of the Company's ships, seeing that not even the English cruisers could overhaul the merchant ship.

At this time the chief cargoes which these East Indiamen took out to the East still included those woollen goods which had been sent ever since the foundation of the first Company, and they continued to bring back saltpetre, but now tea was becoming a much more important cargo. But in addition to that tea which came home in the Company's ships and paid custom duty, there was a vast amount brought in by smugglers. And one argument used to be that this had to be, because the East Indiamen brought back chiefly the better, higher priced kind, compelling the dealers to send to Holland for the cheaper variety.

The East Indiamen's captains were not above engaging in the smuggling industry, at any rate as aiders and abettors. One of the methods was to wait until the ship arrived in the Downs. Men would come out from the Deal beach in their luggers and then take ashore quantities of tea secreted about their person. This was the reason why the Revenue cruisers were told to keep an especial watch on the Company's ships when homeward bound, because of "the illicit practices that are continually attempted to be committed by them." So notorious indeed and so ingenious were the methods to land goods without previously paying duty, that the Revenue cutters were ordered to follow these bigger ships all the way up Channel, keeping as close to them as possible as long as they were under sail, and when the East Indiaman came to anchor, the cutter was to bring up as near as possible to her. This was to prevent goods (such as silk and tea) being dropped through the ship's ports into a friendly boat that had come out from the beach, a practice that was by no means unknown on board these merchant craft home from the Orient.

Just as there was serious friction sometimes between the Revenue cutters and the ships of his Majesty's navy concerning the wearing of pendants, so these incidents were not unknown to happen to the ships of the Honourable East India Company. As an instance, Captain Balchen, R.N., during the year 1726 wrote to the latter complaining that one of their ships had hoisted a broad red pendant at the main topmast head. There was certainly no possible defence, and the Company were compelled to reply that they were "entire strangers" to the complaint, and would give directions to prevent this occurring again. But otherwise these East Indiamen were treated with far more respect than any other merchant ships. No finer ships other than men-of-war sailed the seas. On arriving at their port in India they were always saluted, and their captains ranked as Members of Council, being saluted with thirteen guns when they landed, and the guard turning out when they entered or left the fort. No one, in fact, other than officers of the Royal Navy received such respect. Under the captain were from four to eight officers in the bigger ships, who all wore uniforms, the duties on board being carried on with just the same discipline as in a man-of-war.

Some of the Company's servants were making handsome profits even when the Company itself was doing badly. Eastwick mentions the name of a purser who had such nice little perquisites out of his office that he left the service and became owner of a ship which traded between London and Calcutta. She was a ship of no mean size, for she carried thirty cabin passengers and 300 lascars, together with a large mixed cargo of the value of £13,000. And you may judge of the profits from the passenger source alone when it is stated that one of these cabins cost four hundred guineas for the voyage. The affairs of the Company had for some years been in a rather bad way. Instead of being able to pay to the Government the stipulated sum of £400,000 a year, the directors were actually compelled to ask the Government for a loan of £1,000,000. This was in the year 1772. The affairs of the Company were brought before Parliament, and a Committee exposed a series of intrigues and crime. It was to remedy this rotten condition of things that in June of 1773 two Bills were introduced, of which one authorised the loan just mentioned, and the other, celebrated as the India Act, effected most important changes in the Company's constitution and its relations to India. A Governor-General was appointed to reside in Bengal, to which the other presidencies were to be made subordinate. A supreme court of judicature was inaugurated at Calcutta. The salary of the Governor was to be £25,000 a year, and that of the Council members at £10,000 each, the chief judge receiving £8000 a year. From this time forth the Company's affairs were brought under the control of the Crown, all the departments were reorganised, and all the territorial correspondence had to be laid before the British Ministry.

It was certainly high time that the Company's affairs were taken in hand. Our present inquiry is concerned only with its merchant shipping, so we may confine ourselves strictly thereto. Had it not been for the wonderfully popular taste which the United Kingdom had now shown for tea, the Company's ships would have been compelled to cease trading with the East. When, in 1773, the Company's charter was once more renewed, a grant was made of a monopoly also to China. From about the middle of the eighteenth century, however, the Company had become more of a military than a trading concern, yet the latter was anything but insignificant. Enormous tracts of land had been obtained in India. The governments of the native princes were corrupt, and the East India Company was strong. The British Government was some thousands of miles across the sea, so gradually but surely, without much interference, the Company had obtained a strong grip on the natives. From that followed extortion, and when the Company's servants returned home they came with fortunes, even though the Company itself was doing badly.

In the year 1772 the East India Company were employing fifty-five ships abroad, aggregating 39,836 tons. At home they owned, and there were being built for its service thirty ships of an aggregate of 22,000 tons. In 1784 the number of its ships at home and abroad was sixty-six. The chief object of the inquiry into the Company's trade with the East by the Committee just alluded to was apparently to see if the ships could be built and run more cheaply than under the present method of chartering. It was seen from the evidence of Sir Richard Hotham that the existing method of freighting the Company's ships could be improved upon to effect greater economy, for whereas the Company were paying in the year 1772 as much as £32 a ton for the carriage of fine goods, this expert witness expressed himself as willing to bring goods from any part of the East at £21 a ton.

The result of this inquiry was that important changes had to be made. The Company began to put its shipping business into proper condition. The Company decided to build for its own use a number of bigger ships than they had been wont to use, and thus those wonderful East Indiamen, for which the eighteenth century will ever be famous, came into being. They were of 1200 to 1400 nominal tons, though their real measurement was greater than this. Such ships began to be built about the year 1781, though in earlier days, as the reader is aware, the ships had recently averaged between 400 and 500 tons, not exceeding the latter figure. The new type, of course, did not entirely drive the smaller ones straight off the sea, but the two classes existed side by side. We alluded just now to the terrible national evil of smuggling. This vice had reached amazing limits during the eighteenth century, and the country was in such a state of alarm, and honest traders complained so bitterly of the disastrous effects on their prosperity, that in the year 1745 a beginning was made of an inquiry by a Parliamentary Committee into the causes of smuggling and the most effectual methods to stop it. We have seen that tea, because of its recent popularity, was especially an article beloved by these smugglers. We need not enter further into this inquiry, but evidence showed that one of the best means of ending this illicit trade would be to reduce the duties, thus not making it worth while for the illicit trader to carry on his work. Now when Pitt did reduce the duties on various Indian productions, but especially on tea, it was found that a complete change was made in the demand for this commodity. Many thousand more pounds' weight were now required, the sales were trebled, and thus there was a much greater shipping business. The export trade to China now began to be most important also, and the Company was prospering.

But before we proceed any further we must just see the conditions which were in existence up to 1773 in regard to the method of chartering ships by the Company from the owners. It was agreed that these hired ships were to be surveyed by the Company whenever the latter desired, and it is typical of the times that the proviso had to be inserted that the Company's surveyors "are to be civilly treated." In order that the ship might be efficiently armed, the commander and owners were liable to a fine of £40 for each gun that was wanting. If any of the guns were sold, the owners and commander were to be fined £100 for each gun, and the commander to be dismissed the Company's service. The commander was also to obey the Company's orders during the voyage, as well as their agents and factors. In order to encourage the seamen, the Company agreed to reward them when the ship returned to the Thames from the East Indies at the end of the voyage—that is to say, if they had been able to prevent any wilful damage to the Company's property, or save them from being lost, a reward suitable for the benefit was to be made. If a seaman were to lose his life in defending the ship, his next of kin was to receive £30. If he lost a limb, he himself was to have the same sum. If he received minor wounds he was to be given some smaller monetary reward and to be "cured of his wounds" at the Company's expense.

The Company expressly forbade these hired ships from calling at places other than those which it ordered, or to take any foreign coin or bullion, goods or provisions at any place short of her consigned port. The cargo was to be disposed in the best manner to prevent damage, and so that the working of the ship and her efficient defence would not be interfered with. Pepper was not to be shot loose between decks or the freight would not be paid for. If the ship should touch at St Helena or the island of Ascension she was not to sail without the permission of the Governor and Council. Nor was she to touch at Barbadoes, or any American port, or any of the western islands, or even Plymouth, without orders or some unavoidable danger of the sea, under a penalty of £500. The commander, chief and second mates were to keep journals of the ship's daily proceedings, from the time when she first took in cargo in the River Thames to the time of her return and discharge of her cargo in England. Wind, weather, and all the remarkable transactions, accidents and occurrences during the voyage were to be noted in these journals, as also of everything received into the ship. These journals were to be delivered up to the Company afterwards, on oath, if required.

No unlicensed goods were to be carried in the ship nor any passengers to be taken without permission. The ship was to have her full complement of men during the voyage, and none of these crews was to be furnished by the master or officers with money, liquor, or provisions beyond the value of one-third of what the wages of such seamen should amount to at that particular time. The paymaster (who was appointed by the Company and owners jointly) was to pay the seamen's wives one month's wages in six. The commander was to have the use of the ship's great cabin, unless it were required for the Company's servants voyaging out or home. It was the duty of the part-owners or the master to send in the ship always the sum of £500 in foreign coins or bullion for use in the case of extraordinary expenses during the voyage. The commander was also to be supplied with £200 a month for paying wages and provisions while in India or China. And whenever lascars were hired, the Company were to pay for their hire. We shall refer to the subject of these lascars again presently, but we may now go on to witness the development of the Company's shipping after the inauguration of those reforms at which we hinted just now.

CHAPTER XIII

THE EAST INDIAMEN'S ENEMIES

The East India Company had recovered from their period of desolation. They had set their house in order, had been granted a further extension of their monopoly, were opening up a good trade with China, and had received fresh capital for their operations in wider spheres. The trade of the East was practically now in the hands of England, the Dutch East India Company having suffered very heavily, and the French East India Company after languishing had come to an end in 1790. Although there had been formed the first Danish East India Company as far back as 1612, and a Spanish Royal Company for trading with the Philippines incorporated in 1733 and an Ostend East India Company incorporated by the Emperor of Austria in 1723; yet the last-mentioned had become bankrupt in 1784, and now the English East India Company, after many vicissitudes, was left practically the sole surviving trading power in the Orient.

Under Pitt's Act the directors of the English Company were allowed to superintend their shipping and matters of commerce as before, yet the Board of Control exercised its influence both in England and India. Each year the Company settled the number of ships to be built and their sizes. For instance, in 1784, as they saw that at least four more ships would be required, they ordered six to be built. The keels were to be laid down within six months, and the ships were to be launched within twelve months of the laying of the keel. The following year they decided to have three sets of shipping with about thirty ships in each class, so leave was given for eight ships to be built. Tenders were therefore advertised for in January 1786, much to the indignation of the owners, who complained that this advertisement was directed against their interests. They denied that hitherto their rates for freight had been exorbitant, and protested that they had embarked on immense shipbuilding programmes expressly for the Company's benefit. The Company therefore replied, inviting them to send in tenders, which was done, the same rate being offered as in the preceding season—viz. £26 a ton to China direct, £27 for coast and China, Bombay £28, coast and bay £29. On 9th June of that year a tender was offered the Company to build a 1000-ton ship at £22 a ton for the first two voyages, and £20 for the third and fourth voyages.

Up till the year 1789 the size of the Company's recent big ships had been from 750 to 800 tons. But in this year it was decided to build five ships of from 1100 to 1200 tons. The following May the Court resolved that from past experience ships could quite well make three voyages without stripping off their sheathing. And, further, those ships which had been accustomed to make the fourth trip their repairing voyage might with perfect safety perform even six voyages. A by-law of 1773 had restricted the employment of ships for more than four voyages, but this was now modified, and instead of four voyages agreements were entered into with the owners for the ships to run six.

It was decided also by the Company in the year 1789 to allow the commanders and officers of their ships to fill, freight free, all such outward tonnage as might be unoccupied by the Company, and to allow the Company's servants and merchants residing under the Company's protection in India to fill up such homeward tonnage as might be unoccupied by the Company, at a reasonable freight. When we come to the year 1793 we have to deal with an important Act of the reign of George III., which had far-reaching effects. The Company's charter was extended until 1814, but provision was made for opening up the Indian trade to private individuals, and thus the long-lived monopoly of the Company was doomed. At length the agitations of the Liverpool and Bristol shipowners to be allowed to participate in the East India trade were to have some sort of effect, though it was far from what was desired. However, one of the conditions of the renewal of the Company's exclusive privilege under this Act was that any of the Company's civil servants in India, and the free merchants living in India under the Company's protection, might be permitted to send to Europe on their own account and risk in the Company's ships all kinds of Indian goods with the exception of calicoes, dimities, muslins and other piece-goods. And "for insuring to private merchants and manufacturers the certain and ample means of exporting their merchandize to the East Indies, and importing the returns for the same, and the other goods, wares and merchandize, allowed by this Act, at reasonable rates of freight," the Company was ordered to set apart at least 3000 tons of shipping every year. The charge was to be £5 a ton on the outward voyage in times of peace, and. £15 homeward. But in the time of war the rates should be increased if the Board of Control approved. It was further stipulated that his Majesty's subjects might be allowed to export from England to India any produce or manufactured goods except military stores, ammunition, masts, spars, cordage, pitch, tar and copper. But in all cases of exports and imports in this Anglo-Indian trade the goods must travel in the Company's ships. These vessels, provided under the Act, thus became known as "extra East Indiamen," and sometimes in reading books of voyages and travel of this period you will find the narrator informing the reader that he travelled to the East on board the "extra" East Indiaman so-and-so. It may be stated at once that though the Act was obeyed, it produced little result, for considering that the Company still had such a powerful monopoly of trade in the East, it was quite impossible for home merchants to compete with such a corporation. Most manufacturers and merchants declined to avail themselves of this privilege, full well realising beforehand how useless it would be. However, the Company fulfilled their obligation to provide this additional tonnage, though it entailed a heavy expenditure without much benefit to the public. The people who benefited most were the servants of the Company, who, being homeward bound, were able to bring back to England Indian produce that would find a ready market here.

In the year 1793 the Company had only thirty-six vessels of 1200 tons each and forty of 800 tons each. This of course represented the whole of the British shipping trading to the East. Some idea of the shipbuilding programmes of the next few years may be gathered from the following facts, bearing in mind that the Company were trading to China as well as to India, and that both big and moderate-sized ships were deemed necessary. Thus in October of 1793 the Court decided that sixteen ships of from 700 to 800 tons were necessary, and one of 1200 tons for the annual imports from India in their regular commerce; and that fifteen large ships of 1200 tons would be required for imports from China. When a ship became worn out by age, accident or inability, an advertisement was published, describing the size of the ship required, inviting tenders and specifying the rate of freight to be paid for six voyages, the ship to be commanded by the captain of the ship whose bottom was worn out. In December of the following year it was resolved that ships of 1400 tons were the most suitable for the Company's trade to China, but that these ships should be tendered at 1200 tons only. So also the regular ships (as distinct from the extra East Indiamen) which brought home their rich cargoes from Bengal and Madras were not to exceed 820 tons and to be chartered at 799 tons. It was further settled that ships of from 480 to 520 tons were the most suitable craft for bringing home what were known as "gruff" goods—that is, cargoes of Indian goods consisting of such raw materials as cotton, rice, sugar, pepper, hemp and saltpetre. The silks, muslins, tea and fine goods were carried in the Company's larger ships, which carried also the passengers. From the latter quite a large revenue was obtained, as soon as the Company's rule in India became fully established.

The public were still very jealous of the Company's private monopoly, and the country was deluged by pamphleteers and tractarians giving vent to this indignation. However, some benefit had been obtained by a reduction in the freights, and it was brought about in the following manner. The suggestion was made that great advantages would result if India-built ships were employed by the Company for the spare freight which was lying ready for shipment to Europe. English oak was getting scarcer, and therefore dearer, and could ill be spared so long as the Royal Navy continued to be wooden walls: whereas out in India the Company owned inexhaustible forests. So from the year 1795 India-built ships were for the first time allowed to take exports and imports. They were commonly known as "country-built" ships, and in the year mentioned twenty-seven of these craft were despatched from India with cargoes of rice. The cost of engaging these ships was at £16 a ton for rice and other deadweight goods and £20 a ton for light goods, the ships to arrive and discharge in the Thames. As a result a saving in one season alone was made of £183,316 in respect of freights. But there occurred some keen disappointment to the owners of these India-built ships. The arrangement had been that, having delivered the goods mentioned in the Thames, they should be allowed to take back to India whatever merchandise they cared to put aboard. Many of these ships had been built as a speculation, their owners believing that they would be taken into the Company's regular service and so be employed permanently. Notwithstanding that they had been warned against any such supposition, it came as a bitter grief to them when they realised that after the Company's immediate requirements were completed the services of these ships were no longer required; but for all that the day was now not far distant when trade to India was to be thrown open altogether. It is the last straw which breaks the camel's back, and the load which had been accumulating ever since the year 1600 was soon to reach the point when something would have to give way.

It should be explained that this was one of the most critical periods in the whole of England's naval chronicle and therefore of her very existence. The Battle of the Glorious First of June had been fought in 1794, and in this same year Martinique had been captured from the French. The year 1795 was to be even still more replete with naval doings. Ships and men were required as they had never been wanted before, and it was just in this respect that the existence of the East India Company was of the greatest direct benefit to the country and the navy. It must always be to its honour that the Company which had for so long enjoyed the privilege of the Indian monopoly was on this especial occasion to have the privilege of assisting the nation in a most valuable manner. At the opening of the year France possessed advantages which she had never previously enjoyed. She had made peace with Prussia, she had reduced Holland to submission and made a treaty with the latter, the result of which was that the Dutch fleet of about 120 ships was placed at France's disposal. These were well-built craft, manned by excellent crews who were seamen to their finger-tips. As against this, England was in a condition of isolation and there was a tremendous amount of work to be done and too few ships at hand. For Brest had to be watched, and the Mediterranean fleet had to look after the French based on Toulon. Admiral Duncan had to be sent across the North Sea to prevent any Dutch ships from emerging out of the Texel, but in the southern part of the world something much more historic was destined to occur, for the Cape of Good Hope was captured from the Dutch, and just at the time when our success hung in the balance a strong squadron of East Indiamen arrived with a reinforcement of British troops. The result was that against this force the Dutch could no longer stand. The Dutch settlement (and incidentally a brig belonging to the Dutch East India Company) now became British.

Never had the East India Company been more useful to the navy than in this year. Ships and seamen cannot be got by the mere signing of documents unless they already exist, and it was lucky for the nation that such fine, stout craft, accustomed to long voyages and fighting, manned with such able crews, should already be at hand under the East India Company. At the time of which we speak no fewer than six of their finest vessels were taken into the nation's service straight away. Eight others which had not quite finished building were also assigned to the Government. In addition to these fourteen handsome craft, the Court of Directors also decided on the 13th of March to raise 3000 men at their own cost for the Royal Navy. This meant a loss of £57,000, but the nation needed it and the Company did their duty. During the ensuing July the Company further decided that fourteen East Indiamen should be placed at the disposal of the Government in September ready to carry troops across the ocean—a work for which they were extremely well fitted—and we have just seen to what advantage this was done. England at this time was distressed by the scarcity of corn, but in order to relieve this distress in some measure large quantities of rice were brought home by twenty-seven ships which the Company purposely added to their fleet for the emergency, and these were the India-built ships of which we spoke just now. Thus in more ways than one, but certainly to the utmost of their ability, the East India Company had come to Britain's aid when she was passing through a time of great crisis.

During this year the seas which wash the Indian coast were really unsafe to merchantmen by reason of the presence of both French and Dutch cruisers and privateers. The British naval strength in those waters was very inadequate, and we had suffered some naval disasters which were neither a credit to our seamanship nor likely to maintain our prestige as gallant sea-fighters. The whole of the Bay of Bengal was being scoured by French men-of-war ready to fall upon any merchant craft that dared show herself. The privateers were both numerous, well manned, well armed, well commanded and very fast sailers. The consequence was that the East Indiamen never completed their voyages without having some excitement. Nor were pirates exterminated; especially along the Malabar coast, where they had many fastnesses, their strongholds being protected by forts. These men feared nothing, and had actually come out and defeated English, French and Dutch men-of-war that had been especially sent out to punish them, in some cases even capturing their enemy's ships. A French 40-gun frigate had been compelled to haul down her colours to these robbers of the sea: one of the East India Company's ships, armed with twenty guns, had also been taken after a fair fight, and three Dutch men-of-war. For some years they were crushed by the wholesome effect of a regular expedition which the English had sent against them, but after a few years they broke out again in their piracy and by the year 1798 they were freely capturing European ships.

On at least one occasion, however, they made a serious mistake, which might have been even still more grievous for them but for a piece of luck. It happened that H.M.S. *Centurion*, a 50-gun frigate, was cruising in the neighbourhood, and her the pirates mistook for a merchantman, for the East Indiamen were very similar in appearance to the frigates of the Royal Navy. One of the favourite devices of these rovers was to creep up under cover of darkness and wedge the rudder of the ship they intended to attack, their victim being thus rendered unable to manœuvre. In the present instance they had succeeded in carrying out this tactic to the *Centurion*, and then surrounded the ship and began their attack. The frigate was certainly surprised, but she soon had her guns loaded and brought them to bear on the pirates, and so punished them with a hot fire, which had not been expected, that they were glad to take to flight. It was only the fact of the wedged rudder which prevented the *Centurion* from being steered in pursuit and capturing their craft. However, it was a lesson to them in the future, and they attacked only when they were certain of their victim.

Of the privateers which hung about in Indian waters, one of the most notorious was the *Malartic*, which had captured two of the East Indiamen, *Raymond* and *Woodcot*, of 793 and 802 tons respectively. Whenever it was known that this ship was in the offing, no merchantman dared put to sea. She eventually captured the *Princess Royal*, an 805 tonner, and other East Indiamen, but was herself finally taken by the Company's ship *Phœnix*. So great was the relief occasioned by this deliverance that Captain Moffat, the *Phœnix's* commander, was afterwards publicly presented with a sword of honour. But an even more dangerous privateer was the *Confiance*. This was a very beautiful ship, and the envy of every captain who set eyes on her. Captain Eastwick, who knew her well, and to whose account I am indebted, described her as follows:—"She sat very low upon the water, and had black sides with yellow moulding posts, and a French stern all black. She carried a red vane at her maintopgallant masthead, very square yards and jaunt masts, upright and without the smallest rake either forward or aft. Her sails were all cut French fashion, and remarkable, having a great roach and steering sail, very square. There was not a ship in those seas that she could not overtake or sail away from. It was the custom of her commander, Captain Sourcouff, to ply his crew with liquor, and they always fought with the madness of drink in them."

It was this ship which attacked the East Indiaman *Kent*, and after a heavy engagement killed or wounded no fewer than sixty of the merchantman's crew, with the result that the latter was forced to haul down her flag. When the news of this occurrence reached Calcutta, two of the Company's frigates were sent in pursuit of the privateer, and both coming up with her began to attack with such determination that it was certain the *Confiance* would have to yield. This, however, she refused to do, and though she had only twenty-two guns, her captain fought his ship with great gallantry, and even though his losses were necessarily great, he was able at the end to escape by the speed of his ship. The *Kent*, however, was retaken from the clutches of the *Confiance* and brought into Calcutta, and a few years later the *Confiance* herself was also captured. And you may imagine with what joy the news of her capture was received when it was reckoned that within one single twelvemonth not less than £2,000,000 worth of British shipping had been captured or sunk by the French privateers or men-of-war.

And there was the curious incident of the *Lord Eldon* being nearly captured right on the doorstep, so to speak, of her home. This ship was an East Indiaman outward bound to India. At the moment of which we are speaking she had backed her sails and was lying off the Needles hove-to, as she awaited some passengers who had been delayed in joining her. But whilst she was thus hove-to a sea fog suddenly came down. Not far off was a French privateer hovering about, and this was the chance of a century. Under cover of this fog he approached the East Indiaman unobserved, so that he came right alongside. When the men on board the *Lord Eldon* discovered this big ship close up to them in the haze they were alarmed, but not for the reason that you might suppose. It did not occur to them that she was a privateer, but they assumed she was one of the King's ships and was now about to impress the East Indiaman's crew into the navy in the manner that we saw in an earlier chapter. As the crew had no desire to come under impressment, they at once hid, with the result that the privateer's men had no difficulty in coming on board the *Lord Eldon*. The captain was below at the time, and hearing a noise and clamour came on deck to see what it was all about: and then to his amazement found that his ship was in the hands of the enemy. However, he was not one easily to be daunted, even by such a surprise as this. His life was made up of things unexpected, and knowing that his men were well drilled he called to them to repel boarders. They at once responded to the command and came out from their hiding-places, and after a sharp fight drove the invaders overboard. One Frenchman had even got possession of the *Lord Eldon's* wheel, but the East Indiaman's captain killed him with his own hand, cutting off his head with one stroke of the sword. In a very short time the privateer, who was now more surprised than the crew of the merchant ship, hurriedly made sail and disappeared into the fog. The incident well shows the fighting efficiency of the commanders and men of the Company's vessels at this period.

During the early part of the eighteenth century about a dozen or fifteen of the Company's ships would sail to the East Indies from London, but this average gradually rose till, about the year 1779, there were about twenty vessels going out each year. But thereafter the numbers increased to such an extent that in some years there were as many as thirty or forty: and in the year 1795 as many as seventy-six did the voyage. After that date the numbers became again normal, so that up to about the end of 1810 the average was more like forty or fifty. But even this meant a great deal of trade from which the country and Company were to benefit largely.

CHAPTER XIV

SHIPS AND MEN

Bombay had been first so called by the Dutch, meaning Good Bay. Owing to its spaciousness, excellent depth of water and other facilities it was well designated. By the end of the eighteenth century it had its dry and wet docks and every facility for careening and repairing ships, being of great utility to the Company's merchant ships and its navy as well. Its dockyard was furnished with all kinds of necessary stores. Here there was always on hand plenty of timber and planking, here anchors could be forged, here new cables and ropes were made of all kinds. The cables were of hemp, but for the smaller ropes the external fibres of the cocoanut, so abundant in India, were made up into that inferior type of rope known as kyah or coir.

We called attention on another page to the introduction of India-built vessels into the Company's service. India of course is famous for its teak, and every shipman knows what excellent material this wood is for building craft, owing to its hardness and durability. The vessels which Bombay built were fine, stout ships and excellently finished, and Indian shipbuilders even constructed some battleships and frigates for the British navy which were in every way splendid vessels. One vessel named the *Swallow,* which was built out here and launched in April 1777, was actually in use till she was lost on a shoal in the Hooghly in June 1823. But during this lengthy period of usefulness she had served in many seas and in various capacities. She was first employed as one of the Company's packets between India and England. After that she was in the Bombay Marine, or the East India Company's navy. After that she again resumed service as one of the Company's merchantmen, where she remained for many years. About the beginning of the nineteenth century she was sold to the Danes, and from Copenhagen proceeded to the West Indies, where she was arrested as a prize by a British man-of-war. She was then employed in the King's service and became a sloop-of-war, and afterwards sold out of the service to some merchants. In this capacity she again made several voyages between London and Bombay, and eventually brought her fine career to an end as stated.

The East Indiaman "Swallow."

This vessel was of about 700 tons, and armed with eighteen guns. She is here seen in the year 1788 in different ways—hove-to for a pilot, under plain sail, and before the wind under all sail.

(By kind permission of the P. & O. Steam Navigation Company)

Before the close of the eighteenth century the Battle of the Nile had been fought and won. The importance of this to India was tremendous. For had the result been otherwise Napoleon would have possessed himself of all that the English East India Company had done there. Our Anglo-Indian trade would have come to an end, and the ships which are the subject of our present study would have been no longer required, or else compelled to sail under the French flag. Nelson, in fact, had despatched a messenger overland to the Governor of Bombay, informing the latter of the arrival of the French in Egypt, for he knew well that Bombay was the objective of the enemy if they could get there. However, Nelson's victory at the Nile quite altered all this, and when the East India Company afterwards voted the gallant admiral the sum of £10,000, it was to show how deeply indebted was this corporation for the welcome relief from catastrophe.

Before we leave the eighteenth century we have to consider some of the more important changes and developments which were taking place. We have seen that the size of these East Indiamen had gradually increased during the century. About the year 1700 the biggest vessels were under 500 tons. Some were even much smaller, as, for instance, the *Juno*, of 180 tons, and the *Success* and the *Borneo* of similar size, but there was also the *Arabella*, of only 140 tons, and the *Benjamin*, of 160 tons. Between the years 1748 and 1772 all the Company's merchant ships are of one size—499 tons. There are very few exceptions indeed to this, and in those few instances you get an occasional ship of 180, 300, 350, 370 or 380 tons. Otherwise there is nothing but this stereotyped 499-ton ship year after year, season after season. This curious fact has puzzled many people, including those who in later days served in the Company's service. Why was it?

The answer is quite simple, and I give it on the authority of an old skipper contemporary with these ships, named Hutchinson, who at one time of his life had been a privateer. The reader will remember that in an earlier chapter I drew attention to the slackness of morals and general spirit of irreligion which were notorious of the mid-eighteenth century, at any rate so far as English people were concerned. Naturally enough this spirit spread to the ships of the East India Company, so that the corruption ashore had its counterpart afloat. Now these craft, when they were of 500 tons and over, were compelled to carry a chaplain. And it was just in order to be able to dispense with the latter, and so save expense, that the owners used to cause these ships to be rated at 499 tons, and so keep within the letter of the law. These 499-ton ships carried a captain, four mates, a surgeon and a purser. They would sail from the Downs about January or March of one year, proceed to India or China, and then be back again in the London river by June or July of the following year, though sometimes they were away for much longer periods. When homeward bound they had called at Portsmouth—where the more wealthy passengers went ashore and proceeded home by road—and the Downs, they eventually made fast to moorings at one of three places—Blackwall, Deptford and North-fleet.

We spoke, also, some time back of what were known as "hereditary bottoms," by which it was meant that an owner who had been accustomed to charter one of his ships to the Company had a proprietary right to supply other ships when this one had been worn out. Thus one finds, for instance, a ship called the *Brunswick* built on the bottom of the *Atlas*, the *Hindostan* built on the bottom of the *Grosvenor*, and so on. This went on for year after year, so that you could make out a kind of genealogical tree of East India ships. It was a very clear instance of eighteenth-century monopoly which would be hard to beat. But this principle of perpetuity came to an end on 6th February 1796, when open competition was introduced. There can be no question that this decision, together with that of abolishing the sale of commands, was all for the good of the service. The Company themselves recognised that it was the only way in which they could have an efficient fleet, always ready and consisting of vessels built on the best principles, inspected during construction by the Company's own surveyors, and commanded by officers "of acknowledged character, talents and experience," and various by-laws were passed to this effect. The following list will afford the reader some idea of the size and dimensions of these East Indiamen ships at the close of the eighteenth century. The difference between the burthen tonnage and the chartered tonnage is noticeable:—

Name of Ship	Length		Beam		Burthen Tonnage	Chartered Tonnage
	ft.	in.	ft.	in.		
Ganges	149	0	43	6	1502	1200
Hope	144	0	43	6	1471	1200
Neptune	144	0	43	6	1468	1200
Hindostan	144	0	43	6	1463	1248
Walmer Castle	144	0	43	6	1460	1200
Warley	144	0	43	6	1460	1200
Earl of Abergavenny	144	0	43	6	1460	1200
Royal Charlotte	144	0	43	6	1460	758
Coutts	144	0	43	6	1451	1200
Cirencester	144	0	43	0	1439	1200
Arniston	144	0	43	0	1433	1200
Glatton	144	0	43	0	1432	1200
Thames	144	0	43	0	1432	1200
Ceres	144	0	43	0	1430	1200
Cuffnells	144	0	43	0	1429	1200
Earl Talbot	144	0	43	0	1428	1200
Nottingham	130	0	40	0	1152	1152
Dorsetshire	134	0	42	0	1200	1200
Alfred	134	0	41	0	1221	1189
David Scott	134	0	42	0	1257	1200
Alnwick Castle	133	11½	42	0	1257	1200
Exeter	132	0	41	0	1265	1200

Carnatic	132	0	40	6	1169	1169
Boddam	128	0	38	6	1021	1021
Albion	125	0	38	0	961	961
Royal Admiral	120	2	37	10	914	914
Belvidere	123	0	38	8	986	987
Earl Howe	117	10	37	4¾	876	876
Sulivan	116	0	35	0	876	876
Middlesex	116	0	35	0	852	852
Princess Charlotte	102	0	33	6¾	610	610
Earl of Wycombe	101	10¾	34	5¾	643	655
Princess Mary	93	11	34	5¾	643	462

The science and art of shipbuilding in England during the eighteenth century were very defective compared with France. But during the last decade of this, and the early part of the nineteenth century, improvements were taking place. Papers were being read before the Royal Society, treatises were being published, a number of valuable experiments were being made and the best lessons of the French were being studied. To all this must be attributed the better type of East Indiaman which was to follow. The continued demand for tea made it necessary to have fine, big ships which could get the cargoes of this perishable commodity to London as soon as possible. It was always reckoned that an 800-ton ship would be able to bring home about 750,000 lb. of tea, and a 1200-ton ship nearly 1,500,000 lb. Some idea of the increased popularity of this commodity in England will be ascertained when it is stated that during the year 1765 five million lbs. were brought home and sold by the Company. By 1784 the average was about six million lb., the following year this figure was more than doubled, and by the end of the century it was nearly twenty-four million lb. There was, therefore, every need for fine, big ships of good lines. And by an Act of 1799 the Company were restricted from employing in their service any ships but those contracted for six voyages to India or China and back. Whenever they wished to have more ships built, they were to give public notice of this by advertisement four weeks ahead, inviting tenders for building and freighting.

But in the year 1803 the Company were empowered to engage ships for two additional voyages, making eight in all. Two reasons were given for this innovation. First, if was found that the ships now being built were of such a character that they could be repaired and refitted to perform these two additional voyages with great advantage. And secondly, it was contended that if fewer ships were built, this would "be the means of lessening the consumption of ship-timber." It will be recollected that in the year 1803 Napoleon had openly and intentionally insulted the British Ambassador, and that in the month of May war was again declared, and both nations made elaborate preparations for the resumption of hostilities, the British taking time by the forelock and sending squadrons to watch Brest and Toulon. All this warlike activity on sea made it not any easier for the East Indiamen to go about their lawful business. In effect it meant that they must be fitted out with even greater care and that they must be armed as strongly as ever they could be. And this, in turn, meant that the cost to the owners of the ships was much increased. "War extraordinaries," as they were called, were always a source of keen dispute during those anxious years, between the Company and the shipowners, and in this present case the Company were authorised to pay higher rates owing to the increased expense to the owners.

But such was the improvement in the class of vessel now built that in the year 1810 they were allowed by Act of Parliament to engage ships even beyond the allotted eight voyages, provided that after being repaired they were found fit for service. The Company were also allowed to take up by private contract certain other ships in order to bring home the cargoes from China and India. Under this class were chartered vessels which had taken out to New South Wales convicts and stores. The East India Company had already come to the country's aid again during that year, 1803. Ten thousand tons of shipping did they lend to the State for six months free of charge, though this meant a loss to the Company of £67,000. These ships were employed in guarding the British coast against the threatened invasion by the French; and in other ways they were found very useful to the Admiralty.

In peace time they would go out to India with troops and stores, calling at St Helena on the way, and then return home with cargoes from China and India. In the last-mentioned territorial waters they were almost as likely to be annoyed by the attentions of the press-gangs as they were in English waters, for his Majesty's ships out there were sadly in need of men. Repeated complaints were made by the Company in regard to this, even as they had previously complained of what used to take place at home. But repeated and indignant representations proved ineffectual. Captains of the Royal Navy must have men for their ships, and the distance between England and India was too great for much interference under this category, so things went on pretty much as before.

It will have been noticed from the list of the East India Company's ships given on an earlier page in this chapter that the size had immensely increased. Big ships always necessitate big accommodation when they reach port. These particular craft were far and away the biggest merchant ships in the world, for no other trade either required or could afford such vessels. This being so, the East Indiamen when they now arrived in the Thames were compelled to lie many miles down the river, since there was no accommodation for them higher up. But this was to subject them to a grave risk. They came home with most valuable cargoes which meant not only very much to the Company, but were actually of some national importance. As they lay out in the river a good deal of pilfering went on, and the loss was very serious, not merely to the Company and the shipowners, but to the State, which lost a good deal of customs duty thereby, since the goods thus pilfered were then smuggled ashore. It was therefore realised that the only remedy was to have a sufficient area of wet docks in which the ships could be loaded and unloaded. A number of gentlemen therefore decided to form a joint-stock company with a capital of £200,000 in order to provide wet docks to be enclosed by proper walls and ditches, and communicating with the Thames. These docks were to be appropriated solely for the ships in the India trade, who should pay a duty of 14s. a ton in the case of a registered English ship, and 12s. a ton for every India-built ship navigated by lascars. It was ordered that the hatches of every ship arriving from India or China should be locked down before the ship reached Gravesend, and the captain, and one of the two officers next to him in command, must remain on board until such time as the ship was moored in the docks, and the keys of the hatches handed over to an officer of the East India Company. Of the thirteen directors of these docks, four must be directors of the East India Company.

The result of this was that the East India Docks, so well known to all who take any interest in the port of London, were brought into being. During the early part of the year 1914, whilst alterations were being made in connection with the elaborate scheme for the improvement of London's shipping facilities, the original foundation-stone of the undertaking was discovered. This had been laid as far back as 4th March 1804. It had been submerged in the import dock, but was revealed at the base of one of the old quay walls, from which it slightly projected. On its top were found recorded the names of Mr Joseph Cotton, who was then Chairman of the East India Dock Company, and of Mr John Woolmore, the deputy chairman. The inscription stated that the stone had been laid by Mr Joseph Huddart, F.R.S., and the names of the engineers, Mr John Rennie and Mr Ralph Walker, were added. After the dock was opened there were for many years seen therein the pick of the world's shipping. But now, with the overwhelming conquest of the steamship the whole aspect has been quite changed. Gone are those fine old wind-jammers, gone is the romance of these ships from the Orient, gone is the stately, naval system under which these vessels were run, gone are the handsome opportunities for making fortunes which were then open to the captains and officers of the mercantile marine.

In some years these ships were very unfortunate. The years 1808 and 1809 were particularly unhappy for the Company's craft. Ten homeward-bound East Indiamen were lost, and with them vanished over a million sterling. The months of November 1808 and March 1809 were notoriously stormy. Even such big craft as the *Britannia* (1200 tons) and the *True Briton* (1198 tons) were lost during this period. The former went down off the South Foreland on 25th January 1809. The latter had parted company from the Bombay ships on 13th October in that year, whilst sailing in the China seas, and was never heard of again. The *Admiral Gardner* had set forth from the Downs on 24th January 1809, and also foundered off the South Foreland on the same day as the *Britannia*. The *Calcutta* parted company with the other East Indiamen off Mauritius on 14th March 1809, and was never seen again. Other ships were captured by the enemy, some were blown up, others ended their days by fire, some ran ashore, but as a rule these old East Indiamen managed to get their freights into the London river with safety.

About the year 1809 the rates of insurance between Bengal and England were £7, 7s. for the regular East Indiaman, and £7 on her cargo. In the case of "extra" ships the premium was £9, 9s. on the ship and £9 on the cargo. India-built ships were not insured at all, but the cargo was insured at £15, 15s. If the Company's ships were convoyed home, then the "extra" craft were charged only £1 from Bengal to St Helena, and another £1 from St Helena to England. If there were more than one ship then only 19s. was charged in both cases, but India-built ships in these instances were charged £2, 10s.

Commodore Sir Nathaniel Dance.

(By courtesy of Messrs. T. H. Parker Brothers)

The number of ships employed for the India and China trade during the years 1803 to 1808 will be found indicative of the Company's activities. These varied from forty-four to fifty-three, and their burden from 36,671 to 45,342 tons. They ran great risks sometimes, but in spite of occasional casualties they were often more than able to look after themselves, when no naval force could be spared to convoy them. One of the most famous instances on record is that in which the exploits of a certain Captain Nathaniel Dance figured prominently. This gallant commander was in charge of the Company's ship *Earl Camden*. This vessel was of 1200 tons charter, and had sailed from England in the season of 1802-1803. She had put into Torbay, and left there on 4th January 1803, and proceeded to Bombay and China. On the last day of January in the following year she had filled up her holds and began her return voyage from China. With her sailed also fifteen other East Indiamen, named respectively the *Warley, Alfred, Royal George, Coutts, Wexford, Ganges, Exeter, Earl of Abergavenny, Henry Addington, Bombay Castle, Cumberland, Hope, Dorsetshire, Warren Hastings* and *Ocean*. And inasmuch as Captain Dance was the senior commander he acted as commodore for this China fleet. In addition to these sixteen vessels a number of other vessels were put under his charge to convoy them as far as their courses were the same. These vessels included a dozen "country" ships.

The "country" trade, by the way, was the trade between India and the East as far as China and Manila. It was largely carried on by civil servants of the East India Company and the free merchants living under the Company's protection. In effect the Company resigned this trade to these people, the scope of this commerce to the westward extending as far as the Red Sea, the principal commodities being indigo, pepper and cotton. Of the East India Company's ships the *Ganges* was a fast-sailing brig, which was to be employed by Dance in any way that might tend to the safety and convenience of the fleet until it had passed through the Straits of Malacca, when he was to send her on to Bengal.

On the 14th of February at daybreak the *Royal George* made a signal to the commodore that she had sighted four strange sail to the south-west. Thereupon Dance signalled that the *Alfred, Royal George, Bombay Castle* and the *Hope* should run down and examine them. It happened that among the passengers aboard Dance's ship was Lieutenant Fowler, R.N., and the latter, who had recently been commander of the *Porpoise*, offered to go in the *Ganges* brig and, getting quite close up to the strange craft, examine them carefully. To this the commodore assented, and away she went too. After a while Dance learned by signal that the four strange vessels were none other than a squadron of the enemy, consisting of a line-of-battle ship, two frigates and a brig. At one P.M. Dance signalled to his scouts to return, and formed the line of battle in close order. Now this merchant captain was a decidedly able tactician, and it is most interesting to note the way he disposed his forces for battle.

Repulse of Admiral Linois by the China Fleet under Commodore Sir Nathaniel Dance.

(By courtesy of Messrs. T. H. Parker Brothers)

When the enemy saw that they could "fetch" in the wake of the East Indiamen, they went about, but the commodore held on his course, keeping under easy sail. About sunset the enemy were close up to the rear of the English fleet, and as Dance momentarily expected his rear ships would be attacked, he stood by to succour them. But as the day ended no attack came, and the enemy hauled off to windward. Meanwhile the commodore sent Lieutenant Fowler in the *Ganges* to station the twelve country ships to leeward of the line of East Indiamen, so that the latter were between the enemy and the country ships. This was duly carried out and Mr Fowler returned, bringing with him some volunteers from the latter to help work the East Indiamen in the fight. All night long the ships lay in their line of battle, and at daybreak the enemy were descried about three miles to windward hove-to. The English ships now hoisted their colours and offered battle. The enemy's four ships hoisted French colours. These ships consisted of the *Marengo*, an 84-gun ship with 1200 men; the *Belle Poule*, 44 guns and 490 men; the *Semilante*, 36 guns and 400 men; and the *Berceau*, 32 guns and 350 men. The *Marengo* was seen to be flying the flag of a rear-admiral. In addition there was an 18-gun brig under Dutch colours.

At nine A.M., as the enemy showed no signs of engaging, the commodore formed the order of sailing and resumed his course, still under easy sail. But the enemy now filled his sails and edged towards the China fleet. At 1 P.M. it was obvious that the rear-admiral's intention was to cut off the English rear, so Dance made the signal to tack and bear down on him and engage him in succession, the *Royal George* being the leading ship, the *Ganges* second, and the *Earl Camden* (flagship) next. This was done and then under a press of sail the British ships ran towards the enemy—a very magnificent sight for those privileged to behold it. The enemy then formed in a very close line, and opened fire on the first ships, but this was not returned until the distance was much reduced. The *Royal George* had to bear the brunt of the engagement, being in the van, and in consequence suffered, but she got as close as she could to the enemy. As soon as their guns could have effect, the *Ganges* and *Earl Camden* opened fire, and the rest of the ships were ready to go into action as soon as their guns could bear. But before this was possible the French rear-admiral had taken alarm, the enemy hauled their wind and made away to the eastward, with every stitch of sail they could set. They had been beaten—and by merchantmen.

Dance then made the signal for a general chase. This was at 2 P.M., and the retreating enemy were pursued for two hours, but as the commodore feared that further pursuit would take his fleet too far from the Straits, and that his first duty was to preserve his ships rather than give the enemy any further beating, he made the signal to tack, and at 8 P.M. anchored for the night, so as to be able to make for the entrance of the Straits in the morning. The casualties were confined to the *Royal George*, which had lost one man killed and one more wounded. Her sails and hull had received many shot, but both the *Ganges* and the *Earl Camden* were practically untouched. The enemy's gunnery was distinctly bad, the shot falling either short or over.

Every man who took part in this extraordinary engagement had done his duty handsomely. Captain Timins of the *Royal George* had taken his ship into action most gallantly, but every ship in the English line had been cleared and prepared for action, anxious to have the opportunity of showing their worth. As the enemy had now long since disappeared there was nothing for Dance to do but continue on his homeward voyage. From Malacca he despatched Fowler in the *Ganges* brig to Pulo Penang, asking the captain of any of his Majesty's ships to convoy this exceedingly valuable fleet—the value of the sixteen ships together with their cargoes and private property amounting to nearly eight million pounds sterling. It was learned at Malacca that the squadron which had just been encountered was that of Admiral Linois, comprising a battleship, two heavy frigates, a corvette and the brig.

On the 28th of February, whilst in the Straits of Malacca, Dance's fleet fell in with two of his Majesty's ships, *Albion* and *Sceptre,* and the *Albion's* captain was prevailed upon to take charge now of the fleet, considering its national importance, and on the 9th of June these treasure ships reached St Helena, still under the convoy of the two British men-of-war. There the latter parted company from the merchantmen, and instead H.M.S. *Plantagenet* convoyed them to England, where they arrived early in the month of August. The news of this successful engagement, the circumstance that an enemy's fleet had been put to flight and chased by a fleet of East Indiamen caused the greatest acclamation in London. The Patriotic Fund Committee presented Commodore Dance with a sword of the value of £100, and a silver vase of the same worth; to Captain Timins a sword of the value of £50, and each of the other captains, as well as to Lieutenant Fowler.

As for the directors of the East India Company, they showed their appreciation of the gallantry and the preservation of their property in the most handsome manner. Setting aside about £50,000 they rewarded Commodore Dance with the sum of 2000 guineas, and a piece of plate valued at 200 guineas. To Captain Timins 1000 guineas and a piece of plate valued at 100 guineas. To Captain Moffat 500 guineas and a piece of plate valued at 100 guineas. The other thirteen captains were each awarded 500 guineas and a piece of plate valued at 50 guineas. The chief officers received each 150 guineas, the second officers 125 guineas, and so on down to the boatswains, who got 50 guineas, and the seamen and servants 6 guineas each. The Company also presented Lieutenant Fowler with 300 guineas and a piece of plate, as well as 500 guineas to the captain of the *Plantagenet,* who had convoyed them home from St Helena.

Commodore Sir Nathaniel Dance was offered a baronetcy, which he refused, but accepted a knighthood: and thus ended the last chapter in an incident that was the pride and subject of yarning among the men of the East India Company's service for many a long day. It certainly shows the British merchant sailor at his best—ready for a fight, going into the engagement gallantly, and yet all the while remembering that his first duty is to his owners and to get ships and cargoes safely to port without unnecessarily wasting valuable time.

CHAPTER XV

AT SEA IN THE EAST INDIAMEN

The first decade of the nineteenth century had been very unfortunate for the East India Company. There had been the losses of those ships already mentioned, owing to disasters at sea. This meant not only the loss to the Company of the rich cargoes, but of the advances to the owners amounting to thousands of pounds. The French war had also not merely interfered with the coming and going of the merchant ships, but it had thrown the whole of Europe into such a state of bewilderment that commerce generally was paralysed, and therefore the trade in Indian goods to the different parts of the Continent was exceedingly curtailed. Notwithstanding all that had been done by the Act of 1796, and the superintendence which was exercised over the Company, the latter was anything but prosperous. It had been engaged in hostilities with the Mahrattas and other Eastern powers. The result had been the acquisition of vast territory which was shortly to be for the good of the British Empire. But the immediate result of all this was that the Company's finances were in a crippled condition. Later on we shall see what a wholesale effect the abolition of the monopoly had on the Eastern trade, dating from the year 1813: but before we come to that I desire to give the reader a fair account of the conditions of life in the East Indiamen of the first part of the nineteenth century. We shall presently proceed to examine these in greater detail, but it will greatly assist the imagination if we look into contemporary accounts left behind by officers who put to sea in these craft.

And first of all let us take the account of that Captain Eastwick whom we introduced to the reader on an earlier page. This time he was proceeding to India, not in his capacity of mercantile officer, but as a passenger. Nevertheless his ripe knowledge and experience were of the greatest value to these East Indiamen, as will be seen. It was a tedious business in those days to get down to Portsmouth, where the wealthier passengers used to join the East Indiamen. Eastwick was taking out to India his sister-in-law on a visit to her brother-in-law, Colonel Gordon. The journey was made to Portsmouth by road, of course, and those who have motored along this Portsmouth road scarcely realise how tedious and risky the journey was in those days. In the month of January 1809 Eastwick and his sister-in-law set out on their journey with a good deal of luggage and jewellery, as well as a hundred pounds in money. They had to cross Hounslow Heath, which was then infested with robbers, and there was every probability of the post-boys being held up, the horses shot and the passengers relieved of their possessions. However, in the present case the journey to Portsmouth was made without adventure, where it was learnt that the *Neptune* East Indiaman would not sail for another ten days.

This was a vessel of 1200 charter tons, and one of the largest of the East India Company's fleet, being employed for the voyage to Bombay and China, this being her sixth trip thereto. She was owned by Sir William Fraser, Bart., and commanded by Captain William Donaldson, under whom were a chief officer and three mates, a surgeon and a purser. After the *Neptune* and her fellow-ships of the Company's fleet had at last got under way a storm came up—the reader will remember that this year, 1809, was notorious for its virulent weather—and as a result the *Henry Addington,* another East Indiaman of about the same size, got driven to the eastward round Selsey Bill and struck the Bognor Rocks to the north-eastward of the Bill, and it was only with difficulty that she got off and reached Portsmouth again. This storm had dispersed the whole of the Company's fleet outward-bound, and the *Neptune* had found herself in the vicinity of the Channel Islands, where she was in extreme danger. Captain Donaldson ordered the second mate to go aloft and help to take in the foretopsail, but this the officer refused to do, and he was instantly "broke."

Eastwick thereupon volunteered to fill his place, and this offer was gladly accepted temporarily, the *Neptune* eventually sailing across the English Channel once more and let go anchor on the Mother Bank (to the west of Ryde, Isle of Wight). Here the ship was refitted for a second attempt, and the second mate had his place now taken by a Mr Richard Alsager, who had lately been M.P. for Surrey. At length the *Neptune* was ready for sea once more, the heavy weather had given way to beautiful summer, and the wind was fair for making a quick passage down the English Channel: so on 21st June the East India fleet weighed anchor and proceeded, consisting of the *Neptune, Henry Addington, Scaleby Castle* and the *True Briton*. These ships were all pretty much of the same size, though the *True Briton* was of 1198 charter tons. So fine did the weather continue that when the fleet was two days out from England the captain of the *Neptune* gave a dance on board to the passengers of *all* the ships, and the following evening another dance was given by the captain of the *Henry Addington*. Fortunately the passengers were safely rowed across the ocean to the entertaining vessel, and back. But most people will agree with Eastwick's criticism of this foolish proceeding. "I did not consider it prudent at such a season of the year to do these things at sea."

So the voyage continued as far as Table Bay with everything in their favour. After rounding the Cape, the *Neptune,* the *Scaleby Castle* and the *True Briton* shaped a course for Bombay, but the *Henry Addington* was compelled to stay behind in order to repair a bad leak that had broken out afresh. This was doubtless a relic of the incident on Bognor Rocks. Whilst approaching Madagascar Captain Donaldson invited the other two captains to come on board and dine with him, and during the conversation the subject came up of the disagreeable weather met with during the south-west monsoon on going into Bombay. Eastwick offered that if no pilot were available he would take the squadron in, and this the three captains accepted. The next day they encountered just that experience which the reader will remember occurred to some of the first English sailors when bound to India. For a heavy clap of thunder—"so loud it sounded as though a hundred great guns were going off"—broke over the *Neptune* and an extraordinary flash of lightning took place, and so close that Eastwick declares he saw many electric balls darting into the water. The chief officer was on watch at the time, and came running aft. He announced that the ship had been struck in the foremast and that the lightning had knocked down four of the men. It took the crew afterwards sixteen hours to repair the damage, get up the new foretopmast, foretopgallant mast and yard, for the original ones had been rendered useless.

As the squadron approached Bombay they got into the south-west monsoon, with very thick, dirty weather and a tremendous sea running. It was when they were just a day's sail off Bombay that the captain of the *True Briton*, who was acting as commodore of the squadron, made the signal: "Will Eastwick stand by his promise?" This was immediately answered by the affirmative signal, and then the commodore ran up another: "*Neptune*, go ahead, and lead the way." So, although a passenger, Eastwick had the honour of taking the squadron into Bombay harbour and never picked up a pilot until ready to let go anchor.

But even more illuminating than Eastwick is a man named Thomas Addison, who was born on 18th December 1785, and made a dozen voyages in the old East Indiamen, entering the service as a midshipman of the *Marquis Wellesley* in February 1802, and eventually rising to fifth mate, and so to first mate by May 1817. There are of course plenty of log-books and journals still existing, but one has to wade through many pages before one finds anything of real interest. In the case of Addison, however, there is so much in his journals that reveals to us the life and the incidents on board these old ships of the Company's service that we cannot feel other than grateful that the MS. still exists. After his death these journals eventually passed into the hands of a Norfolk rector, who was good enough to place them in the hands of the Navy Records Society, and a few years ago they were edited by Sir John Laughton and published under the auspices of that Society. It is to this source that I am indebted for the information which is afforded by Addison, though space will not allow of more than a brief outline of his experiences.

He was able to obtain a berth in the Honourable Company's "Maritime Service" (as it was called, in contradistinction to the Company's Marine) owing to the influence of a Mr Edmund Antrobus, a teaman and banker in the Strand. The latter took the sixteen-year-old youth and introduced him to a Mr Matthew White, who was the managing owner of the ship *Marquis of Wellesley*, by whom the midshipman's appointment had been granted. She was a vessel of 818 charter tons and was now about to start on her second voyage to India, her commander being Captain Bruce Mitchell. Mr White gave Addison a letter of introduction to the chief officer, named Le Blanc, and after the boy had completed his sea-going kit he was taken down to the ship at Gravesend by Mr Antrobus. Addison was now handed over to his future messmates, and then began his initiation. As so many of these old-time ceremonies have long since passed away, it may not be out of place to say Addison was sent up into the mizen top, outside the futtocks, where according to custom he should have been seized up to the rigging by a couple of seamen, had he not received the tip to promise them beforehand a gallon of beer. "In lieu of which, by the by, five gallons was afterwards demanded of me by my messmates, stating that the mizen top was their sole prerogative. This is a very old usage practised on board all ships, considered a fair claim from all strangers on first going aloft."

In addition to the captain, there were the chief officer, three mates and a large crew. In all there were thirty officers and petty officers, the whole complement amounting to 151, which nowadays would be thought enormous for a ship of her size. The men received two months' wages in advance before sailing, and in February 1802 made sail down the Thames from Gravesend under the charge of one of the Company's pilots, who brought her safely into the Downs, where the wind was blowing hard from the south-west, sending in a high sea. Addison was destined at once to have excitement, for about sundown, whilst his Majesty's frigate *Egyptienne* was coming to anchor in the Downs, she had shortened sail and left herself too little way to shoot ahead of the Indiaman, with the result that she fell broadside on to the *Marquis Wellesley's* bows, tearing away the latter's cutwater and bowsprit, bringing down the foretopmast also, making in fact a clean sweep of the ship forward. The merchantman was lying to a single anchor at the time, but although it blew most of a gale during the night the ship rode it out all right, and next morning, the weather having moderated, the frigate's commander sent some hands on board to give the ship a temporary refit. After this the Indiaman proceeded to Portsmouth, where she was fully repaired alongside a man-of-war hulk. On the 4th of March she went out of harbour and anchored at Spithead, where she took on board a number of his Majesty's dragoons, as well as forty-nine of the East India Company's troops and their wives for India. The next day, having received the Company's packet from the India House and the despatches for Bengal and Madras, she weighed anchor in the afternoon and proceeded down Channel.

The last of old England was sighted the following day, and then anchors were unbent and all harbour gear stowed away for the long voyage. Madeira was sighted on the 14th of that month—not a bad passage for a sailing ship—and on the 4th of April the Equator was passed, where the usual ceremonies of crossing the line were undergone. "It being my own and Newton's [a young messmate's] first trip into Neptune's dominions, we underwent the accustomed and awful ordeal of shaving by the hands of his Majesty's barber, thereby rendering us free mariners of the ocean." On 24th April they were off the Cape of Good Hope, and on 21st June sighted Ceylon, and three days later arriving at Madras, "Found Admiral Rainier's squadron riding here, consisting of eight sail. Shortly afterwards a sham fight took place with the fleet and shore, followed by a grand illumination displayed from ships as well as the shore, likewise fireworks and rockets, in commemoration of the Peace of Amiens."

The *Marquis Wellesley* left Madras again in February 1803, after visiting ports on the coast, and in July fell in with an American bound from Gibraltar to Boston, and learned from her that war had been declared between England and France, so cartridges were filled and every preparation made on board the East Indiaman for defending herself. On the nineteenth of that month a strange sail appeared. The Indiaman made her private signal, but the stranger did not answer and sailed away. But at midnight she returned and was coming up fast, so the Indiaman at once prepared for action, Addison acting as powder-monkey. But presently she was found to be H.M. frigate *Endymion*, and sent a boat to the Indiaman in charge of a lieutenant and pressed eight of the merchant ship's men, for the frigate had captured so many prizes that he had more prisoners on board than all his ship's company. But before the mouth of the English Channel was reached the *Marquis Wellesley* was to have further exciting experiences. A few days after the previously mentioned incident, two ships were descried one morning while the people were at breakfast. At first Captain Mitchell bore up to assist one which was flying English colours, but one of the passengers (apparently of the sea-lawyer type which still survives) protested "against the legal propriety of such proceeding on the part of an Indiaman volunteering her services in such an affair," so Mitchell put his ship again on her course, much to the indignation of a choleric colonel, for the ship with the English colours was subsequently captured.

Later on a large ship hove in sight on the weather bow and stood down towards the *Marquis Wellesley*. It was now night and the latter at once cleared for action and showed two tiers of lights. The stranger was hailed seven times before it could be ascertained that she was H.M.S. *Plantagenet* with a sloop-of-war as tender in company. Her captain came on board and complimented Captain Mitchell on the good arrangements made for the defence of the ship, and as he walked round the decks the men remained at quarters. He was good enough also to compliment Mitchell on the clever manner in which he had manœuvred his ship to prevent a raking broadside, but before leaving he "impressed a few hands from us."

On the 1st of August the Indiaman anchored in the Downs, and one of the Company's pilots came aboard and took charge of her, bringing with him a number of "ticket-men" to work the ship up the Thames. These were men who were sent from a man-of-war in place of such as had been impressed. On the third of the month the ship had reached her moorings off the Gun Wharf, Deptford, and four days later discharged the ship's company and hired gangs to deliver the cargo. And then came the final, dramatic touch to this voyage: "Shortly afterwards found that Mr White, managing owner of the *Marquis Wellesley*, had become bankrupt and was unable to pay the ship's company."

Addison's first voyage had thus begun and ended with adventures. He had got back in the summer of 1803 and soon began to prepare for a second voyage. Through the good offices of his friend Mr Antrobus he once more obtained a berth as midshipman, this time in the *Brunswick*. The latter was a ship of 1200 charter tons, and was about to make her sixth voyage out to Ceylon and China. On being introduced to Captain James Ludovic Grant, the latter made him senior midshipman and his coxswain, as none of the other youngsters had yet been to sea. The midshipmen were allowed a cabin, servant and every comfort, and though Captain Grant was regarded as a martinet and disciplinarian, yet he was by no means unpopular among Addison's messmates, "supporting his mids as officers and gentlemen." "There were five of us; two were stationed as signal midshipmen, as he was commodore; the other three in three watches, one in each. I was in the latter; never allowed to quit the lee side of the quarter-deck, except on duty or on general occasions of reefing or furling. Two of us dined with him every day, and nothing could exceed his politeness and kindness at table."

Captain Grant had served as midshipman in the Royal Navy in the *Prince George* with the Duke of Clarence, who at the time we are speaking of was now George III. Grant had reached the rank of lieutenant in the navy, and was serving aboard a frigate in the West Indies in the year 1786. The captain died and then it was decided to continue the cruise, Grant as first lieutenant, and a brother officer named Hugh Lindsay as captain. However, when at length they reached England their conduct was so badly criticised that they had to resign their commissions. Both officers therefore did the next best thing and joined the East India Company's service, Grant being now commander of the *Brunswick,* whilst Lindsay had the *Lady Jane Dundas,* a vessel of 820 tons.

During the month of February, then, the *Brunswick,* having taken on board her cargo and stores, dropped down the Thames to the Lower Hope, where she received on board passengers and the remainder of her crew, who received their usual advance. Colonel Hatton and staff of the King's 66th Regiment came on board, together with about 350 privates: and a little later the ship sailed to Portsmouth. Here she remained till the 20th of March, when she came out of harbour and ran across to the Motherbank, where she anchored. Here the whole fleet of East Indiamen, together with their naval convoy, were assembled. This consisted of nine ships—his Majesty's frigate *Lapwing,* and the Company's ships *Brunswick, Marquis of Ely,* Addison's former ship the *Marquis of Wellesley,* the *Lady Jane Dundas* (Captain Hon. Hugh Lindsay, Grant's old shipmate), the *Marchioness of Exeter,* the *Lord Nelson,* the *Princess Charlotte* and the *Canton.* The captain of the *Marquis Wellesley* was now Charles Le Blanc, who had been "chief" when Addison first went to sea.

It must have been a magnificent sight to have witnessed this fine fleet getting under way and setting their canvas that afternoon at a signal from the frigate. Under close-reefed topsails they ran down the Solent and past the Needles with a fresh breeze from north by east. Four and a half hours after leaving the Motherbank they had dropped their pilot in the English Channel, and by eleven that night they were nine miles off the Portland lights, with a gale working up and thick, hazy weather. This caused the fleet to be scattered and topsails were taken in, but towards morning the weather moderated. Getting into the north-east trade-wind the *Brunswick* soon reeled off the miles, though the units of the fleet were still much dispersed, thus making it much easier for the enemy to inflict injury if met with.

On the 7th of April Addison has this entry in his journal:—

"Trimmed ship by the head with 200 pigs of lead. The missing ships rejoined the convoy with two whalers. On a Saturday (weather permitting) constantly exercised great guns, and small arms frequently, with powder blank cartridges. My station at quarters was aide-de-camp to the captain."

And then there are several instances of the way discipline was maintained on board in those days of flogging:—

"9th. John McDonald, seaman, was punished with a dozen for insolence to the boatswain....

"12th. Punished T. Botler, seaman, with a dozen for neglect, etc."

A view of the East India Docks as they appeared in the early nineteenth Century.

(By courtesy of Messrs. T. H. Parker Brothers)

On the following day the frigate parted company with the fleet to return to England, so the *Brunswick* became commodore ship. On the 23rd of June the squadron was in the Mozambique Passage, and at daylight espied a strange brig to the south-east. Sail was therefore made, the *Lord Nelson* having been signalled to chase with the *Brunswick*, and the *Dundas* to lead the fleet on a north-east-by-north course. At 7 A.M. the brig tacked, and half-an-hour later the *Brunswick* also tacked. At eight o'clock Grant ordered his squadron to heave-to, and at noon was coming up fast with the brig. Half-an-hour later he had reached her and found her to be the French *La Charlotte* of four guns and twenty-nine men. She had left the Isle de France twenty-eight days previously and was bound for the Mozambique. She was now a prisoner, and Commodore Grant accordingly sent on board the *Brunswick's* second officer, Mr Benjamin Bunn, Addison, five seamen and twenty soldiers in the cutter to take possession of her. Her captain, a lieutenant, a midshipman and ten seamen were brought off to the *Brunswick*, and at three in the afternoon the brig was taken in tow, but two hours later she was cast off. Eventually, after the captains of the other English ships had come aboard and joined in a consultation, Grant decided that the prize was not worth keeping. So all her cargo of muskets were thrown into the sea, and afterwards she was handed over again to her French captain, who went aboard her with his men, very thankful to be allowed to take possession once more.

About the middle of June the East Indiamen reached Trincomalee and saluted H.M.S. *Centurion* with eleven guns, which respect was returned. But it is typical of the time that the following day a lieutenant came off from the *Centurion* and pressed ten of the Indiamen's men, and a little later three more seamen deserted and joined H.M.S. *Sheerness*. Having disembarked the troops and baggage, assisted by the boats of his Majesty's ships, the *Brunswick* once more put to sea, and two days later brought up in Madras Roads, where she saluted the fort with nine guns, and received a similar salute in return. Here also a lieutenant from H.M.S. *Wilhelmina* came aboard and pressed four more men. Here the *Brunswick* remained some weeks, landing the Company's cargo, taking on board cotton and other goods for Captain Grant's own account—on a later page the reader will learn how much cargo a captain was allowed to ship for himself—and after the vessel's rigging had been refitted, and her hull painted, she prepared for sea.

Meanwhile the Company's ships which had come out with her bound for Bengal had sailed to the north, but on the 13th of August H.M. frigate *Caroline*, which was now to convoy the East Indiamen bound for China, made the signal for the fleet to unmoor, and then proceeded on the voyage. The fleet went through the Singapore Straits, the convoy being kept in close order of sailing as Admiral Linois was known to be cruising in the China Sea. It was now September, and the reader will recollect that in February of that year his squadron had been put to flight by Commodore Dance. The East India squadron now consisted of the Company's ships *Brunswick, Glatton, Cirencester, Walmer Castle, Marquis of Ely, Thames, Canton, Winchelsea*, ten country ships, and convoyed by five of his Majesty's ships—the *Caroline, Grampus, La Dédaigneuse, Russell* and *Dasher*, the first-mentioned being the commodore's ship.

Arrived at the mouth of the Tiger, permission was obtained from two mandarins to pass, as was the custom in those days when China was still so little open to the European. And the way the fleet was able to navigate the river by night at the last quarter of the flood is most interesting. Two Chinese pilots had been taken on board the *Brunswick*, and in order to denote the channel across the bar by night a row of fifty boats with lights was placed on one side, and another fifty on the other, the ship of course to sail between. When the *Brunswick* was about in mid-channel one of the pilots sang out "port littee," while the other contradicted him by shouting "starboard littee." Captain Grant was not the man to be humbugged in this manner, so he kicked one of these men overboard, and the other immediately jumped after. The lights were at once put out and the *Brunswick* grounded on the bar. The tide soon began to fall, and in spite of carrying out a kedge she refused to budge. So the top-gallant yards and masts were sent down, the guns were put into the launches which were sent by the other ships of the fleet, and eventually next day the *Brunswick* was floated at high water, but at once swung round and took the ground again, and the tide ebbed out.

In order to lighten her forward, the bower anchors were made fast between boats, and the stream anchor was taken out in the launch ready for the next flood, and with the last quarter of that tide she came off; the hawsers were slipped, and while the anchors were being recovered Captain Grant backed and filled across the channel and finally came to anchor again.

Addison tells us of an interesting custom in the Company's service at that time. For each season the senior captain was allowed £500 "table money," as we should call it, for public dinners and various expenses, the second captain in seniority being allowed £300 for the same purposes. The ships took their turn to act as guardship, naval fashion, and whichever ship's turn it was so to act on a Sunday, the captain was to attend on board together with his surgeon. And during the whole day, up till eight o'clock in the evening, one of his sworn officers was to row guard up and down the fleet, after which he was to make his report to the senior ship. But when the viceroy and the leading Chinese authorities made their visits to these English ships in state they were received with great ceremony, which is curiously absent from the modern merchant ship.

Many hundred local craft would put off to the East Indiamen. The English captains were on board to receive them, the yards were manned and every possible display was made. An officer was first sent in full uniform to compliment the great man—John Tuck, as the English sailor nicknamed him, owing to the fact that in the fore end of his boat he kept gallows to tuck up any unfortunate who displeased him. Having come alongside the East Indiaman, the great man always refused to trust his valuable life to the ropes and accommodations supplied for entering the ship, but used his own long ladders. Business was duly contracted, and then he would make a present to the ship's company of bullocks, flour, fruit and a vile, maddening spirit of a most intoxicating nature, which the men were made to exchange for something better. After this the captains all dined together on board a large chop boat.

The fleet remained here from October till the first day of 1805, and then got under way with fine cargoes of teas for England. But the *Brunswick* never reached England. Doubtless owing to the damage sustained when she got aground on the bar she developed a serious leak, and made for Ceylon and Bombay, where she was docked and repaired, her tea being sent to England in another ship. The *Brunswick* was now sent back to China again with a cargo of cotton, which would have been a very lucrative affair. But there was a good deal of trouble with the crew, many of the men deserting to the warships, until at last Captain Grant sent every man he had in the launch on board a British frigate. The latter's captain selected from these all that were worth having and then sent the rest back to the *Brunswick*.

When the latter set sail from Bombay for China on 1st July 1805 she was very ill-manned, consequent on nearly the whole of the ship's company having been pressed by the navy. There were not twenty European seamen on board to work this big ship. The guns had to be manned by Chinamen, with only one European seaman at each. For the rest lascars had to be relied upon. In such a weak condition she put to sea, together with a couple of country ships, keeping as near each other as possible. But a few days later at break of day two strange sail were discovered to the eastward. The *Sarah* made a signal that the strangers looked suspicious. Later on the *Brunswick* perceived that one was a line-of-battle ship and the other a frigate. But the *Sarah* signalled that she thought they were friends. However, the *Brunswick* was much less credulous and had already cleared for action, hoisting her private signal (which was not answered) and hoisting her British colours. The stranger presently answered by showing St George's colours. The line-of-battle ship then tacked in order to get into such a position as to rake the *Brunswick* from aft. The frigate passed to leeward and exchanged St George's colours for the French national colours, giving the *Brunswick* a broadside as she passed. This was immediately returned, but as the ship was heeling over at a great angle, the lee guns could not be elevated sufficiently to do any damage to the enemy.

But the *Brunswick* was clearly to be out-manœuvred. The frigate went about just astern of the Indiaman, and as she was then observed to be coming on fast, Captain Grant kept his ship as full as possible, hoping to be able to run her ashore. The frigate, however, approached at such a pace, and the line-of-battle ship was also so close that the *Brunswick* would assuredly have been sunk by the line-of-battle ship's broadside before taking the ground. After consultation with his officers Grant was reluctantly compelled to strike his colours and surrender to the enemy off the coast of Ceylon. A boat came off—and then, well the line-of-battle ship was none other than Admiral Linois' *Marengo*, and the big frigate was the *Belle Poule*, which had fought and run away the previous year from Commodore Dance. Linois was stationed in those Eastern waters for the express purpose of harassing and cutting up our trade, avoiding the British ships-of-war. Any modern strategist would tell you that whilst this kind of hostility is very annoying to the power attacked, it cannot afford any lasting good. The same kind of folly was attempted, you will remember, by the Russians interfering with Japanese merchantmen in the East during the late war, and the practical value of this measure was nil.

However, Linois may have remembered that he who fights and runs away will live to fight another day. He had been compelled to fly before Dance, but this time he got his revenge. You may ask what England was doing to leave those seas unpoliced. The answer is that as a matter of fact Indiamen had to rely on naval convoys when they could be got, and Rear-Admiral Sir Thomas Troubridge, who had been one of Nelson's captains at the Battle of the Nile, was actually escorting, in H.M.S. *Blenheim*, eleven more Indiamen. The two courses were converging and presently we shall see them meet.

Needless to say, it was with great grief that Captain Grant, all his officers and midshipmen (excepting the chief officer and surgeon) were put on board the *Marengo*, whilst the frigate went in pursuit of the *Sarah*. The latter, however, ran herself ashore with all sail set, but the crew were saved. Admiral Linois received Captain Grant with every courtesy, and the *Brunswick* was ordered to a rendezvous nearer the Cape of Good Hope. Before the month was out, when a fog which had settled down lifted for a while, the *Marengo* suddenly found herself close to a large convoy of Indiamen. The former instantly cleared for action and firing began. It was Troubridge with his convoy! But nothing much came of this, and the contending forces separated during the night. To cut the story short, Addison and his shipmates were landed in South Africa, whence they were taken to St Helena by an American brig. From there they reached England in a British frigate, landing at Spithead, and so making their way to London. As for the poor old *Brunswick*, she drove ashore on the South African coast, and so ended her days.

If Addison had been unfortunate in the ending of his first voyage, so in this he was again unlucky. "According to the Company's law," he writes in his journal, "having been captured by an enemy, or the ship in any way wrecked or destroyed, the captain, officers and crew forfeit their pay and wages, consequently we have no claim upon the owners of the late *Brunswick* for at least twenty months' hard duty on board of her." However, he was now wedded to the sea, and the next time he went in his first ship, the *Marquis Wellesley*, as fifth mate, with Charles Le Blanc as captain, and in her he served during the following years till he went as second mate in another of the Company's ships. I make no apology to the reader for giving so much detail in this connection, for Addison's and Eastwick's accounts tell us just those intimate details which show the risks of many sorts which had to be encountered in the old days when the sailing ship was still far from perfect, and those handsome, fast China tea-clippers had not yet come into being to startle the world with their record runs. No doubt the captains of these East Indiamen of which we are speaking were often hated by their men for their severity: but those were no kid-glove days, and a voyage was not a thing of certainty as with the modern liner, which maintains a punctuality almost equal to that of a passenger train. If a captain retired after a few voyages with a nice little fortune, he certainly deserved it. For he was a long time before he reached a command, and there was scarcely a day during the whole of those long voyages when he was not plunged into some sort of anxiety. Anything might happen; from having his sails blown out of his ship and carrying away his best spars to losing the ship herself, her cargo, her men. Every force seemed to be up against him—gales of wind, uncharted seas, coasts and rivers, privateers, warships of the enemy: even the warships of his own country snatched out of his vessel his best men. And then, to add insult to injury, he came home to find either his managing owners gone bankrupt or a by-law which prevented him from receiving his hard-earned pay.

The "Thames," East Indiaman, 1,424 tons.

This was one of the finest vessels employed in the East Indian trade.

Yes, taking it by and large, he deserved his good luck when it came his way;

but when it was absent, he did his best and more for the British capitalist and merchant princes than the latter ever cared to acknowledge. In the history of Eastern development and civilisation the shipmaster of these old Indiamen ought to occupy a high place of respect and admiration. He has left behind a magnificent example for his successors to follow.

When a passenger in the olden days joined an East Indiaman as she lay in the Downs he had to be rowed off by one of the Deal boatmen. These "sharks" often made a fine thing out of such passengers, for the latter were completely at the mercy of the former. In calm weather the boatman was willing to row the passenger aboard for the sum of five shillings (or more if he could get it). But in the case of dirty weather and the nasty lop which gets up here with onshore winds the passenger had to pay as much as three guineas and sometimes even five: it was all a question of bargaining between himself and the boatman. Inasmuch as the passenger had to get aboard the big ship at all costs, and since the only method possible was to employ one of these Deal boatmen, the competition was solely between the boatmen themselves. But these fellows were so closely bound together, owing to the ties of relationship and their co-operation in extensive smuggling, that the passenger could scarcely help being fleeced.

Having at last arrived on board, weary of his coach drive from London, drenched with the sea-spray scooped up by the Deal galley, the passenger bound for India in those days set forth with not the light heart and eagerness with which the modern traveller embarks on an East-bound liner. If contemporary accounts are to be trusted, the mere anticipation was a kind of terrible nightmare. The passenger often enough would retire at once to his cot, and remain there for days prostrate with sea-sickness. The cuddy would not see him at meals until the Bay of Biscay had been passed and finer, warmer weather encountered. Some of the Company's cadets bound out to enter this corporation's Indian army were utter scamps, and the only way to get them out of their cots was to cut the lanyards which kept the latter up. Before they had reached the Equator they had begun to find their sea-legs, and they were compelled to take part in the usual ceremonies of crossing the line. In the accompanying illustration will be found one of these young gentlemen undergoing this initiation in one of the East Indiamen ships.

These ships, because of their bad lines and clumsy proportions, could scarcely rely on keeping up an average of more than three or four knots an hour, and their performances when compared with the voyages of the celebrated clippers in the mid-nineteenth century show the essential difference in the capabilities of the old and the new types respectively. Let the following table show how slow the old-time craft were. The reference is to an East Indiaman which left the Thames in 1746, and after voyaging to the East arrived off Scotland in 1748:—

Left England, September 20, 1746.
Arrived at St Helena, December 25, 1746.
Left St Helena, January 14, 1747.
Arrived at Batavia, April 19, 1747.
Left Batavia, June 9, 1747.
Arrived in China, July 8, 1747.

Left China, January 12, 1748.
Arrived at St Helena, April 4, 1748.
Left St Helena, April 25, 1748.
Arrived off Scotland, July 9, 1748.

Even one of the Company's own ships—the *Thames*—which was not as fast as the China clippers presently to be started by private firms, performed the voyage between Canton and England in 115 days a little time before the East India Company lost their China monopoly. This vessel left Canton on 18th November 1831, arrived at St Helena on 28th January 1832, and was in the English Channel on the following 13th March.

An anonymous writer who flourished about the middle of the eighteenth century, on whose authority the details of the length of voyages have been given above, has left us a detailed account of a voyage to the East Indies about this time. I need not try the patience of the reader by following the entire journey, but it will suffice if we, so to speak, voyage with this traveller from England as far as St Helena. The account, which is written with great restraint, leaves the reader every opportunity to imagine the discomforts and trepidations which were the essential conditions of the long journey to the Orient in those days.

"On Thursday the 30th of July 1746, I set out from London for Gravesend, where I was agreeably entertained to see a great number of people on board the vessel, in which I was appointed to go to the East Indies, and the vast preparations, and quantities of provisions, on board, to supply the necessities of so long a voyage.

"Next day several young people came on board, inlisted to go in the service of the East India Company, where they were to remain for the space of five years at least....

"On the 2d of August we weighed anchor, passed the Nore, saluted the *Royal Sovereign* with nine guns, and came to an anchor in the Downs on the 3d. As the wind was variable, we were obliged to come to an anchor every now and then. On the 5th, at night, we passed Dungeness lighthouse, and, on the 8th, anchored in St Helen's road [Isle of Wight].

"On the 10th we received on board our treasure from Portsmouth, and, among the rest, a fine large stone-horse, designed as a present from the Company to the Sultan of Benjar, an Indian Prince on the island of Borneo. After taking in more fresh provisions, we weighed anchor, and made the best of our way towards Plymouth. On the 29th we came to an anchor in Cawson [Cawsand] Bay, where, not caring to break upon our store, we sent our long-boat ashore for fresh water. Here we were to wait for a convoy. We were supplied at this place with plenty of bread, fish, etc., in small boats, rowed by a parcel of the stoutest and most masculine women I ever saw.

"On the 5th of September we had very thick weather, with hard gales of wind from S.W. so that we were obliged to lower our fore and main yards, and give great scope of cable, and even to strike our topmasts.

"On the 6th in the morning the weather abated; but, in the evening of that day, it blowed very hard. We heard the *Norfolk* fire several guns as signals of distress. She had parted her cable, and had run adrift before it was discovered: and she was obliged to anchor within the beacon, on the east side of the Sound, in foul and rocky ground. But, by the assistance of some of the men of war, she was again brought to an anchor in Cawson Bay.

"From the 7th to the 16th we were employed in putting everything in order aboard, and, on the 17th, the *Mermaid* man of war was appointed our convoy, and gave a signal for unmooring the same night.

"On Sunday the 20th of September we got under sail, the wind at NNE. When at sea, we cleared our ship fore and aft, and exercised our great guns and small arms....

"On the 27th we parted with our convoy, and made the best of our way for the island of St Helena, for which we had several stores on board."

And so they proceeded on their journey to the south. On 9th October, when in lat. 37° 32′ N., and long. 22° 16′, "we were now beginning to feel the hot climate, so that the allowance of water, with the greatest economy, was little enough to quench thirst. We put an awning on the quarter-deck, to keep off the scorching heat of the sun."

As to the kind of shipmates this traveller had, the following statement is sufficiently illustrative:—

"We could hardly put a stop to the frequent thefts that were committed by the soldiers, though every day one or two of them were tied to the shrouds, and severely whipt. It is indeed the less to be wondered at, as these wretches, who go as soldiers in the company's service, are for the most part the scum of the three kingdoms, and generally go to India to screen themselves from justice at home. By their laziness and inactivity, they were over-run with vermine, and began to complain of swellings in their legs, soreness in their bones, and other symptoms of the scurvy. To prevent their infecting the ship's company, they were brought up on deck, put into a large vessel of hot water, brushed with scrubbing brushes, and all their clothes and bedding thrown over-board....

"On the 2d of December, we had a large swelling sea, with easterly winds. At five in the morning we were surprised with a large waterspout, within three ships-length of our starboard-side. It had no sooner passed our ship, than a sudden puff of wind laid us gunwale to, which was over before we could lower our sails. We had frequent dewfalls in the night, which are very dangerous, and often mortal, if they happen to rest on the naked breast or body of a man, while asleep on the deck. A great deal of our salted pork was so rotten, that we threw several casks of it over-board.

"On the 17th, had cloudy weather, employed our cooper to set up all the water-casks, which we had knocked down as soon as they were empty, for the sake of room.

The "Windham," East Indiaman, with the fleet sailing from St. Helena under convoy of His Majesty's Ship "Monmouth."

(By courtesy of Messrs. T. H. Parker Brothers)

"The 22d, we kept a good look-out for St Helena, and found ourselves to be in Lat. 16° 6′, and, on the 23d, we observed several pigeons flying about the ship, a sure indication that we were near land." This island they eventually sighted the following morning, and arriving off the fort saluted the Governor with nine guns, everyone in the ship being heartily relieved to see land once more. It should be recollected of course that St Helena had long been in the possession of the East India Company, and its geographical position was of great convenience to the ships bound to or from the Orient, giving opportunities for obtaining fresh supplies and drinking water. The illustration which is here reproduced shows the appearance of St Helena at the time of which we are speaking, together with a contemporary East Indiaman lying at anchor.

Such, then, is the kind of life which had to be endured on board these vessels, depicted as we have shown by men of entirely different interests and tastes—the captain, the midshipman and the passenger. But if these voyages were unpleasant and even risky, it is to them and the determination of those on board that the wealth of the East India Company was due, and the fortunes of so many private individuals as well. Ocean travel in those days was not pleasure, but a long-drawn-out martyrdom, except for a very few and in exceptional weather. To-day, even the worst-appointed liner would seem luxurious to the voyager of the eighteenth century, although more comfortable deep-sea ships were not to be found than those which flew the naval pennant of the Honourable East India Company.

CHAPTER XVI

CONDITIONS OF SERVICE

We have seen something of the lives of the officers and men in the Company's ships at sea: we desire now to learn more of their conditions of employment—what was their uniform, what were their rates of pay, privileges, pensions according to their different ranks, the kind of accommodation for the passengers, the nature of their cargoes, and so on. In other words, we are to endeavour to fill in those details of the picture already roughly sketched.

Dating back from the time of the first East India Company, the commanders were always sworn into the service. So likewise were the first four officers. Before being allowed to proceed to his duty on board, an officer had to sign a contract for performing the voyage, and a petition for his "private trade" outwards. As the latter was so very lucrative to him, it may be well to give details. Particulars had to be sent in this petition to the Committee of Shipping of the East India Company, giving the dead-weight of the articles they proposed to take out to the East. These consisted of almost anything, from wines to carriages. This "private" trade allowed to the commanders and officers of the East India ships, allowing them to participate in the Company's exclusive monopoly, did not permit woollen goods and warlike stores, but otherwise the ship's officers could reap a fine income by taking out English goods and bringing back Eastern products which would be sure of a market at home.

There was a proper schedule, and the following were the officers and petty officers enabled to avail themselves of this privilege:—Commander, chief mate, second mate, third mate, purser, surgeon, surgeon's mate, fourth mate, fifth mate, sixth mate, boatswain, gunner, carpenter, four midshipmen, one midshipman (who was also the commander's coxswain), six quartermasters, commander's steward, ship's steward, commander's cook, carpenter's first mate, caulker, cooper, armourer and sailmaker. Reckoned for a ship let for 755 tons and upwards, the commander was allowed as much as 56 tons, or 20 feet of space, for all articles (excepting liquors) which weighed more than they measured were reckoned according to their weight. The chief mate was allowed eight tons, the second mate six tons, and so on down the list, even a midshipman being allowed a ton, the purser three tons, the surgeon six, and each quartermaster as much as a midshipman. In the case of the China ships only, if it was not practicable to invest in goods to the following amounts respectively, the Company allowed them to carry out bullion to make up the amount:—Commander, £3000, chief mate, £300, and so on down to carpenter, £50.

Homeward-bound East Indiamen were similarly allowed privileges to their officers. Ships lading from India might not bring back tea, china-ware, raw silk, or nankeen cloth: and ships lading from China might not bring back China raw silk, musk, camphor, arrack, arsenic or other poisonous drugs. But otherwise the commanders of China ships were allowed homeward 38 tons, the chief mate 8 tons, the second mate 6 tons, and so on down to the carpenter 1 ton. But the other homeward ships allowed the commander 30 tons or thirty-two feet, the chief mate 6 tons or sixteen feet, and so on down to the carpenter, who was allowed thirty-two feet. These importers, of course, had to pay the customs and also three per cent. to the Company for warehouse room on the gross amount at the sale of the goods in the case of Indian products, and a bigger percentage in the case of goods from China. But the wily old commanders were not always content with these privileges. The reader is doubtless familiar with the word dunnage. This consists of faggots, boughs, canes or other similar articles, which are laid on the bottom of a ship's hold and used for stowing the cargo effectively. Now when it was found that there was a good demand in London for Eastern bamboos, ratans, and canes a commander would see that his dunnage consisted of a very ample amount of these realisable articles, and far beyond what was necessary for the protection of the cargo. The result was that the Company had to step in and make very strict regulations to stop this abuse, so that if the dunnage did not seem absolutely necessary and *bona fide* it was charged against the amount of tonnage allowed to the commander and officers.

Tea was allowed to be brought home from China and Bencoolen according to a schedule, the captain being allowed as much as 9336 lb., down to the carpenter, 246 lb., but a big percentage was charged on its sale value. Piece-goods were allowed to be brought home on paying the customs and £3 per cent. for warehouse room. These articles were disposed of at the Company's sales, which took place in March and September. Although the importation of china-ware was reserved to the Company, yet "as the Company do not at present import any China-ware on their own account" they allowed their officers to do so, "during the Court's pleasure," provided it was brought as a flooring to the teas and did not exceed thirteen inches in height. This made, therefore, another source of revenue to the officers, for as much as 40 tons of this ware could be permitted in the 1400-ton ships and 30 tons in a 1200-tonner. The commander could also bring home two pipes of Madeira wine in addition to the above allowances.

When outward bound the chief, second, third, fourth and fifth mates, the surgeon and his mate, the pursers, boatswains, gunners and carpenters were allowed as indulgence a liberal amount of stores, consisting of wine, butter, cheese, groceries, pickles, beer and also spirits for the respective messes. In the case of "extra" ships the commanders and officers were usually allowed 5 per cent. of the chartered tonnage, but the chief mate was always allowed three tons, the second mate two, the third mate one ton, and the surgeon two. The fourth officers and pursers in these ships were not acknowledged in this respect. As regards indulgence in stores, the chief mate, second mate and surgeon were allowed the same amounts as in the regular ships just mentioned, but the third mate was allowed not quite so much.

On the whole, it will be seen that every officer and petty officer of an East Indiaman, whether trading to India or China, had the opportunity of putting by very handsome perquisites, and so you can now easily believe Eastwick's statement that a purser friend of his had retired and bought a ship for himself. But, of course, in addition to all these "privileges," everyone received his salary or wages. The following is a list of the monthly pay to the commander, officers, petty officers, "tradesmen" (*i.e.* coopers and the like), and the able-bodied seamen, called foremast men. It will be found that this makes up a complement of 102 men, such as were employed in one of the big regular East Indiamen. The pay in the case of "extra" ships will be given after this list:—

Monthly Pay on Board a Regular East Indiaman

Commander	£10	0
Chief Mate	5	0
Second Mate	4	0
Third Mate	3	10
Fourth Mate	2	10
Fifth Mate	2	5
Sixth Mate	2	5
Surgeon	5	0
Purser	2	0
Boatswain	3	10
Gunner	3	10
Master-at-Arms	3	0
Carpenter	4	10
Midshipman and Coxswain	2	5
4 Midshipmen, each	2	5
Surgeon's Mate	3	10
Caulker	3	15
Cooper	3	0
Captain's Cook	3	5
Ship's Cook	2	10
Carpenter's 1st Mate	3	5
Carpenter's 2nd Mate	2	10
Caulker's Mate	2	15
Cooper's Mate	2	10
6 Quartermasters, each	2	10
Sailmaker	2	10

Armourer	2	10
Butcher	2	5
Baker	2	5
Poulterer	2	5
2 Commander's Servants, each	1	5
1 Chief Mate's Servant	1	0
1 Second Mate's Servant	0	18
1 Surgeon's Servant	0	15
1 Boatswain's Servant	0	15
1 Gunner's Servant	0	15
Captain's Steward	2	0
Ship's Steward	2	10
2 Boatswain's Mates, each	2	10
2 Gunner's Mates, each	2	10
1 Carpenter's Servant	0	15
50 Foremast Men, each	2	5

In the case of an "extra" ship the commander received £10 a month, the chief mate £5, the second mate £4, the third mate £3, 10s., the surgeon £5, the boatswain £3, 10s., the gunner £3, 10s., the carpenter £4, 10s., the two midshipmen were paid £2, 5s. each, the cooper and steward got £3, the captain's cook £3, 5s., the ship's cook £2, 10s., the boatswain's mate and the gunner's mate were each paid £2, 10s., the carpenter's mate and caulker £3, 15s., the two quartermasters received each £2, 10s., the two commander's servants £1, 5s. each, and the thirty foremast men £2, 5s. each. As to the last-mentioned, a vessel of from 400 to 500 tons carried twenty foremast hands. A ship of 500 to 550 had thirty hands, and the next size, from 550 to 600 tons, carried thirty-five. A 600 to 650 tonner had forty men, and a 650 to 700 tonner forty-five men. But a 700 to 800 ton ship had fifty-five men, and an 800 to 900 tonner sixty-five of these hands. The Company's rule was that regular vessels of 750 to 800 tons were to carry a total complement of 101 officers and men. A 900-ton ship was to carry 110 men, a 1000-ton ship 120 men, a 1100-ton ship 125 men, and a 1200-tonner 130 men.

Five supernumeraries were allowed to be carried, of whom two were to be allowed to walk the quarterdeck. No commander was allowed to increase the number of midshipmen under pain of being suspended for three years. This was to prevent him from taking a raw young officer out of consideration for a monetary reward. In order to act as a safeguard, if any person borne on the ship's books as part of her complement were discharged in India, China or St Helena without permission of the Company, or if the commander were to act in collusion and allow him to quit his vessel, the commander was liable to a fine of £300. Nor could he bring home or carry out any passenger or person without the directors' leave.

Owing to the fact that the men out of these East Indiamen were so frequently pressed into the British men-of-war whilst in the East, it was often enough necessary to ship a lot of lascars in order to get the vessel home at all. But these feeble-bodied men were accustomed only to voyages of short duration, and that in the fine weather season. They could not bear the cold, neither were they dependable when the East Indiaman had to defend herself against a privateer, pirate or enemy's warship. Ignorant of the English language, they were not easy to handle. It was always reckoned that eighty or ninety of them were not quite the equal of fifty British seamen, and for every hundred of them employed four British seamen must be also. It was the India-built ships which were manned almost exclusively by these lascars, and a new problem arose, for these fellows used to remain behind in England, where their condition became piteous. There was an obligation that these lascars were always to be sent back to India, but in practice many of them "are turned off in London, where they beg and perish." So wrote Macpherson in 1812. "The appearance of these miserable creatures," he remarked, "in the streets of London frequently excites the indignation of passengers against the Company, who, they suppose, bring them to this country and leave them destitute," whereas, in reality, these Easterns actually preferred to sink into degradation in our land rather than return to their own. Many of them never reached England, or, if they did, died on the return voyage: for the bad weather off the Cape of Good Hope and the rigours of the English climate caused considerable sickness and death.

English gentlemen who had been for some years under the Company in India, either in a civil or military capacity, were often wont to bring black servants home with them, and after these servants had been some time in England they were discharged. The result was that, under the terms of their obligation, the Company were put to great expense in sending them back to their native country. It was with a view to protecting themselves from this possibility that the Company used to cause the master of such a servant to take a bond in India as security for the cost of returning these coloured people, these bonds being sent to the commander of the ship in which the master and his servant was travelling to England. Otherwise, the commander was ordered by the Company to refuse to have the black man on board.

Before an officer could become commander of one of the Company's ships it was necessary that he should be twenty-five years old and have performed a voyage to and from India or China in the Company's regular service as chief or second mate, or else have commanded a ship in the extra service. A chief mate had to be twenty-three years old, have voyaged to India or China in the Company's service as second or third mate. A second mate had to be twenty-two years old and have made a similar voyage as third mate. To become a third mate he had to be aged twenty-one and been two voyages in the Company's service to and from India or China. A fourth mate had to be twenty years old and been one voyage of not less than twenty months to India or China and back in the Company's service, and one year in actual service in any other employ, and of the latter he had to produce satisfactory certificates.

The "Jessie" and "Eliza Jane" in Table Bay, Cape of Good Hope, 1829.

(By courtesy of Messrs. T. H. Parker Brothers)

In the case of the extra ships the commander had to be twenty-three years old at least, have made three voyages to India or China and back in the Company's service, one of which must have been as chief or second mate in a regular ship, or as chief mate in an extra ship. The chief mate must be at least twenty-two, and have made two of these voyages as officer in the Company's regular service. The second mate had to be at least twenty-one and have performed two voyages as officer in the Company's service to India or China and back. The third mate must be twenty years and been one voyage in the Company's service, or two voyages as midshipman in the extra service.

It would not be untrue to say that officers of the early part of the nineteenth century in this service were excellent seamen and fair navigators, but many of them would not be sufficiently expert in navigation nowadays to have entrusted to them the work and responsibilities commensurate with those with which they were charged. It was in the year 1804 that the Company issued the following regulation:—

"That such of the officers as have not been already instructed in the method of finding the longitude of a ship at sea, by lunar observations, do immediately perfect themselves under Mr Lawrence Gwynne, at Christ's Hospital, previous to their attending the Committee to be examined for their respective stations; and that they do produce to the Committee a certificate from that gentleman of their being qualified in the method."

And within six weeks after each ship had arrived home, the commander and officers had to attend a Committee of the Company which dealt with the reasons for any deviation which the ship might have made during the voyage.

As touching the accommodation in these ships, the officers had canvas berths only, laced down to battens on the deck, with upright stanchions, a cross-piece, and a small door, with canvas panels, the canvas being capable of being rolled up. On the gun-deck the chief mate's berth was on the starboard side from the fore part of the aftermost port, to the fore part of the second port from aft, the space being eight feet broad. The second mate was located on the opposite side to correspond, but his space was six inches narrower. Between the second and third ports two similar berths, each six feet long and seven feet broad, were fitted up for the third and fourth mates: and two more for the purser and surgeon between the third and fourth ports. Two others, slightly smaller still, were located between the ports on this deck for the boatswain and carpenter. And no alteration from this was allowed to be made during the voyage. The captain's "great cabin" was in the steerage, and he was forbidden to partition it off in any way without special orders from the Company. When a ship went into action, those canvas berths or cabins of the officers just alluded to were taken down. The reader will recollect the capture some pages back of the *Brunswick* by the *Marengo*. Addison in his journal mentions that when he and his fellow-officers were taken on board the latter they were marched below to the ward-room. He then adds that, "being cleared for action, the cabins were all down, and the whole deck clear fore and aft, open to the seamen."

The full uniform for the commander of one of the Company's ships was as follows:—Fine blue coat, black Genoa velvet round the cuffs, four holes by two's, three outside, one inside. Black velvet lapels, with ten holes by two's. Black velvet panteen cape, with one hole on each side, straight flaps, with four holes by two's. The fore parts were lined with buff silk serge, black slit and turns faced with the same. One button on each hip, and one at the bottom. The buttonholes were gold embroidered throughout and gilt buttons with the Company's crest. The chief mate wore a blue coat with black velvet lapels, cuffs and collar, with one small button to each cuff. The buttons gilt, with the Company's crest. The second, third and fourth mates' uniforms were similar to that of the chief mate, except that the second had two small buttons on each cuff, the third had three, and the fourth had four.

In the extra ships the commander wore a blue coat with black velvet lapels, cuffs and collar, with only one embroidered buttonhole on each cuff, and on each side of the collar. His buttons were gilt with the Company's crest. The chief mate's uniform in these extra ships consisted of a blue coat, single-breasted, with a black velvet collar and cuffs, and one small buttonhole on each cuff, with gilt buttons as before. The second and third mates' were like this with the difference of two or three small buttons on each cuff as mentioned. And it was strictly ordered that officers were always to appear in this uniform whenever they attended on the Court of Directors, their Committees, any of the Presidents and Councils in India, or at St Helena, or the Select Committee of Supra-Cargoes in China.

Some of the officers when they came up to be sworn in before the Court of Directors did not always appear in the prescribed uniform, and the Company sent out a warning against coming into their presence in boots, black breeches and stockings, except in the case of deep mourning. When appearing before the Court of Directors the officers were compelled to wear full uniform, but when attending the Committee they were to wear undress.

Whenever the ship dropped down from Deptford or Blackwall to Gravesend the captain was to be on board. There were two sets of pilots. One took the ship from Deptford or Blackwall to Gravesend, and another took her from Gravesend to the Isle of Wight. Whilst the ship lay at Gravesend the commander was ordered to go aboard her once a week in order to report her condition to the Committee. Before sailing, the ship took on board a sufficient amount of lime-juice to last the crew through the whole voyage. And the commander had strict instructions to see that his new hands—"recruits" the Company called them—wore the clothes which the Company provided, and that the men did not sell them for liquor; also that these men did not desert. For this reason no boats were allowed to remain alongside the ship without having been made fast by a chain and lock—thus preventing any possibility of the men escaping to the shore. No boat was allowed to put off from the ship until every person in her had been examined, lest one of the crew might be in her. And a quarter watch was to be kept night and day to prevent the loss of recruits. If any did desert, then the commander would most probably have to pay the cost which this involved.

During the course of every watch the ship was to be pumped out, and entries made in the log. And as regards divine worship, the slackness of the previous period mentioned in an earlier chapter was no longer tolerated. "You are strictly required to keep up the worship of Almighty God on board your ship every Sunday, when circumstances will admit, and that the log-book contain the reasons for the omission when it so happens; that you promote good order and sobriety, by being yourself the example, and enforcing it in others; and that you be humane and attentive to the welfare of those under your command, the Court have resolved to mulct you in the sum of two guineas for every omission of mentioning the performance of divine service, or assigning satisfactory reasons for the non-performance thereof every Sunday, in the Company's log-book."

From the Company's India House in Leadenhall Street the commander was supplied with charts. These had to be returned at the end of the voyage, together with the commander's journals and track charts. What were known as free mariners must have performed two voyages to India or China and back in the Company's ships, or else have used the sea and been in actual service for at least three years. The reader is aware that many a time the Company's ships were endangered by the naval authorities impressing so many men from them. At last, after many protests, the Admiralty instituted a new regulation, so that, although it was still not possible to abolish this impressment, yet the evil so far as the East Indiamen were concerned was mitigated and controlled. A letter was sent to the Rear-Admiral of the Red on the East Indies station instructing him to order his captains and commanders to conform to this new regulation. A proper scheme was drawn up, showing what officers and men in East Indiamen ships of varying tonnages were to be exempt from impress, though this protection applied only until the ship should reach Europe. However, even if the whole exemption could not be obtained, a portion thereof was better than nothing at all, especially as the Company attributed so many of the losses of their ships to having been deprived of their best men.

In addition to their wages, the men became entitled to a pension from what was known as the Poplar Fund. Any commander, officer or seaman, or anyone else who had served aboard any of these East Indiamen for eight years and regularly contributed to this fund was entitled to a pension. But if a man had been wounded or maimed so as to be rendered incapable of further service at sea, he could still be admitted to a pension even under eight years. The size of the pension was based on the amount of capital which the officer possessed. Thus, if a commander stated that he was not worth £2500, or £125 a year, he received a pension of £100. Similarly, if a chief mate had not been able to amass £1300, or had £65 coming in every year, he was granted a pension of £60. And so the scale descended down to the rank of midshipman, who was granted a £12 pension if he was not worth £400, or £20 a year. Allowances were also made for the widows and orphans of those who had served the Company for seven years.

The "Alfred," East Indiaman, 1,400 tons.

(By courtesy of Messrs. T. H. Parker Brothers)

Before a candidate could be appointed as ship's surgeon, those who had already made one voyage in the Company's service, or acted twelve months in that capacity in his Majesty's service in a hot climate were given priority. After a qualified surgeon had served in one of the extra ships for one voyage to India and back he was eligible for the regular service. Both surgeon and a surgeon's mate had to produce a certificate from the examiners of the Royal College of Surgeons and also from the Company's own physician. The surgeons were allowed, in addition to their salary and their privilege of private trade, fifteen shillings per man on the voyage for medicine and attendance on the military and invalids. But they were no longer required, as part of their duties, to cut the hair of the Company's servants! The assistant-surgeon had to be at least twenty years old, and possess a diploma from the College of Surgeons of London, Edinburgh or Dublin, and a certificate from the Company's own physician.

The gunner and his mate were examined as to their efficiency by the Company's master-attendant, who after approval gave them a certificate. Volunteers for the Company's Indian Navy, otherwise known as the Bombay Marine, had to be between the ages of fourteen and eighteen; for their cavalry and infantry, between sixteen and twenty-two.

To many passengers this voyage to the East was one of terror. Eastwick tells a yarn about an assistant-surgeon in one of these ships. For five days on the way out a great storm had been raging. This had evidently so impressed this surgeon that the night after the storm abated he dreamt that there was a great hole in the ship's side. Jumping out of his cot with alacrity, he knocked over the water-jug, and feeling the cold water about his toes he ran headlong up on deck, clamouring that the ship was sinking. For some time he was believed. The carpenter and some of the officers hurried to his cabin, and meanwhile the passengers had become alarmed and left their cabins, congregating by the boats. The story, however, does not give the remarks of the carpenter and officers when they found the assistant-surgeon had been romancing.

The passengers in these ships were made as comfortable as possible, though they had to pay fairly heavily for the same. We have seen that they were entertained with dances whenever possible. They brought with them on board their servants, their furniture and their wines. But the conduct of some of these passengers became so highly improper at times that the Company found it necessary to frame regulations for the preservation of good order on board, and these had to be enforced strictly by the commander. In the words of the Court of Directors, they bewailed the fact that "the good order and wholesome practices, formerly observed in the Company's ships, have been laid aside, and late hours and the consequent mischiefs introduced, by which the ship has been endangered and the decorum and propriety, which should be maintained, destroyed."

One of the great terrors on board these vessels was the possibility of fire at sea. We shall have the account presently of the loss of the *Kent* East Indiaman in the Bay of Biscay, through that species of disaster, in the year 1825, and there were other instances. It was in order to guard against this possibility that no fire was allowed to be kept in after eight at night except for the use of the sick, and then only in a stove. Candles had to be extinguished between decks by nine o'clock, and in the cabins by ten at the latest. This was before the days when ships were compelled by Act of Parliament to carry sidelights. In fact, just as in mediæval days not even the boatswain was allowed to use his whistle, nor a bell to be sounded, nor any unnecessary noise made after dark, lest the ship's presence should be betrayed to any pirate in the vicinity, so in the case of these East Indiamen, not only were there no sidelights, but the commander was enjoined that the utmost precautions be used to prevent any lights 'tween decks or from the cabins being visible "to any vessel passing in the night."

The passengers used to dine not later than 2 P.M. And such was the authority of the captain that when he retired from the table after either dinner or supper, the passengers and officers must also retire. The captain was to pay due attention to the comfortable accommodation and liberal treatment of the passengers, "at the same time setting them an example of sobriety and decorum, as he values the pleasure of the Court." Any improper conduct of the ship's officers towards the passengers or to each other was to be reported quietly to the captain, and the decision left with the latter. But if anyone thought himself aggrieved thereby, he could appeal to the Governor and Council of the first of the Company's settlements at which the ship should arrive, or, if homeward bound, to the Court of Directors.

And the following brief, common-sense paragraph summed up the whole situation:—

"The diversity of characters and dispositions which must meet on ship-board makes some restraint upon all necessary; and any one offending against good manners, or known usages and customs, will, on representation to the Court, be severely noticed."

We can well believe that those military officers or civil servants of the Company who came on board homeward bound, after spending years in India without benefit to their livers and tempers, if to their pecuniary advantage, and were as ill-accustomed to the conditions of ship life as they were bereft of an adaptable spirit, needed all the tact and patience of the commander and ship's officers to prevent matters being even more uncomfortable than they were. Those who had spent their lives wielding authority in India, and both honestly and otherwise making fortunes, were not the kind of mortals most easy to live with in the confined area of a ship not much over 1200 tons. However, every passenger who came on board was given a printed copy of the regulations, which had been formed for the good of all, and they were told very pertinently to observe them strictly, and the captains had to see that they did as they were told.

Certainly up to the second decade of the nineteenth century, the ships themselves also were in great need of supervision, as to their construction, though there were not many capable critics then in existence. All the Company's ships were of course built of wood, but iron was already being extensively used for the knees. The idea was excellent, but in practice inferior material was actually employed and not the best British iron. And the same defect was noticeable with regard to anchors and mooring chains. Of those various losses which occurred to the East

Indiaman ships about the year 1809, it was thought by some that the cause was traceable to these weak iron knees which had been put into the vessels. A certain Mr J. Braithwaite wrote a letter to the East India Company in December of 1809, in which he stated that he had been employed to recover the property of the *Abergavenny,* which had been lost off Weymouth; and he found, on breaking up the wreck, that many of the iron knees were broken, owing to having been made of such poor, inferior material. This, he noticed, snapped quite easily, and he was convinced that ships fitted with such knees would, on encountering gales of wind, be lost owing to the knees giving way. The East Indiaman *Asia* was thought to have perished owing to that reason.

But there was also another reason why the ships of this period were unsatisfactory. They were built not under cover but outside, exposed to all the weather. But, in addition, there was a bad practice at that time which unquestionably caused a great deal of serious injury to the ship. When the ship was approaching completion, and before the sheathing had been put on, the sides and floor were deluged with water, the intention being to see if there were any shake in the plank, or butt or trenail holes, or if any of the seams had been left uncaulked. If the water poured through anywhere this would indicate that there was need for caulking before the ship was set afloat.

This was all very well in theory, but in practice it was very bad indeed, for the water thus admitted settled down into the innermost recesses, and the result was that the cargoes were always more or less affected injuriously by the damp. Similarly, it injured the ship herself, and dry-rot eventually shortened the vessel's life. Damp, badly ventilated, these old East Indiamen were frequently the source of much anxiety to their managing owners or "ships' husbands," as they were usually called. Then there was another defect. The influence of the Middle Ages was not yet departed from shipbuilding: consequently trenails were still used. This meant that the ship was riddled with holes for the insertion of these wooden pegs. Speaking of an East Indiaman of this time, a contemporary says that thus "she appears like a cullender," and "there is hardly a space of six inches in small ships that is not bored through" by a trenail of one and a half inches in diameter, being only six inches apart from the next trenail. Thus, of course, the timbers were weakened, and at a later date when the ship needed to be re-bored with holes for more trenails on the renewal of decayed planking, there were so many holes in the timbers that the ship was very considerably weakened thereby.

The method of the French in building ships had formerly been to use iron fastenings, but the plank grew nail sick, and the iron having corroded became very weak. Indian-built ships, however, were constructed in such a way that there were no numerous series of holes bored, and thus the hulls remained strong and stout. The planking was secured to the timbers by spikes and bolts of iron, yet—owing to the oleaginous sap of the teak from which they were built—the iron did not corrode as it did in the case of oak-built ships. So about the year 1810 the introduction of metal nails and bolts was advocated in connection with the building of ships.

After the Company had lost their China monopoly the class of ship that was built by the Greens, for instance, was composed of oak, greenheart and teak, and excellently constructed. Mr F. T. Bullen has written of such a ship, the *Lion*, which was launched in 1842 from the famous Blackwall yard. He tells us that this was the finest of all the great fleet that had been brought into being at that yard up to this date: how, decked with flags from stem to stern, with the sun glinting brightly on the rampant crimson lion that towered proudly on high from her stem, she glided down the way amid the thunder of cannon and the cheers of the spectators. She was afterwards given ten 18-pounders, with many muskets and boarding-pikes stowed away in a small armoury in the waist. This famous vessel, so characteristic of the best type of East Indiaman which succeeded the Company's ships, was, in spite of her great size—as she was then regarded—far handier than any of those "billy-boys" which used to be such a feature of the Thames. "There was as much intriguing," says Mr Bullen, "to secure a berth in the *Lion* for the outward or homeward passage as there was in those days for positions in the golden land she traded to. Men whose work in India was done spoke of her in their peaceful retirement on leafy English country-sides, and recalled with cronies 'our first passage out in the grand old *Lion*.' A new type of ship, a new method of propulsion, was springing up all round her. But whenever any of the most modern fliers forgathered with her upon the ocean highway, their crews felt their spirits rise in passionate admiration for the stately and beautiful old craft whose graceful curves and perfect ease seemed to be of the sea *sui generis*, moulded and caressed by the noble element into something of its own mobility and tenacious power."

Like many other of the later-day East Indiamen, she was eventually taken off the route to India and ran to Australia with emigrants. With her quarter-galleries, her far-reaching head, her great, many-windowed stern, she would seem a curious kind of ship among twentieth-century craft. But she held her own even with the new steel clippers, and made the round voyage from Melbourne to London and back in five months and twenty days, including the time taken up in handling the two cargoes, finally being sold into the hands of the Norwegians, like many another fine British ship both before and since her time. The last act of her eventful life came when she crashed into a mountainous iceberg and smashed herself to pieces. It was a sad end to a ship that had begun so gloriously.

CHAPTER XVII

WAYS AND MEANS

THERE was a fixed rate of passage-money, and it was thought necessary to forbid the captains to charge passengers any sum above that specified for their rank. These were the respective rates, including the passage and accommodation at the captain's table.

General officers in the Company's service were charged for the passage from England £250, colonels or Gentlemen of Council £200, while lieutenant-colonels, majors, senior merchants, junior merchants and factors had to pay £150. Captains were charged £125. Writers in the Company's service paid £110, subalterns the same, assistant-surgeons and cadets £95. If any of the two last mentioned proceeded to India in the third mate's mess, the latter was not to demand more than £55 for the passenger's accommodation. The money was paid direct to the paymaster of seamen's wages at his pay office in London, who handed these respective sums over to the commander or third mate. In the case of military officers who were in his Majesty's service and not in the East India Company's army, the charges were slightly different. Thus general officers were charged £235, colonels £185, lieutenant-colonels and majors £135, captains and surgeons £110, subalterns and assistant-surgeons £95, for the voyage out.

For the homeward voyage the commanders of these East Indiamen were allowed to charge 2500 rupees from Bombay for lieutenant-colonels or majors, 2000 rupees for captains, and 1500 rupees for subalterns when returning to Europe, either on sick certificate or military duty, whether in his Majesty's or the Company's service. Regular East Indiamen were bound, if asked, to receive on board at least two of the above officers, and in this case the larboard third part of the captain's great cabin, with the passage to the quarter-gallery, was to be apportioned off for their accommodation. In the case of an extra ship one such officer was bound to be carried if the commander were requested, and he was to be accommodated with a cabin on the starboard side, abaft the chief mate's cabin, and abreast of the spirit-room. His cabin was to be not less than seven feet long and six feet wide. If the whole of one of his Majesty's regiments were returning to England, the entire accommodation in the ship might be allotted as the Government in India deemed advisable, the sums for the officers being paid to the commander as just mentioned. Factors and writers homeward bound from Bombay were charged 2000 and 1500 rupees respectively.

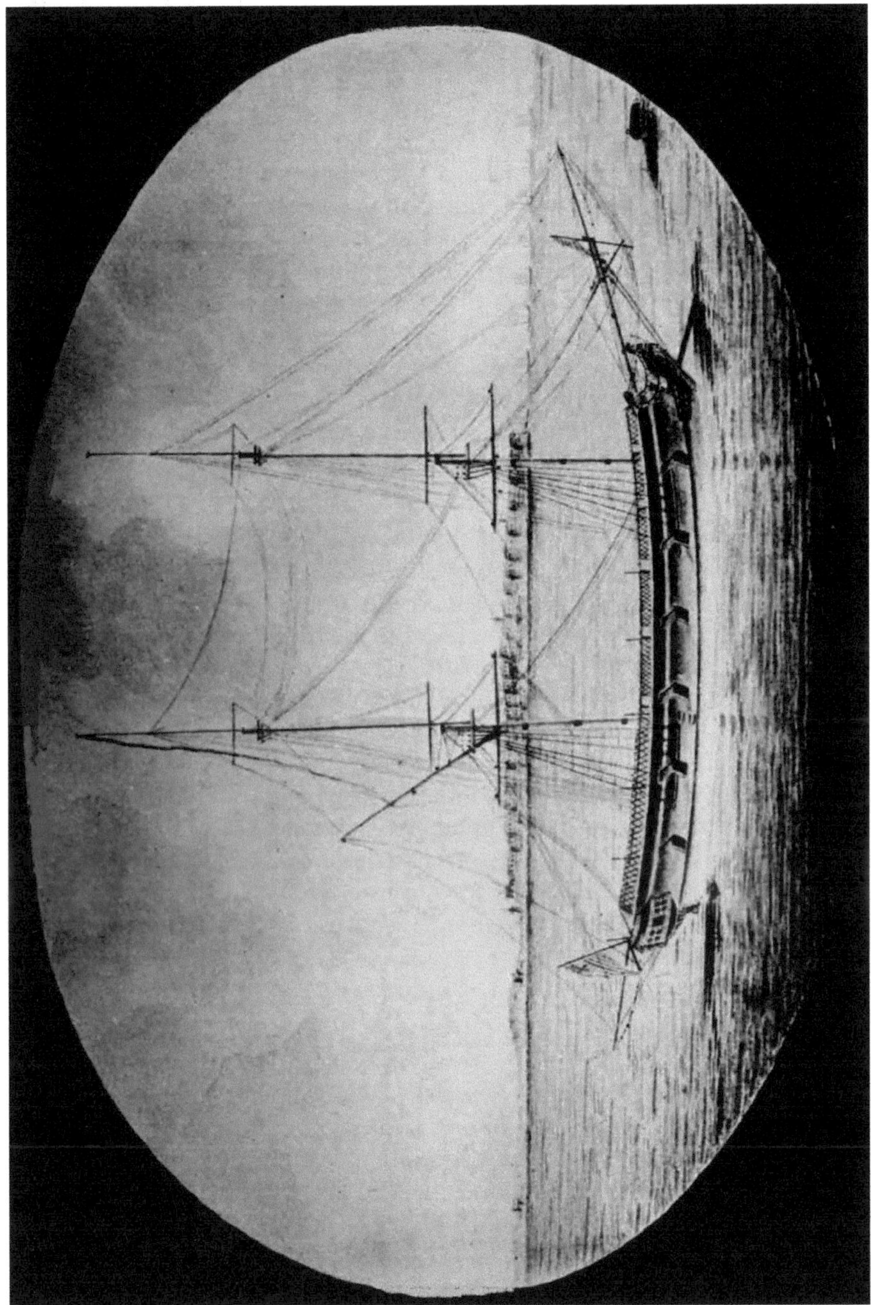

The East Indiaman Cruiser "Panther," known as a "Snow," lying in Suez Harbour on August 15th, 1794.

(From a sketch in the Journal of William Henry, a Midshipman serving in her at the time)

Under no circumstance was a commander allowed to receive any gratuity above these sums, and to give effect to this he had to enter into a bond for £1000 before being sworn in. Similarly the third mate was equally forbidden to exact more than the sums mentioned under his category.

Some idea of the victuals which were carried on board a 1200-ton East Indiaman may be gathered from the following. Recollect that, of course, there was no such thing as preserved foods or refrigerating machinery in those days, but during these long voyages the passengers and crew were not pampered with the luxuries of a modern liner. The accommodation was lighted with candles and oil-lamps, the food was plain, the cooking very English. Beside the amounts which an Atlantic liner takes on board for her short voyage these figures seem insignificant: and there were none of those manifold articles for serving up the food in an appetising manner. For the strong, the healthy and vigorous, this plain, substantial living was all right: but for invalids, for delicate women, and for children naturally terrified of the sea and unable to settle down to life on board, the voyage was certainly not one long, delightful experience.

For the use of the commander's table 11 tons of ale, beer, wine or other liquors were carried in casks or bottles, allowing 252 gallons or 36 dozen quart bottles to the ton. There were also 40 tons of beef, pork, bacon, suet and tongues, 28 tons of beer (additional to the above), 350 cwt. of bread, 30 firkins of butter, 500 gallons of spirit for the commander's table, 1040 gallons of spirit for the ship's company, 20 cauldrons of coals, 50 dozen candles, 50 cwt. of cheese, £65 worth of "chirugery and drugs," 6 cases of confectionery, 134 cwt. of flour, 21 cwt. of fish, 80 cwt. of groceries, 130 gallons of lime-juice, 50 bushels of oatmeal, 300 gallons of sweet and lamp oil, 500 bushels of oats, 15 tons of potatoes, 5 barrels of herrings and salmon, 2 chests of "slops" for the seamen to obtain new clothes, 11 hogsheads of vinegar, 6 chests of oranges and lemons and 70 tons of drinking water. In addition, 63 barrels of gunpowder, 6 tons of iron shot, 6 tons of iron for the store, 5 cwt. of lead shot, 20 barrels of pitch, 6 cwt. of rosin, 7 tons of spare cordage, 2½ tons of sheet lead, 30 cwt. of tobacco, 20 barrels of tar, 3 barrels of turpentine and quantities of wood were also carried for the boatswain's, gunner's and carpenter's stores.

As to the passengers' baggage, Gentlemen in Council were allowed to bring three tons or twenty feet of baggage, two chests of wine being included as part of this baggage if returning to India. Their ladies were allowed to take one ton of baggage if proceeding with their husbands: but if proceeding to their husbands two tons. General officers were allowed the same as Gentlemen in Council, colonels were allowed three tons, but only one chest of wine, and so on down the scale. When a first-class passenger to-day goes aboard a liner he finds that his state-room contains everything that is required in the way of furniture: but had he lived in the days of the East Indiamen he would have to have taken on board a table, a sofa (or two chairs), and a wash-hand stand. This much he would have to acquire, and this much he was allowed. But in addition to bedding, sofa, table and two chairs, members of the Select Committee could take three tons of baggage, supra-cargoes two and a half tons and writers proceeding to China one and a half tons.

If there was no duty payable on the baggage it could be shipped at Gravesend:

but if otherwise it went aboard at Portsmouth. No other articles than wearing apparel and such things as were really intended for the use of the respective passengers on the voyage, including "musical instruments for ladies" and books, were allowed to be taken as baggage.

The East India Dock Company, which we have seen was a subsidiary company of the East India Company, was governed by twelve directors, and the three dock-masters lived at the docks. Before the vessels were allowed to enter the dock they had to be dismantled to their lower masts, take out their guns, ammunition, anchors and stores while they lay at moorings. Before being permitted to enter, a report had to be made by the captain to the dock-master of the amount of water the ship was leaking every twelve hours for the previous three days. Whatever stores remained in her after coming into the basin had to be discharged before she was allowed to go into the inner dock. But all ships from the East Indies or China unloaded their cargoes within the docks, except in the case of the biggest ships, which had to unload some of their goods in Long Reach, so as to lessen the draught of water. Outward-bound East Indiamen used to load either in the dock or in the river below Limehouse Creek. Gunpowder was always unloaded before entering dock, and the Company's servants would superintend the unloading of the cargoes when finally moored alongside the wharf. The goods were then taken away by the Company's "caravans," the tea being conveyed to the Company's warehouses without being weighed at the docks.

Tea, of course, was not the only, though the principal cargo which these ships were bringing home. To give a complete list of the commodities would take up too much space, but we may be allowed to mention the following as being among those commonly found in the hold of a homeward-bound East Indiaman:—Aloes, drugs, buffalo hides, bark, coffee, camphor, cotton, cowries, silk, cochineal, coral, elephants' teeth, ebony, green ginger, gum arabic, hemp, Japan copper, china-ware, shells, myrrh, nutmegs, nux vomica, opium, pepper, rice, redwood, spikenard, shellac, sugar, saltpetre, sago, sandalwood, as well as both black and green tea.

The Company had their warehouses in Fenchurch Street, Haydon Square, Cooper's Row, Jewry Street, Crutched Friars, New Street, Leadenhall Street, and elsewhere in London. As to the private trade allowed to the commanders and officers by the Company, we have already shown what spaces were granted in these ships, but it may not be out of place to mention that the goods under this category used to include such articles as the following, which were much in demand in the East:—Carriages, ale and beer, earthenware, hosiery, anchors, books, charts, bar iron, looking-glasses, ironmongery, Manchester goods, cutlery, millinery, hats, clocks, chronometers and watches, boots and shoes, jewellery, saddlery, lead, port wine, stationery, window glass, wines, and so on.

Smuggling still went on even well into the nineteenth century from these homeward-bound ships, and commanders, officers and men were just as bad as each other. The Company and the Board of Customs did their best to stop it by regulations and threats, but there was a certain amount of satisfaction in cheating the State, and good prices were always offered and received for these goods from the East. The officers were always reminded when being sworn in that if they took any part in this illicit trade they would be dismissed the service, but it was most difficult to put an end to the offence, the chief goods illegally thus imported being tea, muslins, china-ware and diamonds: and the professional smuggler was always glad to give what help he could in running his small craft alongside the East Indiaman as she came up the English Channel and anchored in the Downs. It was for this reason that the Company took every care that their ships did not loiter off the British coasts when returning. But very often it happened that, after the officers of these ships had been detected smuggling by the Board of Customs officials, the Company never learned anything of the matter, for although suits were brought against the offending parties the latter used to compound and the matter ended, though not without loss to the Company itself.

The biggest East Indiaman in existence about the year 1813 was the *Royal Charlotte* of 1518 registered tons. She measured 194 feet long, 43 feet 6 inches wide, and had been built as far back as the year 1785. About the same size were the *Arniston* (1498 tons), *Hope* (1498 tons), *Cirencester* (1504 tons), *Coutts* (1504 tons), *Glatton* (1507 tons), *Cuffnells* (1497 tons), *Neptune* (1478 tons), *Thames* (1487 tons) and *Walmer Castle* (1518 tons). There were about 116 ships in the Company's service at the time we are speaking, and these had been built either on the bottoms of other ships, or by open competition (in pursuance of the late eighteenth-century Act which had made this compulsory), or they were those much smaller "extra" ships. Some again had been built as a speculation, and had been taken up by the Company, whilst at least one—the *Thomas Grenville*—had been built at Bombay for the Company in the year 1809. And there were in process of construction in this year four vessels in India, and one in England for the season 1813-1814. The India-built ships were being constructed in Bombay, Bengal and Calcutta, and all these ships were of 1200 tons. The following, which is an example of a tender made under the new system of free and open competition, and accepted by the Company, indicates the prices per ton which were paid for engaging these East Indiamen in September 1796:—

"To China, and the several parts of India.

"*Ganges*, 1200 tons, William Moffat, Esq., for six voyages	£17	10
Surplus tonnage, peace and war.	£8	15
For difference of outfit, difference of Insurance beyond eight guineas per cent., maintaining seamen, returning lascars, and every other contingency and expence	£18	10."

The Company had its own hydrographer, who inspected the journals of the commanders and officers on the arrival home of the ships. Happily some of these are still in existence, and from them we are able to gather a good many details of the work which went on in the ships. Let us take, for example, the journal of Griffin Hawkins, who was a midshipman in the *Triton* during the years 1792-1794. This was one of the more moderate-sized East Indiamen of 800 tons. We have not space to go through the whole of this journal, which occupied a good many large and closely written pages, but it is merely to illustrate the Company's standing orders which we have already chronicled, and to show the preparations which were made in getting these East Indiamen ready for sea, that the following brief extracts are made. You must think of her as lying off Deptford, and in order that you may be able to picture her the more easily, the accompanying sketch of her at anchor by young Hawkins himself is here reproduced. The time of which we are now to speak is the autumn of 1792, when the ship was in hand for the 1792-1793 season.

"Tuesday Oct. 30th ... at 11 A.M. came on board Mr Upham, Inspector, with Mr Bale, Surveyor, overhauld the limbers &c. Left Mr Bale on board. Employed taking in empty butts, and stowing them, also the ship's coals. Chief and fourth officers on board....

"Wednesday 31st.... Received on board the best and smallest bower cables, and sundry stores, filled 43 butts with water. Do. officers.

"Thursday Nov. 1st.... Employed taking in tin and iron, on account of Honble. Company, also the ship's shott and sundry old stores, filling water etc. Do. officers.

"Friday 2nd.... Clapt a mooring service on the small bower cable, set up the rigging for and aft, filling water etc. Do. and 6th officers on board.

"Saturday 3rd.... Employed taking in shot on account of the Honble. Compy. and 45 tons of kentledge for the ship, and also some small stores, filling water etc. Clapt a mooring service on the best bower. 2nd, 4th and 6th officers on board."

On the following Monday the ship took in a quantity of copper as well as sundry stores. On the Tuesday she shipped three new cables, her pitch, tar and chandlery stores. On the Wednesday she saw to her anchors and bent on her cables. On the Thursday her pilot came aboard and took her down the river as far as Gravesend. And finally—to skip over the ensuing weeks—after leaving the Thames and the Isle of Wight, she had to put in to Torbay, quitting the latter not till 13th January 1793. The setting forth of ships was thus a very leisurely, slow business as compared with the dispatch that attends the modern liner.

The tea which came in these ships was disposed of at the quarterly sales, the duty being paid thirty days later. Some idea of the length of time these vessels were away from home may be gathered from one or two voyages at the beginning of the nineteenth century. Thus, the 1200-ton *Glatton* left the Downs for China on 29th March 1802, proceeded to China, disposed of her cargo, took on board a fresh one, and was back at her moorings in the Thames by 24th April of the following year. Another ship, the *Marquis of Ely* (whose managing owner was Mr Robert Wigram, a name that became famous during the clipper period), also of 1200 tons, left Portsmouth on 20th March 1804, proceeded to Ceylon and China, transacted her business, and was back at her moorings in the Thames on 12th September of the following year. Some of the smaller vessels made good voyages too, when we consider that these ships were not well designed nor built with the kind of hull that makes for speed. Their first object was to carry safely a large amount of cargo, rather than to get a small cargo home in the quickest time. Thus, the 600-ton ship *Devaynes* left Portsmouth on 17th September 1808 for Bombay, loaded and unloaded and was back at moorings on 6th July 1810. The *General Stuart*, of the same tonnage, left Portsmouth on the same day and was back in the Thames on

16th April 1810. These passages may be conveniently compared with the hustling days of sixty or seventy years later, when the famous China clipper *Ariel* made her record passage out to China. Leaving Gravesend on 14th October 1866, she arrived in Hong Kong the following 6th of January and was back again in the Thames on 23rd September.

The East India Company had their agents in different ports, both at home and abroad, and it is worth mentioning in passing that the Company's agent at Halifax a few years later on in the century—that is to say, about the year 1830—was that Samuel Cunard who was afterwards to found the great line of Atlantic steamships which still bear his name.

It was in the year 1814 that a most momentous development occurred. Ever since the time of Elizabeth the East India Company had possessed this wonderful monopoly of trading to the East. In spite of the march of time, in spite of all the improvements in commerce and the development of the world, in spite of the spread of industrialism and the growing demands of democracy, in spite of all the vast sums of money which had been on the aggregate extracted from the East, in spite, finally, of the many abuses of which the East India Company or its servants had been guilty, this exclusive privilege of trade had been withheld for over two centuries from the other persons or corporations of the kingdom.

But now all this was banished. For a long time merchant enterprise had realised that Eastern trade would be extended, and that considerably, if it were thrown open and competition were allowed to have its way. So in the year mentioned the monopoly was done away with as regards India. The British public were henceforth allowed to trade with that country unconditionally, except that it must be done in vessels of not less than 350 tons. But China was reserved as the exclusive trading preserve of the East India Company, and the Company still retained the control of the supply of tea, which had become now a common article of consumption, and therefore the importing of this commodity was of great value to this ancient corporation.

It was not without a great effort that the Indian monopoly was done away with. This was a time when the interests of private individuals in high power were considered even more than they would be to-day. The character of social life has changed a great deal since then, so that it is not immediately easy to appreciate the revolutionary nature of this change from a close preserve, strictly guarded for many a generation, to become an open area common to all and sundry of the British nation. The merchants of Manchester, Bristol and Glasgow had been agitating for years: now at last the desired object had been attained. All sorts of arguments were spoken and printed concerning the reasons on behalf of the monopoly. Some of these were utterly ridiculous, and obviously not sufficiently disinterested to appear sincere. The argument of the monopolists was largely of the kind which says practically: "You may not like it, but allow us to tell you that it is really all for your good that we want the monopoly ourselves." Merchants outside the Company were too wide-awake to see it in that light. And when this monopoly was removed in 1814, what was the result?

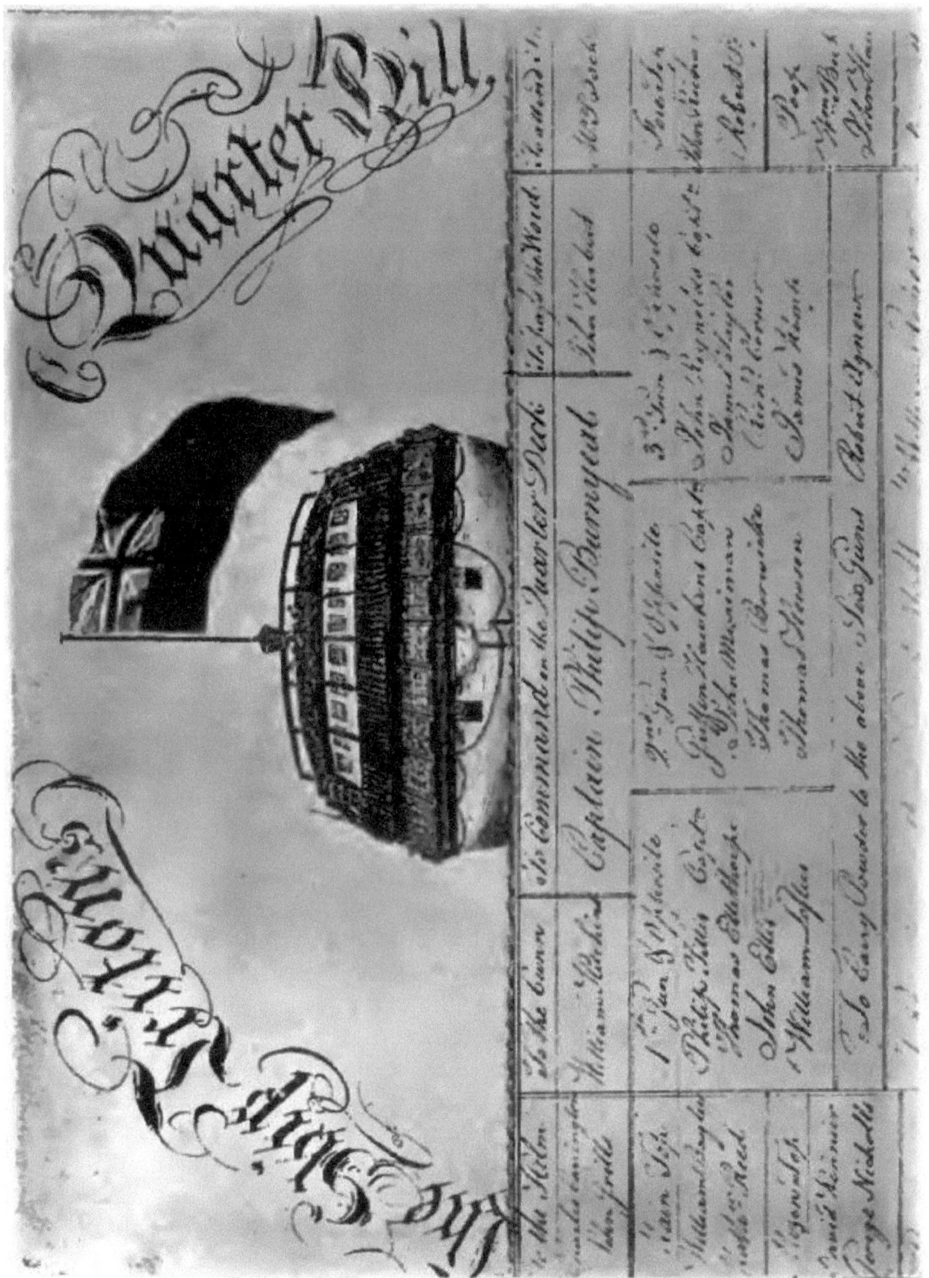

The East Indiaman Triton, rough sketch of Stern.

An Eighteenth Century East Indiaman.

This rough sketch of the East Indiaman "Triton's" stern is from her Quarter Bill, as will be noticed, the date being 1792.

The result was this. As soon as the barrier was thrown down, private shipowners entered, and a number of excellent ships were built for the voyages to India and back. Commerce received a great impetus, and eventually (as had been foreseen) the private traders gained ascendancy over the East India Company, and the trade with India became trebled. The effect of this new element of competition was to cause a reduction in the average rate of freights per ton. The East India Company had been paying £40 a ton for their ships, while better ships could be built and equipped for £25 a ton. By the year 1830 the cost of freights from India to England had dropped to £10 a ton. There can be no doubt that the Company had been managing their affairs with too little regard to economy. Their ships were fitted up with too much expense for the passengers. They were paying £40 a ton as against £25 paid by other traders. The East India Company's ships carried much larger crews than other ships. The former used to have one man to every ten or twelve tons, though the ships engaged in the West Indian trade carried one man to every twenty-five tons. And whilst we are making comparisons let us show how much beamier these East Indiamen were. Four beams to the length was their rule, as compared with five or six beams to the length in the case of the famous Clyde and American clippers which were to come after. To-day in the twentieth century the biggest Atlantic liners have between nine and ten beams to their length. It should be mentioned at the same time that these East Indiamen had necessarily to carry large numbers of men because they must needs be well armed to fight their enemies on an equal footing. But the long years of warfare were now giving way to peace, and instead there was to come a century of industrial progress, invention and commercial development. Privateers, hostile ships, pirates—these were to be withdrawn, and simultaneously the need for arming merchantmen disappeared. It is only quite recently, with the Anglo-German tension, that our merchant ships have begun to be armed again on any extensive scale.

The abolition of the monopoly gave a new impetus to British shipbuilding, and the firm of Scotts, of Greenock, turned out some fine vessels for the East, such as the *Christian,* launched in 1818, the *Bellfield* of 478 register tons—the latter being built in 1820. Both these ships were for the London-Calcutta trade. The Company were of course still trading to India and China, and among the ships which they owned or hired about the last-mentioned date may be mentioned the following. Their biggest ship, then, was the *Lowther Castle,* of 1507 tons. She was built in the year 1811, carried 26 guns and 130 men. Another fine ship was the *Earl of Balcarres,* built at Bombay in 1815. She had the same number of men and guns as the *Lowther Castle,* though of 1417 tons register. Such a vessel was ship-rigged with three masts, triangular headsails and stuns'ls. Still unable to get away from the mediæval influence, the jibboom was "steeved" very high. With her rows of square ports, her figurehead, her enormous anchors, which were stowed over the side by the fore rigging, she was very similar to a British man-of-war of that period. Boat-davits had now come into use, and a boat was thus hung on each quarter.

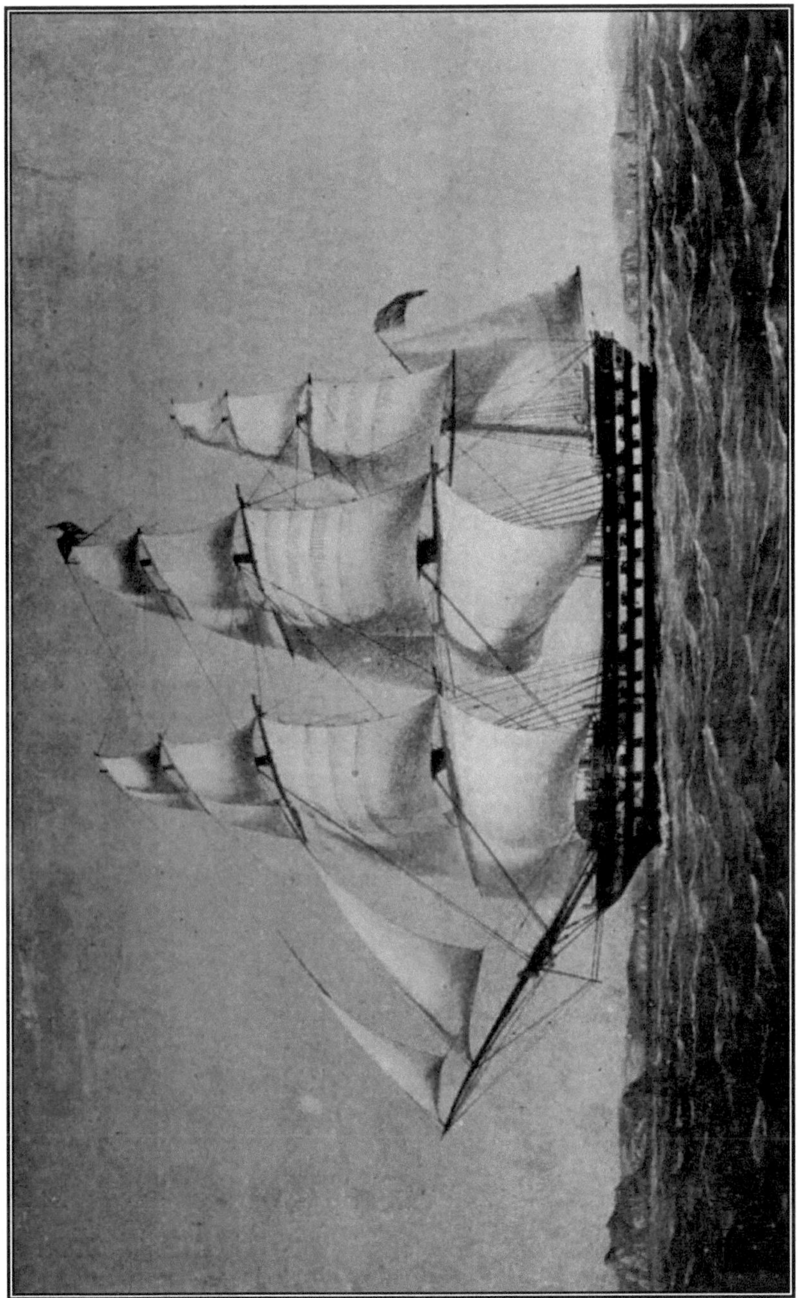

The East Indiaman "Earl Balcarres."

This fine ship was built at Bombay in 1815, and was sold out of the Honourable East India Company's service in 1834. Her tonnage was 1,417, she carried 130 men, and was armed with twenty-six 18-pounder guns.

Contemporary manuscript records of the late eighteenth-century Company's ships show them wearing a long pennant at one mast and a square flag at another. Each of the East Indiamen ships in a convoy would have its own distinguishing pennant. Sometimes this was flown at the main with a square flag at the fore, at other times you find a ship with the square flag at the mizen and the pennant at the fore. And a most elaborate code of signals both for day and night was provided for use between the flagship and the respective units.

Promotion in the Company's own ships was by seniority, though in the case of the ships which the Company hired from private owners for a certain number of voyages, promotion depended rather on ability and influence. The East India Company were wont to appoint commanders to their ships before the latter were completed, in order that they might be fitted out under the captain's personal supervision. Midshipmen had to be between thirteen and eighteen years of age. Pursers were appointed by the commander, subject to the approval of the Committee of Shipping. We have shown that if the pay in these ships was not great, yet the privileges were so lucrative that a commander could afford to retire after four or five voyages with a fortune that would render him independent for the rest of his life. What with being allowed to engage extensively in the Eastern trade, plus the amount of free space allowed them for this purpose on board, and the receipt of passage-money from the various officials who voyaged between England and India, a commander was remarkably unlucky if he had not made about £20,000 in his five voyages in that rank. In some cases his revenue amounted to about £6000 a voyage and even more. This is the figure for what he obtained by honest means. To this must be added in many cases that which he obtained by illicit trade, better known as smuggling. Lindsay mentions the instance of one commander within his own knowledge who in one voyage from London to India, thence to China and so back to London, realised no less than £30,000, this captain having a large interest in the freight of cotton and other produce conveyed from India to China. And, having examined the records of the custom-house, I can assure the reader that whatever a captain made legally he also made additional sums by stealth, to the loss of the nation's customs.

These ships would go out of their voyage to call at foreign, English, Irish and Scottish ports, or to meet with smuggling craft at sea in order to unload some of their goods stealthily, and that was why the Company were so particular in inquiring into the deviations made during the passage. It speaks very little for the honour of some of these captains that, in spite of such handsome remuneration from one source and another, they were always ready to go out of their way to earn a little more by dishonest methods that would bring themselves, their ship and the Company into disgrace. But it is never fair to judge men except when taking into consideration the moral standard of the time: and the less said about the eighteenth and early nineteenth century in this respect perhaps the better. Might was right, and honesty in commerce was a rare virtue. Of course, the mere existence of this trade monopoly was in itself an unhealthy influence, breeding jealousy, corruption, greed and avarice. And this seems to have permeated the Company's service generally, not merely afloat, but ashore. But a better type of man of good family and high character entered the Company's service in the nineteenth century. This, and the rigorous determination of the Company and of the Board of Customs, made smuggling practically non-existent in these East Indiamen.

Let us pass now to a more pleasant subject and see how these ships were worked at sea.

CHAPTER XVIII

LIFE ON BOARD

At 6.30 A.M. in these East Indiamen the crew began to wash down decks, and an hour later the hammocks were piped up and stowed in the nettings round the waist by the quartermasters. At eight o'clock was breakfast, and then began the duties of the day.[5] The midshipmen slept in hammocks also, but the chief mate and the commander were the only officers in the ship to have a cabin of their own.

In no other ships outside the navy, excepting perhaps some privateers, was discipline so strict. The seamen were divided into two watches, the officers into three. The crew had four hours on duty and four hours off. There was always plenty of work to be done. After saying good-bye to the English coast cables had to be put away and anchors stowed for bad weather. Sails were being set, men were sent aloft to take in sail, and sheets and braces required trimming. The East Indiamen from the latter part of the eighteenth century had all been steered by wheels, and the accompanying illustration shows the wheel on board the East Indiaman *Triton*.

The rigging also had to be set up occasionally, and among the confidential signals to be used by these ships when proceeding in a convoy, you will find one which asks permission of the commodore to be allowed to heave-to and set up rigging. In addition, ballast sometimes required shifting, sails had to be repaired, leaks stopped, masts greased, new splices made and so on. This was in normal voyages: but in the case of bad weather there was much more besides.

On Wednesdays and Saturdays the 'tween decks were cleaned and holystoned. The origin of the word "holystoned" has been variously derived. To "holystone" is to rub the decks with sandstone or "prayer-books." When ships, both of the East India Company, his Majesty's navy and other craft, used to anchor in St Helen's Roads (off Bembridge, Isle of Wight, facing Portsmouth) the place was found convenient for two reasons. There was a convenient dip-well close to the shore, which still exists to-day: and this water kept in wooden butts used to keep so well, and unlike much other water did not turn putrid when the ships had been at sea some time, that East Indiamen were actually known to have brought back some of it home quite fresh after being out to the East and remaining in the ship about a twelvemonth. But besides the excellent water, the men used to be sent ashore here to obtain sand for scrubbing the decks. One day it was discovered that there was nothing so good as a piece of the stone of the old St Helen's Church, which had recently been abandoned, the relic of which survives to-day only as a sea-mark. In

[5] For some details in this connection I am indebted to Lindsay's "History of Merchant Shipping," as well as to an article in *The Mariner's Mirror*, vol. i., No. 1.

those sacrilegious days there was little respect for hallowed things, such as churches or graves, and before long every ship that came to these roads would send men ashore as a matter of course to fetch bits of the church and even gravestones in small blocks. The suggestion is that thus when the decks were rubbed with them the work was known as "holystoning," and the blocks themselves called "Bibles" or "Prayer-books."[6]

The men in these East Indiamen were divided into messes, of eight men, their allotted space being between the guns, where the mess-traps were arranged. The 'tween decks had to be kept scrupulously clean, and were inspected by the commander and surgeon. No work was allowed to be performed on Sunday except what was necessary, though manuscript journals rather show that this regulation was not much respected. The crew were mustered in their best clothes, and then everyone that could be spared was present at prayers. Dinner was served at noon, and the passengers were given three courses and dessert, but without fish. There was plenty of wine and beer, and there was also grog at 11 A.M. and 9 P.M. Champagne was drunk twice a week. There was a cow carried, and later on the calf, which was always brought on board with its mother, became veal when the ship had crossed the line and was nearer India. In addition there were also ducks and fowls, sheep and pigs, so that the ship's boats and decks were often mildly suggestive of a farmyard. The crew had grog served out to them at dinner-time and on Saturday nights, when the time-honoured custom of "sweethearts and wives" had not begun to die out. As we have seen from Addison's journals the ceremonies of crossing the line were kept up, and Eastwick has instanced dances: and in addition theatricals were also given on board to relieve the monotony of the long voyage.

The men often employed their dog-watches to "make and mend," or going through their sea-chests, games or amusements. On Saturday nights there would be songs and dancing. When they reached their Eastern port, the men would unload the ship themselves without the assistance of natives. And a ship in those days was far more independent of the shore than even a sailing ship is to-day. There were no better riggers in the world, and steel rope had not taken the place of hemp. We have seen from Addison that in China the crews of the Company's ships rowed guard on Sundays among the ships in the harbour. The number of guns which these ships carried has been mentioned at various dates throughout these pages, and the men were drilled with about as much persistency as in the Royal Navy of that time. The mediæval boarding-pike was still in use, and they were drilled also in musket, cutlass and other small-arms. Also quite naval fashion was the custom of holding courts martial on board, the members being composed of the captain and the four senior officers, the latter having always been sworn when the captain took his oath prior to the ship's sailing from London. Discipline was strict even to harshness and cruelty, and punishments were sometimes inflicted for the merest trivialities. At the same time these crews were not as mild as a porcelain shepherdess, and they were a tough, virile, desperate class as a whole. The reader will recollect Addison's entry in his journal that such and such a seaman was punished "with a dozen" for insolence or neglect. This punishment was

[6] Mentioned in Captain E. du Boulay's "Bembridge, Past and Present."

inflicted over the bare back and shoulders by the brawny boatswain's mate armed with a cat-o'-nine-tails, the victim being triced up by the thumbs. And when it was all over a bucket of salt water washed the blood away. Yes, these men were reckless, they were a coarse lot of dare-devils, they were ever ready to break all the laws and regulations which concerned them. They would desert or cheat his Majesty's customs, knock a man down, drink far more than was good for them, yet for all that they were true seamen to their finger-tips, who could be relied upon to go aloft in all weathers, and the very fellows on whom you could rely when it was a question of nerve and pluck. In battle, stripped to the waist, they would fight with the utmost courage: and when punishment was whacked out to them they bore it like true sons of Britain.

They were kept fairly busy on board, yet as there were so many hands no one could justly complain of being overworked as in the case of the modern man-of-war. They had always plenty of food and grog, and they knew that if they were killed in the Company's service their wives and dependents would be looked after.

As for the ships themselves, they were of course all built of wood. From roughly 1775 to well on into the nineteenth century they were not only rigged, fitted out, manned and handled like the contemporary frigates of the Royal Navy, but they were, in the first place, built after their model, with one exception. The East Indiamen were a fuller-bodied type, but the naval frigates, inasmuch as they were built for speed and not for cargo, could afford to have finer lines. A great deal of valuable room had to be wasted in the excessive amount of pig-iron ballast which these ships had to carry. To call them fast would not be truthful, but then there was no competition before the year 1814, and so there was little need to hurry, and they certainly were not driven. At the approach of night they snugged down, for there was no premium awaiting them, however fast they made the voyage. If, however, they endangered the ship or damaged the cargo they would not only incur the East India Company's displeasure, but detract from their own privileges.

Therefore before darkness overtook them these ships would always take in their royals and fine-weather sails, and the royal yards would be sent down on deck. If bad weather threatened them t'gallantsails and mainsail would also be stowed, and a precautionary reef tucked in the topsails. Thus these vessels never made record-breaking runs, and were never given the opportunity of showing their fullest speed. Caution was the dominating factor, and not speed. In other words, the policy was the exact opposite of the clipper ships which were to follow: but then the clippers were built for speed, and not for fighting. There was in essentials very little difference between the hulls of the time of James I. and of the early nineteenth century, if we omit the somewhat elaborate external decoration which was peculiar to the Stuart times, and give the ships their later triangular headsails, staysails and a spanker instead of the old lateen mizen. The cumbrous hull was really but little modified. Built of English oak, elm, and Indian teak, copper-fastened throughout, the later ships of the Company were strong and well-found, with good spars, stout rigging and canvas. Sometimes they were built by the very men and on the very yard that had witnessed the building of the King's ships.

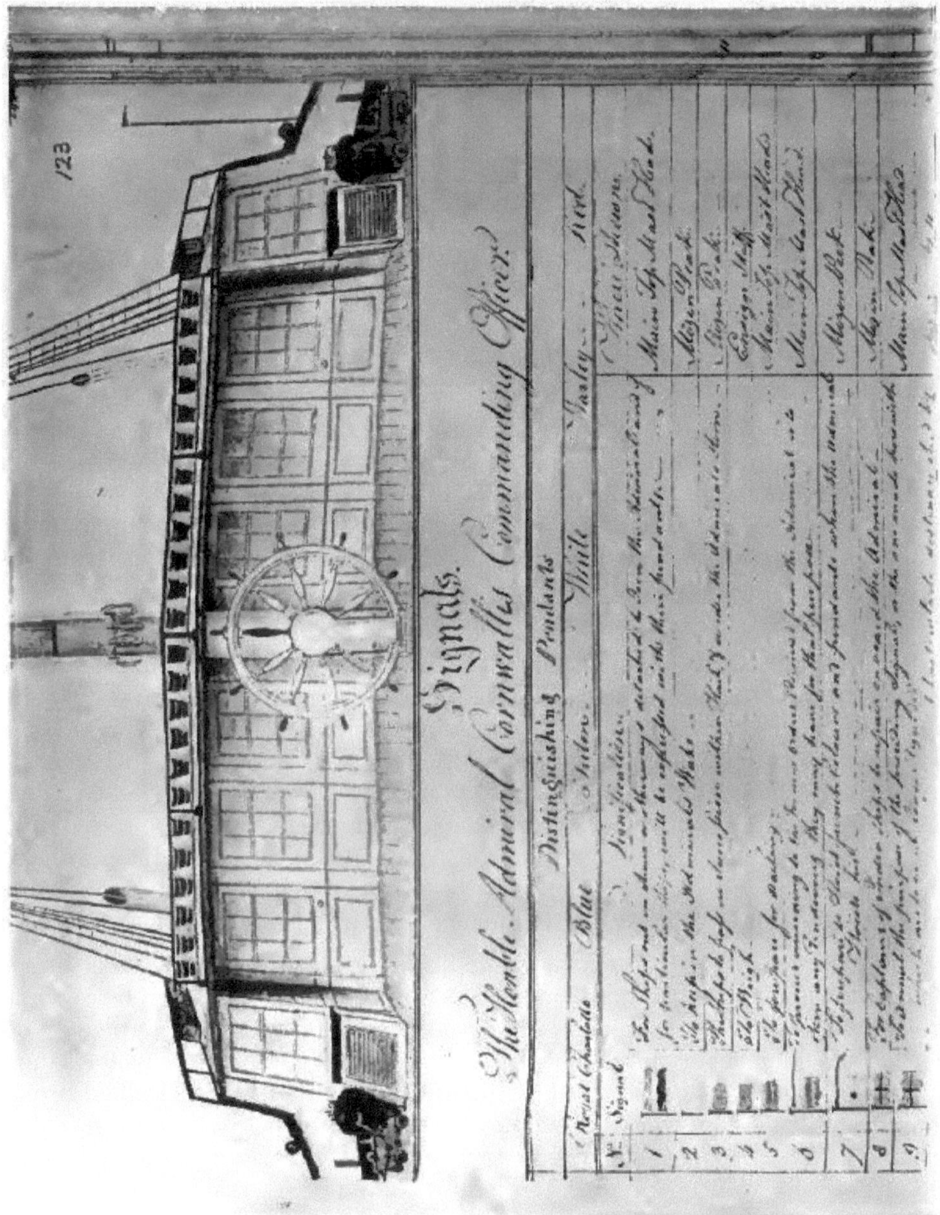

Deck Scene of the East Indiaman "Triton."

This contemporary sketch shows the wheel and mizzen mast and two gun carriages of an East Indiaman of 1792, and is used as a decorative heading to the ship's list of signals employed when convoying.

One of the finest ships ever built for the Company was the famous East Indiaman *Thames*. Happily that great marine artist of the early nineteenth century, E.

W. Cooke, sketched her in all her beauty, and the accompanying illustration shows how she appeared in the year 1829. This was a vessel of 1424 tons, with her general, massive appearance, the strength of her gear, the gun-ports, the decorative stern with its windows—the East Indiaman with all her striking characteristics of picturesque power. A boat hangs in davits on either quarter, the topsails are still single and very deep, with plenty of reef-points, but the hull is certainly unnecessarily cumbrous and clumsy—impressive rather than beautiful, strong rather than fine. But in any case she would have been a pretty tough proposition for a contemporary hostile ship to tackle, especially with such crews as she carried. Compared with her contemporary, the West Indiaman *Thetis* (which is here shown in the act of getting under way off the Needles), the *Thames* is a more powerful fighting ship. But the West Indiamen were essentially more suited for trade, and their capacity for cargo was very great. They were mercantile craft pure and simple.

One of the greatest disasters which ever befell any of these East Indiamen was the loss of the *Kent*. This was a fine new ship which had left the Downs on the 19th of February 1825. She was of 1350 tons, so very similar to the *Thames*. She was bound out to China, calling first at Bengal, and in her were travelling officers, troops, women and children of the 31st Regiment, as well as twenty private passengers and a crew of 148 officers and men.

Favoured with a fine north-east wind the *Kent* made, for her class of vessel, a quick passage down the English Channel, and on the 23rd was out in the Atlantic pitching to the swell. Interrupted occasionally with bad weather the stately ship pursued her way across the Bay of Biscay for another five days, when a heavy gale from the south-west sprang up, and the following morning the weather got worse: the fair wind which had brought them down Channel now headed them and tormented. The bigger sails were taken in, and others were close reefed. Top-gallant-yards had to be struck, and so violent was the gale that by the morning of the 1st of March the vessel had to be hove-to under a triple-reefed main-topsail only. In other words, there was only the merest patch of canvas allowed on her.

She was rolling very badly, and life-lines were run along the deck for the whole watch of soldiers to hang on by. For the women and children below, matters were alarming and unpleasant in those cooped-up quarters. So heavily did the *Kent* roll that at every lurch her main chains were well below the water. Things were bad enough on deck, but below the furniture and other articles had broken away from their cleats and were being violently dashed about both in the cabins and the cuddy. In order to see whether everything was all right below in the hold, one of the ship's officers went down with a couple of seamen, in case anything might have broken adrift and be endangering the hull. He took with him a patent safety lantern, but as the lamp was burning dimly he handed it up to the orlop deck to be trimmed. He then discovered that one of the spirit casks had got adrift, and sent the two men to get some wood to wedge it up. Soon afterwards the ship gave a heavy lurch, so that the officer most unfortunately dropped the lantern. In his eagerness to recover it he let go his hold of the cask, and there was a smash. Instantly the spirits reached the lamp and the whole of the afterhold was in a blaze.

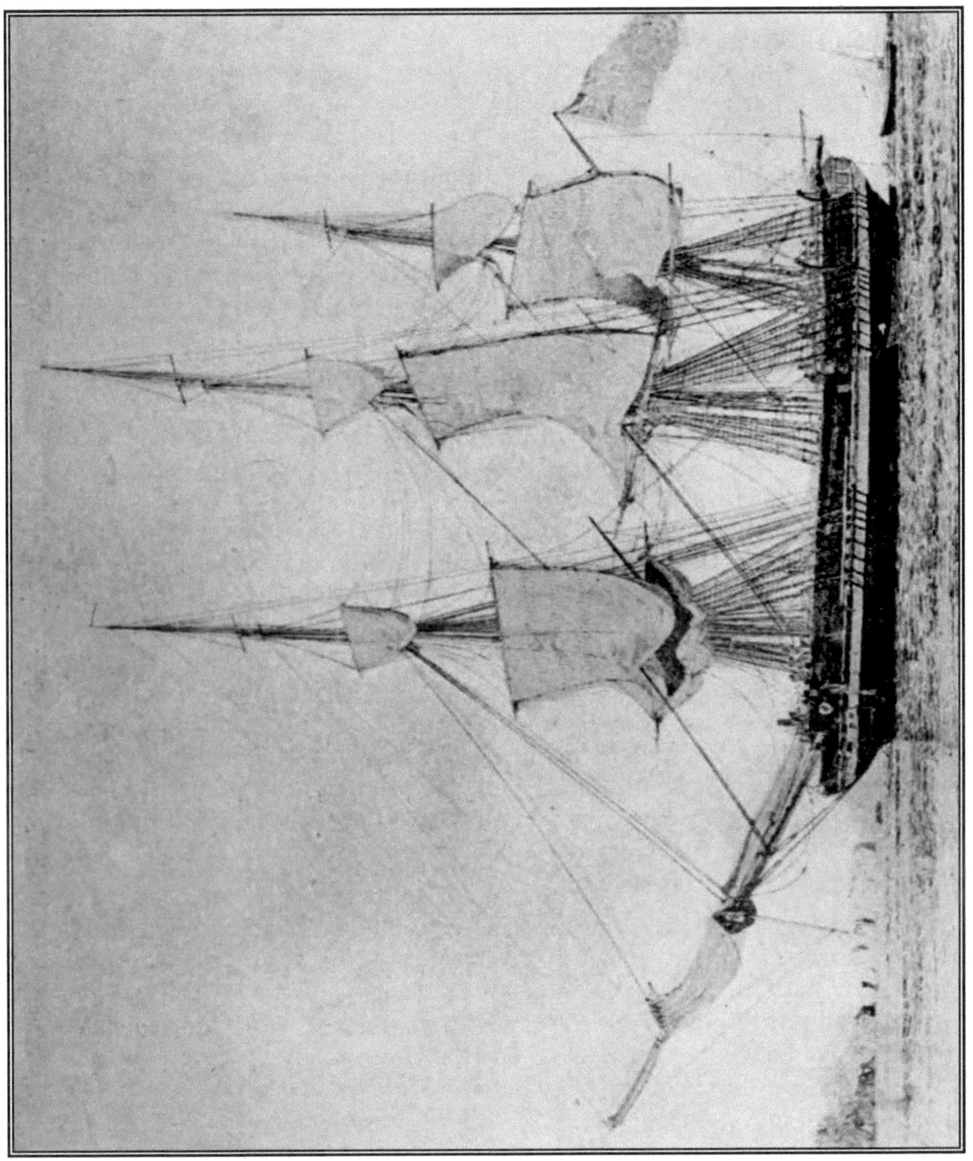

The West Indiaman "Thetis" (Captain Burton).

This shows an Early Nineteenth Century first-class ship employed in the West Indian trade.

Here was a terrible position: a raging storm outside and a raging fire within. Clouds of smoke came up the hatchway and were blown violently to leeward as the wind fanned the flames. The captain of the ship gave his orders, and both the seamen and the troops worked their very hardest with buckets, pumps, wet sails, hammocks—anything in fact that could be employed to put the fire out. But far from decreasing the conflagration was spreading, and smoke came up in volumes from all four hatchways. The captain now ordered the lower decks to be scuttled, the combings of the hatches to be cut, and the ports to be opened, so that all the sea possible might have a free entry. Meanwhile some of the sick soldiers, a woman and several children, unable to gain the upper deck, had perished.

As some of the passengers went below they met one of the mates staggering up the hatchway, exhausted and almost senseless. He reported that he had just stumbled over some dead bodies, who must have perished in the suffocating smoke. With difficulty the lower ports could be opened owing to the atmosphere, but when the passengers at last succeeded the sea came pouring in, carrying chests and bulkheads before it. Happily the tons of water which made their way into the hold checked the fury of the flames and decreased the possibility of explosion, which had been the greatest fear. But now the ship was fairly water-logged, and death from explosion was apparently to give way to death by drowning. Efforts were therefore made to close the ports again, and batten down the hatches and stifle the fire. The occasion was terrifying in the extreme, for it was merely a question as to how long the grave position could be tolerated. Six or seven hundred human beings in the agony of suspense—often more trying than physical pain itself—were on the upper deck. Some had been suffering the pangs of seasickness for days, many had rushed up from below with no time to slip on warm clothes, others were seeking out husbands, wives or children. Some were standing resigned to their fate, while others, as is always the case on such occasions, were indulging in despair and frenzy. Some were saying their prayers, while some of the toughest of the soldiers and seamen took up their positions immediately over the magazine in the hope that when the explosion came at any moment they might be blown into eternity without delay. Every man, woman and child was, to use a fitting expression, "bump up against the inevitable," and everyone acted according to his or her character in this time of crisis.

Meanwhile the seas were making game of the ship, and suddenly the *Kent's* binnacle broke away and was dashed to pieces on the deck. This was taken as a particularly bad omen by some, and the end was being awaited as certain. But just then the fourth mate decided to send a man up to the foretop in case—and it was not even a slender hope—that a distant ship might be descried. With dramatic suddenness the man, after scanning the horizon, began waving his hat and shouting.

"A sail on the lee bow!" he exclaimed, and the announcement was received with three cheers. Flags of distress were at once hoisted, minute guns began to be fired, and setting the three topsails and foresail the *Kent* ran down to the direction of the stranger. This was found to be the brig *Cambria,* of 200 tons burthen, on her way from Falmouth to Vera Cruz with a number of Cornish miners on board. After the *Kent's* signals had been hoisted there followed a further period of suspense. Had the brig seen the signals? Had the sound of the guns reached her in the violence of the gale? But presently the stranger was seen to hoist British colours and to crowd on all sail, in spite of the gale. Her captain was evidently determined to assist if he could.

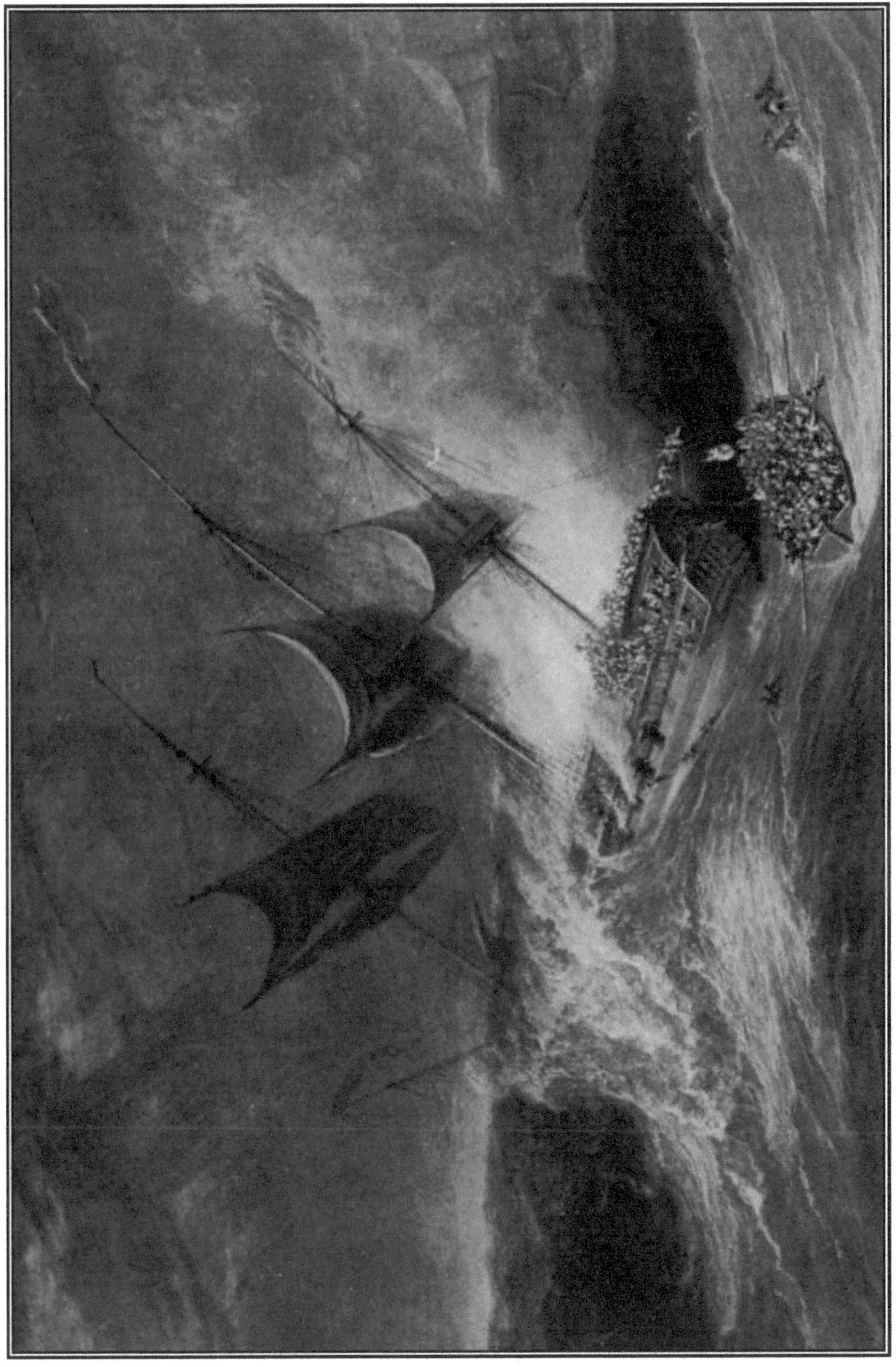

The "Kent," East Indiaman, on fire in the Bay of Biscay.

(By courtesy of Messrs. T. H. Parker Brothers)

There are those who say that the age of miracles has ended, but the good fortune of falling in with the *Cambria* was really far more extraordinary than may seem to the modern reader. To-day the continuous stream of traffic across the Bay of Biscay—liners, men-of-war, tramp steamers and a few sailing ships—is something very considerably greater than at the time of which we are speaking. To-day, if such an occurrence took place in a ship bound for India, there would always be shipping in the vicinity and wireless would summon assistance before very long. But at this time there were no lines of steamships ploughing their regular furrow across the Bay. There were few ocean-going vessels of any sort, and you might cross the ocean time after time without sighting another craft. It was therefore one of those rare instances that the *Cambria* should have chanced to be anywhere in the neighbourhood.

As the ships were lessening the intervening distance, the *Kent's* boats were being got ready. The ship's commander consulted with the colonel and major of the regiment, and provision was made to prevent that dreaded incident in such a case as this, which has sometimes marred the whole picture of self-sacrifice and resignation. Some of the soldiers and seamen in the *Kent* seemed to give evidence of being the ones to rush the boats at the first opportunity. To thwart this, some of the military officers stood over them with drawn swords, and this had a wholesome effect.

The starboard boat was filled with women and children so far as its capacity allowed, these people getting into her through the cuddy-port on that side. The boat was then lowered away into a sea that was so awful that it seemed impossible for the little craft to live many minutes. Even as it touched the water the usual difficulty occurred—and it must have been much worse in those days when there were no patent davits or disengaging gear. The tackle was unhooked only with difficulty, and the boat narrowly escaped being dashed to fragments against the great, heavy hull of the *Kent*. Over the sea the people in the *Kent* watched the load of human lives, now on the summit of a wave crest, now disappearing in the trough. But at length, after this further suspense, strong British arms pulled her alongside the *Cambria*, and the first human being to be lifted into the *Cambria* was an infant of only a few weeks old.

The passage had taken twenty minutes between the sinking and rescuing ships, and after this load had been received on board, the other boat came off. One of the passengers in the *Cambria* who watched the incident afterwards stated that the seas were so big that when the two ships happened to be in a trough of sea at the same time, the *Kent*, great as she was, could not be seen for the intervening mountain wave. The *Cambria* had wisely taken up her position some distance from the *Kent*, fearing that if there were an explosion she might be badly injured. But evidently the *Kent's* boats on their return journey had to row to windward, and this was not easy. Owing to the seas now running these boats could not come alongside the *Kent* again: so the women and children had to be tied together in twos and then lowered from the stern, the boat doing its best to be immediately underneath at the right time. Everyone who has had experience of the sea knows how difficult this must have been, and it happened that many of these poor women were unwillingly ducked several times in the sea before being received half-drowned and half-dead with terror into the boats. Still, not one of this sex was lost thereby, though some of the children perished with exhaustion and shock.

Some of the soldiers behaved with great gallantry, and worked hard to save the women and children, to their own danger. The *Kent* had six boats, but three had been swamped or stove in during the trips between the two vessels. All this time the flames were spreading worse than ever, and as the daylight was drawing to a close it became a race against time, for there were still many passengers on board, although many had been taken off to the *Cambria*. The *Kent's* captain had a rope made fast to the outer end of the spanker-boom, and after walking out to the end of this spar the men had to slip down by the rope into the remaining boats below. Many landsmen, however, dreaded this means of escape so much that they preferred to throw themselves out of the stern windows. Rafts were constructed out of spars, hen-coops and other materials, and acted as a means of reaching the boats. But now night had fallen over the wreck. Some of the baser passengers who remained still on board had drunk themselves speechless: others were prowling about for spoil, whilst the ship's poultry and pigs were turning the ship into a mad farmyard.

As the darkness came down the work of rescue was the more difficult. The *Kent* was now sunk ten feet below her marks, and squalls of wind and rain together with the big seas made her hours of existence fewer. The guns had burst their tackle owing to the action of the flames, and as they fell into the hold exploded. There were still a few people left in the ship, including the captain, but the latter, having in vain tried to persuade the others to leave, left them too terror-stricken and dumbfounded to move. Crawling out along the spanker-boom and steadying himself by the topping lift, he dived into the sea and was picked up by one of the boats. As the last boat left the side of the *Kent*, flames burst through the cabin windows. Some of those who had feared to leave the ship had also a miraculous escape. Driven by the flames, they sheltered as best they could on the chains (where the rigging joins the ship's hull) and stood there till the masts went by the board. They then clung to one of these masts until a ship named the *Caroline*, bound from Egypt to Liverpool, saw the explosion when three miles away and made all sail in its direction, and so picked up fourteen survivors. The captain of the *Caroline* stood by till daylight, but was unable to find any more people.

The magazine (which in East Indiamen ships was placed under the forecastle) had exploded about 1.30 A.M., and portions of the old East Indiaman that had set forth so well with a fair wind now rose into the air like rockets. As for the survivors in the *Cambria*, they had been hauled on board with difficulty by the Cornish miners standing in the chains as the heave of the sea lifted the boats up to that level. The women, surviving children and men were made as comfortable as possible, in spite of the fact that 600 people in a brig of only 200 tons put a somewhat heavy strain on the accommodation at their disposal, with a heavy Atlantic gale blowing too. In a few days all the food and water on board would give out, so, at the risk of carrying away his masts, the captain of the brig drove her for all she was worth before the gale, so that by the afternoon of 3rd March the Scillies were sighted, and soon after midnight the ship had cast anchor in Falmouth harbour. It was another miracle that the *Cambria* arrived in Falmouth when she did, for an hour after she had dropped anchor the wind flew right round to north-east and remained there for several days. This would have meant a head-wind for the brig, and meanwhile in this delay—for those bluff old craft were very slow beating and could not sail very close—many of her passengers must have died of starvation.

At Falmouth the survivors disembarked, being met on the beach by huge crowds, and were hospitably received in the houses of the inhabitants, who also got up a subscription for the relief of the sufferers. A service of thanksgiving was held, and a few days later the passengers and sailors were sent to their homes, the troops embarking for Chatham, while the sick and injured remained in hospital. Notwithstanding that about six hundred had been saved, yet eighty-two had perished in this disaster. Some of the seamen belonging to the *Kent* had certainly behaved in a cowardly manner by refusing to go back and fetch the remainder of their shipmates until they were compelled by the captain of the *Cambria*. It is such instances as these which make one wonder whether those rough characters were always as brave as we have preferred to hope they were.

The captain of the *Cambria* for his fine seamanship and the excellent manner in which he directed the rescue was awarded the sum of £150 from the War Office, with smaller sums to the mate, crew and miners. The East India Company, in compensation for the losses and expenses caused by this rescue, sent the sum of £287, 11s. to the captain of the *Cambria* for payment of the bill of provisions, £287, 10s. on account of the owners for the food of the passengers, and £300 for demurrage. In addition, they presented the *Cambria's* captain with the sum of £600, the first mate £100, and varying sums to the crew and miners. Other presents were also made by Lloyd's, the Royal Humane Society, the Royal Exchange Assurance, and the Liverpool underwriters.

CHAPTER XIX

THE COMPANY'S NAVAL SERVICE

PRIMARILY, of course, the East Indiamen were built fitted out and manned for the purpose of trade: but owing to circumstances they were compelled to engage in hostilities both offensive and defensive. The result was that these ships figured in more fights than any essentially mercantile ships (as distinct from pirates, privateers and other sea-rovers) that have ever been built.

It is necessary at the outset to distinguish carefully between what became known subsequently as the Indian Navy and the Company's merchant ships. The former existed to protect the latter, by suppressing both local and nomadic pirates of all kinds, by convoying East Indiamen and even carrying troops when necessary, and by performing other duties, such as surveying, in addition to existing as a defence against any aggressive projects of rival nations. The Indian Navy evolved from the Bombay Marine. It is not necessary to recapitulate the history of the East India Company and the rise of its mercantile fleet: it is sufficient to state that with the establishment of factories on shore and the passing and repassing of valuable freights over seas frequented by hostile ships some sort of local force was essential. The Portuguese had their Indian Navy, consisting of large, ocean-going vessels and small-draught craft for operating in shallow local waters, the crews being composed of Portuguese, slaves and Hindoos. It was therefore natural enough that the English should soon find it necessary to fit out ships capable of meeting the enemy on a fairly even basis. Furthermore, the Bombay trade had been so much interfered with by the attacks from Malabar pirates that it became essential to build small armed vessels to protect merchant craft. The result was that Warwick Pett, of that famous shipbuilding family which had been building vessels in England from the early Tudor times, was sent out in the seventeenth century to Bombay to construct suitable ships. Local craft were also employed, and very useful they were found in negotiating shallow waters.[7]

Throughout most of the seventeenth and eighteenth centuries the East India Company's cruisers were kept actively employed in suppressing the native pirates who roamed the Indian Ocean and attacked with great daring and ingenuity. They hung about off the entrance to the Red Sea, found a snug base near the Straits of Bab-el-Mandeb, strengthened it with fortifications for the protection of themselves and their shipping, and eventually moved to Madagascar, which was to be a famous base for those notorious eighteenth-century pirates of European and North American origin, whose names are familiar to most schoolboys.

[7] I wish to acknowledge my indebtedness in this chapter to Captain Rathbone Low's "History of the Indian Navy."

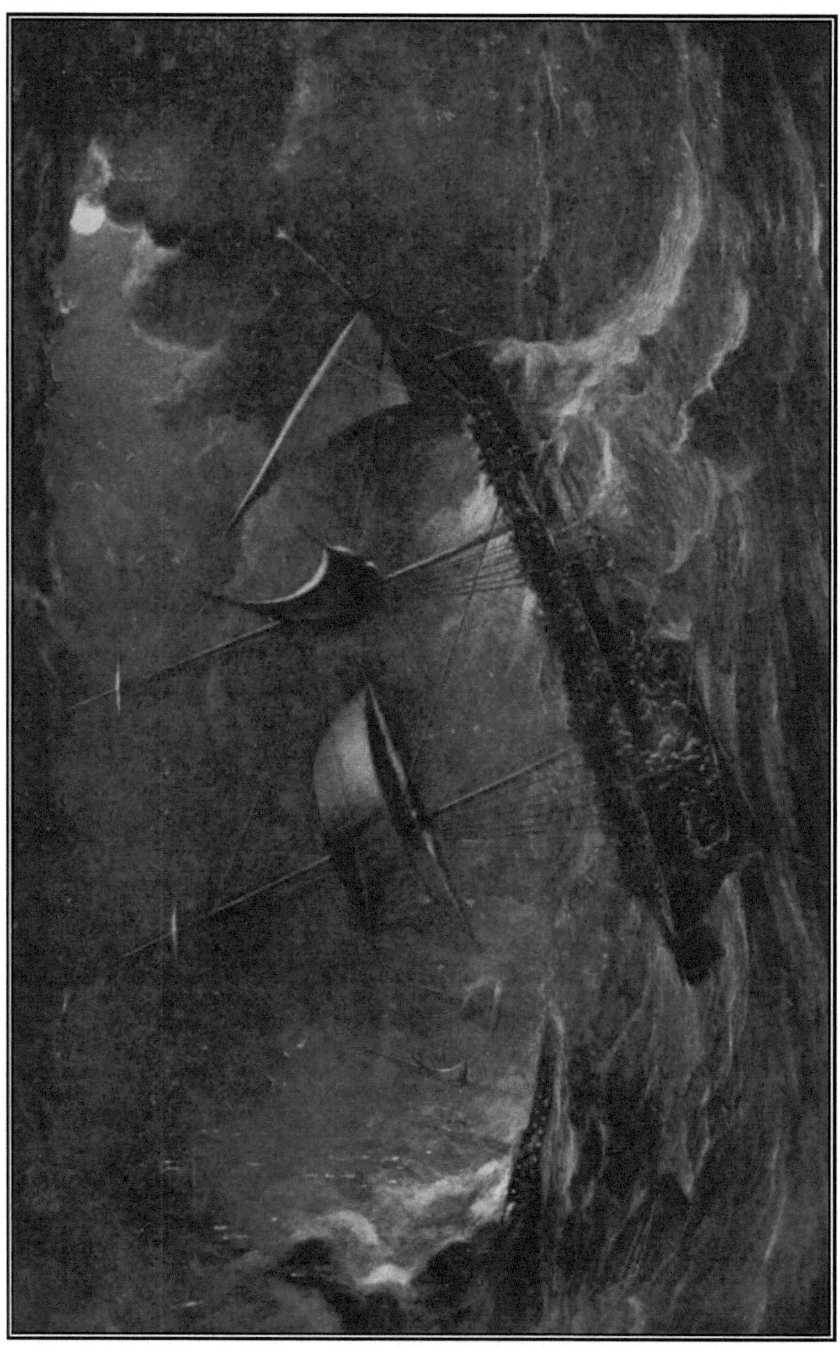

The "Cambria" Brig, receiving on board the last boat-load from the "Kent," East Indiaman, when the latter was being burnt.

(By courtesy of Messrs. T. H. Parker Brothers)

The year 1697 was marked by attacks on the Company's ships, not merely by pirates, but by the French. Three of these East Indiamen were attacked, plundered and burned by pirate craft flying English colours. Two more of the Company's ships were captured by the French, so things were serious enough. The matter was reported to England, and a squadron of four well-armed ships was accordingly sent out to extirpate these robbers of the sea. In fact, the pirate problem became so great that by a mutual agreement the English, French and Dutch eventually agreed to an arrangement for policing the Eastern seas for the purpose of destroying their common foe. Thus the English looked after the southern Indian Ocean, the Dutch were responsible for the Red Sea, and the French for the Persian Gulf.

The English Indian Marine had sometimes to be strengthened by seamen from the Company's merchant ships, and very gallant fighters they proved themselves to be. Arabian pirates roamed about over the whole of the Indian seas, and having become emboldened with success actually built more ships and formed what was in fact a navy of their own. Their ships were well armed and their men were excellent both as seamen and fighters, and as soon as ever the English men-of-war moved off, these pirates, swooping down on coast or ship, would act as they liked.

After the occupation by the English of Bombay and that island becoming a presidency, the naval force there developed under the name of the Bombay Marine, under the command of an admiral, drafts of officers and men being obtained from ships arriving from Europe. For years this service had indeed fought against privateers, pirates, Portuguese, Dutch and French, to defend both ships and factories of the Company. In a smaller, but still an important, degree they had been called upon also to keep out those interloping English ships which had no lawful right to trade with India. Looking back through the first century of the Company's existence, its ships had captured the Island of St Helena in 1601. Eight years later the *Solomon* had defeated several Portuguese ships. In 1612 the Company's fleet had again defeated the Portuguese fleet in India, and the year after this incident had been repeated. In 1616 a valuable Portuguese frigate had been taken and the Dutch severely defeated at Batavia. Four of the Company's ships in 1619 and 1620 defeated yet another Portuguese fleet. The capture of Ormuz in 1622 had been made by the Company's fleet acting with the King of Persia's forces. In 1635 Bombay had been recaptured by the Company's fleet, but it was not till 1662 that England sent out men-of-war to India for the protection of the Company's interests. Therefore, during its first sixty years the Company had to act both as merchants and a naval power without any external aid, such as trade had a right to demand.

If the Bombay Marine was distinctly a small service as regards numbers, it was certainly very gallant, and many a fine incident bright with bravery and daring belongs to its history. During the war with France a number of ships belonging to the Bombay Marine were attached to the Royal Navy on service in the waters that wash the coasts of India, and rendered good service in this capacity. For although the real theatre of war between England and France was not in the Orient, yet some severe, if indecisive, engagements were here fought, and the Company's ships, if smaller in size, were a valuable form of assistance. About the middle of the eighteenth century the Marine consisted of about twenty ships, and these were essential for protecting the progress of the mercantile East Indiamen, for without such convoys it was impossible for those rich freights ever to have traversed the Indian Ocean. It was the Bombay Marine, also, who made surveys of part of the Arabian, Persian, the west coast of Media and other coasts, and all this was to be for the benefit of navigation and trade generally.

By the beginning of the nineteenth century the Bombay Marine consisted of a couple of frigates, three sloops-of-war, fourteen brigs, in addition to prizes and vessels specially purchased for the service, and a few years before that, when Napoleon was contemplating his big scheme in connection with Egypt, which was to be the stepping-stone to India, a naval force was sent from England to cruise in the Red Sea. But, as everyone now knows, the Battle of the Nile prevented these vessels from having any serious work to perform. And when eventually hostilities were resumed, the Bombay Marine had to protect the trade in the Bay of Bengal. This they did with such thoroughness that British merchant ships were singularly free from capture. In spite of the opposition in some quarters, and the prejudice against India-built ships, some of the biggest vessels of the Bombay Marine were built in India, and excellent craft they proved themselves to be.

One of the most interesting incidents connected with the Bombay Marine during the early part of the nineteenth century was that in which the *Mornington* sloop-of-war figures conspicuously. The French privateers, especially *La Confiance* (of which we spoke on an earlier page) and *L'Eugénie,* were most harassing to any craft navigating the vicinity of the East Indian coast. The commander of the *Mornington* was Captain Frost, and he was determined to bring *L'Eugénie* to book. For a time the latter evaded him, and he then hit upon a smart idea. He succeeded in altering the *Mornington's* appearance so that even her own builder would scarcely have recognised her. In order to prevent any suspicion of her seeming a warship, Captain Frost added to his ship a false poop, so that she looked just like a country ship. He changed also the painting of the hull and added patches of dirty old canvas to the sails, and after a while she seemed to be anything but the smart sloop-of-war which she really was.

When this transformation had been completed, the *Mornington* took up her position to cruise about the track where the French ship was likely to be hovering, and before long the look-out aloft espied the privateer. The *Mornington* then continued her game of bluff and altered her course as if she was anxious to get away from the Frenchman. The latter, unsuspecting, began to work up towards the English ship, and by sunset was getting quite near. After darkness had fallen the *Mornington* ran under easy sail, and presently the Frenchman hailed, asking the ship's name, ordering them to heave-to. Too late the privateer discovered that he had been ensnared and fired into the *Mornington,* mortally wounding a seaman and injuring the running gear. Captain Frost now determined to injure the enemy's rigging and sails aloft, and thus cripple him to such an extent that *L'Eugénie* would not be able to get the windward berth. So chasing him he blazed away at the Frenchman. It was an exciting chase and lasted for three hours. So anxious was the privateer to escape that she threw overboard guns and boats and spars as she went: but at the end of this time the *Mornington* had come up alongside and the

Frenchman's captain hailed and begged the Englishman to cease firing as they had surrendered. Very shortly the privateer became an English prize, though she was found to be so crippled that she could not beat to windward. But it was a great relief when the news reached India that this mosquito craft had been taken away from any further possibility of preying on the peaceful merchant ships; and by the irony of events she who had formerly spent her time in attacking these trading craft was now to become their protector, for the Government added her to the service and the command was given to the senior lieutenant of the *Mornington*.

The Bombay dockyard by the end of the second decade of the nineteenth century was building such big warships as a '74 and '84 gun line-of-battle ship, the latter being of 2289 tons. Other big warships were also being constructed, and even those most conservative of sailormen who had always believed exclusively in oak were able after trial to concede that better ships than these Indian teak craft could not be desired. And the men and officers were like their ships. Continuously they seemed to be subject to service, and always they came through it well. French and Dutch, pirates of the Indian Ocean or the Persian Gulf, privateers of France, England or America, it was much the same; the Bombay Marine had to do its work, being hurried here and there to fight and conquer. And when the short intervals of respite occurred these hard-worked people took up again their surveying duties between those distant regions of the Cape of Good Hope and the Sea of Japan and northwards to the Red Sea and the Persian Gulf. At the close of the Burmese War the officers and men of the Bombay Marine received the thanks of both Houses of Parliament, for no fewer than five of the Company's cruisers had served throughout the campaign.

But the time was at hand for a series of changes in the Bombay Marine. First of all we must call attention to the law passed in the year 1826 by which it was decreed that henceforth any naval force that was sent out from England by his Majesty to the East Indies on the representation of the East India Company's Court of Directors, for the purpose of hostilities against native powers, was to be paid for by the Company. The Marine Board which controlled this Company's naval force consisted of the Superintendent, the Master-Attendant, the Commodore of the Harbour and the senior captain. To be Commodore at Surat or in the Persian Gulf, or Master-Attendant at Calcutta was also to enjoy one of the plums of the service reserved for those who had served long years. But after twenty-two years' service an officer could retire with the following pay:—

Master-Attendant and Commodore	£450 a year
Captain of the First Class	360 a year
Captain of the Second Class	270 a year
First Lieutenant	180 a year

If an officer were to retire after ten years' service, owing to ill-health, he was granted one-half of the above allowance. But except from the cause of ill-health no officer was allowed to come home on furlough under ten years.

During the year 1827 the whole condition of the Bombay Marine was inquired into, and as a result the service was changed from a Marine established purely for war purposes into something of a curious character. The officers were embodied into a regiment called the Marine Corps, and a regular packet service was established. The larger warships of the service were made more efficient, new ships were added, and a uniform approximating more to that of the Royal Navy was sanctioned. Finally, from the 1st of May 1830 the Bombay Marine was changed to the Indian Navy, and this in turn came to an end in the year 1863. Beginning as an adjunct of the East India Company it rendered a varied and important series of services during a period extending over two and a half centuries. It had combated the hostility of the Portuguese and Dutch in those early days when the English Company was struggling to get a secure foothold in India. It had made history along the Persian Gulf, it had inflicted punishment on privateers and pirates, it had protected the mercantile East Indiamen, it had assisted the British navy wrestling with the French foe in the Orient. The Company's cruisers were, in fact, excellent fighting ships for their size, commanded by gallant officers and well manned by able crews. And when at last this service was abolished, many were the indignant outcries against such a step. However, it had long survived the existence of the Company's maritime service, both as regards India and China, and a new order of things in India had already begun to be inaugurated. The story of the East India Company's navy, as distinct from its maritime or mercantile service, is that of a comparatively small force doing wonders for two and a half centuries, showing great gallantry, enterprise, and enduring much hardship. Its last years were conspicuously marked by red tape, yet the time had clearly come for a change, and the last link was snapped that had connected the old East Indiamen of historic memory with the period of steamships and the modern men-of-war. Sentiment is an excellent thing in its way, and one of the undoubted forces of the world, yet when it comes into collision with efficiency it is not the latter which must give way. To-day the Royal Indian Marine contains just as gallant and able a personnel as in the past, and the name of Lieutenant Bowers of this service, who died in Captain Scott's expedition to the South Pole, will at once be remembered.

CHAPTER XX

OFFENCE AND DEFENCE

We have made reference during the course of our story to the grave risks which were run by the mercantile East Indiamen in regard to pirates and privateers. It will now be our duty to give some instances of these and to show that if the captains and officers of the Company's ships received big rewards for their few voyages, they were certainly entitled to a high rate of remuneration considering the dangers which had to be encountered as regards ships, cargoes and human lives. The very essential basis of overseas trade is that trade-carriers shall be able to go about their lawful business with some certainty of not being attacked on the way. To-day, if a war broke out between our own and some other country possessing a navy, the merchant ships would be so endangered that they would either have to remain in port or else wait till our cruisers could convoy them.

To a certain extent this happened in the time when the East Indiamen flourished. But some say that to-day privateering could not be revived, and in any case piracy, if not quite dead in the East (and for that matter off the north coast of Africa), has been so heavily crushed, thanks to the good work of the Royal Navy, that it would not avail much against our big modern liners and freight-carriers. But in the days with which this present volume is concerned, piracy was a very real, flourishing concern: and quite apart from all the long-drawn-out hostilities between our country and other powers this remained an eternal source of anxiety to an East Indiaman captain. If he could not meet the pirate on an equal footing the end would come quickly and decisively, for the pirate captains were often enough of British origin and just as fine seamen and fighters as any in the employ of the East India Company.

Take the case of Captain John Bowen, who about the year 1700 used to cruise over the Indian Ocean between the Malabar coast and Madagascar, making piracy his serious trade. One day he fell in with an English East Indiaman homeward bound from Bengal under the command of a Captain Conway. In a very short space of time she had been overcome, made a prize of, taken into port, and both her hull and her cargo put up for sale to the highest bidders, which consisted of three merchants glad to obtain the spoil at their own price. A little later on the East Indiaman *Pembroke,* having put into Mayotta for water, and being promptly boarded by the boats of the pirates, whose men killed the chief mate and one seaman, the ship was taken. Some idea of the experiences which beset the East Indiamen may be gathered from a letter dated from Bombay on 16th November 1720 by a certain Captain Mackra, who was in command of one of the Company's ships.

The "Vernon," East Indiaman, 1,000 tons.

(By courtesy of Messrs. T. H. Parker Brothers)

"We arrived on the 25th of July last," he writes, "in company with the *Greenwich*, at Juanna, an island not far from Madagascar. Putting in there to refresh our men we found fourteen pirates who came in their canoes from the Mayotta, where the pirate ship to which they belonged, viz, the *Indian Queen*, two hundred and fifty tons, twenty-eight guns, and ninety men, commanded by Captain Oliver de la Bouche bound from the Guinea Coast to the East Indies had been bulged [*i.e.* "bilged"], had been lost. They said they left the captain and forty of their men building a new vessel to proceed on their wicked designs. Captain Kirby and I concluding that it might be of great service to the East Indian Company to destroy such a nest of rogues, were ready to sail for that purpose on the 17th of August, about eight o'clock in the morning, when we discovered two pirates standing into the bay of Juanna, one of thirty-four, and the other of thirty-six guns. I immediately went on board the *Greenwich*, where they seemed very diligent in preparation for an engagement, and I left Captain Kirby with mutual promises of standing by each other. I then unmoored, got under sail, and brought two boats ahead to row me close to the *Greenwich*: but he being open to a valley and a breeze, made the best of his way from me: which an Ostender[8] in our company, of twenty-two guns, seeing, did the same, though the captain had promised heartily to engage with us, and I believe would have been as good as his word, if Captain Kirby had kept his. About half-an-hour after twelve, I called several times to the *Greenwich* to bear down to our assistance, and fired a shot at him, but to no purpose: for though we did not doubt but he would join us because, when he got about a league from us he brought his ship to and looked on, yet both he and the Ostender basely deserted us, and left us engaged with barbarous and inhuman enemies, with their black and bloody flags hanging over us, without the least appearance of ever escaping, but to be cut to pieces. But God, in his good providence, determined otherwise: for notwithstanding their superiority, we engaged them both about three hours: during which time the biggest of them received some shot betwixt wind and water, which made her keep off a little to stop her leaks. The other endeavoured all she could to board us, by rowing with her oars, being within half a ship's length of us above an hour: but by good fortune we shot all her oars to pieces, which prevented them, and by consequence saved our lives.

"About four o'clock most of the officers and men posted on the quarter-deck being killed and wounded, the largest ship making up to us with diligence, being still within a cable's length of us, often giving us a broadside, there being now no hopes of Capt. Kirby coming to our assistance, we endeavoured to run ashore: and though we drew four feet more of water than the pirate, it pleased God that he struck on a higher ground than happily we fell in with: so was disappointed a second time from boarding us. Here we had a more violent engagement than before: all my officers and most of my men behaved with unexpected courage: and, as we had a considerable advantage by having a broadside to his bow, we did him great damage: so, that had Captain Kirby come in then, I believe we should have taken both the vessels, for we had one of them sure: but the other pirate (who was still firing at us) seeing the *Greenwich* did not offer to assist us, supplied his consort with three boats full of fresh men. About five in the evening the *Greenwich* stood

[8] That is to say a ship belonging to the Ostend East India Company.

clear away to sea, leaving us struggling hard for life, in the very jaws of death: which the other pirate that was afloat seeing, got a warp out, and was hauling under our stern.

"By this time many of my men being killed and wounded, and no hopes left us of escaping being all murdered by enraged barbarous conquerors, I ordered all that could to get into the long-boat, under the cover of the smoke of our guns: so that, with what some did in boats, and others by swimming, most of us that were able got ashore by seven o'clock. When the pirates came aboard, they cut three of our wounded men to pieces. I with some of my people made what haste I could to King's town, twenty-five miles from us, where I arrived next day, almost dead with the fatigue and loss of blood, having been sorely wounded in the head by a musket-ball.

"At this town I heard that the pirates had offered ten thousand dollars to the country people to bring me in, which many of them would have accepted, only they knew the king and all his chief people were in my interest. Meantime I caused a report to be circulated that I was dead of my wounds, which much abated their fury. About ten days after, being pretty well recovered, and hoping the malice of our enemy was near over, I began to consider the dismal condition we were reduced to: being in a place where we had no hopes of getting a passage home, all of us in a manner naked, not having had time to bring with us either a shirt or a pair of shoes, except what we had on. Having obtained leave to go on board the pirates with a promise of safety, several of the chief of them knew me, and some of them had sailed with me, which I found to be of great advantage; because, notwithstanding their promise, some of them would have cut me to pieces, and all that would not enter with them, had it not been for their chief captain, Edward England, and some others whom I knew. They talked of burning one of their ships, which we had so entirely disabled as to be no farther useful to them, and to fit the *Cassandra* in her room. But in the end I managed the affair so well, that they made me a present of the said shattered ship, which was Dutch built, and called the *Fancy*: her burden was about three hundred tons. I procured also a hundred and twenty-nine bales of the Company's cloth, though they would not give me a rag of my own clothes.

"They sailed on the 3rd of September: and I, with the jury masts, and such old sails as they left me, made a shift to do the like on the 8th, together with forty-three of my ship's crew, including two passengers and twelve soldiers: having no more than five tuns of water aboard. After a passage of forty-eight days, I arrived here on the 26th of October, almost naked and starved, having been reduced to a pint of water a day, and almost in despair of ever seeing land, by reason of the calms we met with between the coast of Arabia and Malabar.

"We had in all thirteen men killed and twenty-four wounded: and we were told that we destroyed about ninety or a hundred of the pirates. When they left us, there were about three hundred whites and eight blacks in both ships. I am persuaded had our consort of the *Greenwich* done his duty, we had destroyed both of them, and got two hundred thousand pounds for our owners and selves: whereas the loss of the *Cassandra* may justly be imputed to his deserting us. I have delivered all the bales that were given me into the company's warehouse, for which the governor and council have ordered me a reward. Our governor, Mr Boon, who is extremely kind and civil to me, had ordered me home with the packet: but Captain Harvey who had a prior promise, being come in with the fleet, goes in my room. The governor had promised me a country voyage to help to make up my losses, and would have me stay and accompany him to England next year."

This Captain England was a notorious sea-pirate and had made many a capture of an innocent merchant ship, and now commanded the *Victory*, which as the *Peterborough* he had previously captured. He used Madagascar as his base for attacking East Indiamen, though he had sailed into most of the seas of the world on the look-out for his victims. It was only after remaining a short time at Madagascar that they had proceed to Juanna and fallen in with the two English East Indiamen and one Ostender. Captain Mackra was certainly lucky to have got off with his life and also with even a crippled ship to reach India. But England, villain that he was, respected Mackra as a brave seaman, and with difficulty succeeded in restraining the pirate crew from exhausting their fury upon the East Indiaman captain. In fact this generosity towards Mackra was eventually the undoing of England, for the crew considered the treatment had not been in accordance with the severe traditions of pirates, and England was deprived of his command.

Captains of the East Indiamen had to be masters of resource no less than able tacticians and shipmasters. In the month of January 1797 the French Rear-Admiral Sercey was splendidly outwitted by the captain of one of the East India Company's merchant ships. It happened on this wise. Admiral Sercey was commanding a squadron of six frigates and was returning to the Isle of France. When he was off the east end of Java he descried what appeared to be a considerable force, and before the day had ended counted himself very fortunate to have escaped them. That, indeed, was how it appeared to him. But looked at from the opposite point of view we have to consider half-a-dozen homeward-bound East Indiamen all richly laden, and not one of them a warship. The commodore of this merchant squadron was Captain Charles Lennox, whose ship was the *Woodford*. On the morning of the day mentioned he was alarmed to see Admiral Sercey's frigate squadron and feared for the safety of the Indiamen under his own charge. Here was a dilemma indeed. These six merchantmen were not the equal of the six frigates in a fight: therefore an engagement must be avoided. But, on the other hand, if the merchantmen attempted to crowd on all sail and run away this would be an admission of inferior strength and the Frenchman would be bound to attack at once.

So with much ingenuity Lennox devised a piece of bluff. In order to deceive Sercey, the English commodore hoisted the blue flag of the French Rear-Admiral Rainier at the mizen, and made all the other five ships to hoist pennants and ensigns to correspond, for it must be remembered that in appearance a French frigate and one of the Company's East Indiamen were very similar at a distance. In addition he had the audacity to detach two of his ships and send them on to reconnoitre the French squadron. These approached the French reconnoitring frigate *Cybèle*, and the latter's captain, having had a good look at the enemy, made the signal at her mast-head, "The enemy is superior in force to the French," and crowding on sail rejoined Sercey's squadron. The French admiral therefore caused his ships to make sail and escape, though when one of his vessels—the *Forte*—had the misfortune to carry away her maintopmast he was more than surprised to notice that the English did not continue their chase. But inasmuch as the captain of the *Cybèle* had assured him that the enemy's force consisted of two line-of-battle ships and four frigates he felt that he was justified in retreating and declining fight. So it came about that the six East Indiamen were able to congratulate themselves on escaping, and the French rear-admiral was no less pleased to have avoided an engagement. But you may judge of the latter's anger and chagrin four weeks later when, on arriving at the Isle of France, he learned that Admiral Rainier had not been near the straits (where the East Indiamen were sighted), and that therefore six rich merchant ships which ought to have been captured had been allowed literally to slip through his fingers.

From time immemorial the Indian Ocean and the Gulf of Persia had been the happy hunting-ground of pirates, and the mouth of the Red Sea, from its strategical position, was another favourite resort. There is on record an incident belonging to the year 1696, when the pirates attacked a Bombay ship commanded by an Englishman named Sawbridge, whose cargo consisted of Arab horses for Surat. The pirates were able to seize the ship, whereupon Sawbridge began to expostulate with them as to their manner of life. On this they ordered him to be silent, but as he continued to speak they took a sail-needle and twine and sewed his lips together, keeping him like this for several hours with his hands tied behind him. They then at length unloosed both his hands and his lips and took him on board their own ship, and having successfully plundered Sawbridge's vessel they set it on fire, burning both her and the horses. Sawbridge was set ashore at Aden, together with his people, but it is not surprising to learn that he soon died.

Now the pirate in this case was not an Oriental, but that notorious blackguard Captain Avery, who certainly knew better. The pirates, however, of whom we are now to speak as enemies of the East Indiamen ships were those Easterns who dwelt on the Arabian side of the Persian Gulf and were known by the name of Joassamees. They were seamen by nature and occupation, trading with their vessels to Bussorah, Bushire, Muscat and India. Finding that to plunder the big merchant ships which now came to the Persian Gulf was a profitable concern, they applied themselves with great assiduity to that task, and became even more ambitious. About the year 1797 one of the East India Company's warships was lying at anchor in the inner roads of Bushire (on the Persian side of the Gulf). Her name was the *Viper* and she carried ten guns. Anchored in the harbour were some Joassamee dhows, but as they had always respected or feared the British flag no hostile measures had been taken against them by British ships. The commanders of these dhows had applied to the Persian agent of the East India Company for a supply of gunpowder and cannon shot, and as the agent had no suspicion of their intentions he furnished them with an order to the commanding officer on board for the quantity required.

The captain of the *Viper* was ashore at the time in the agent's house, but as the order was produced to the officer on board the powder and shot were delivered and the dhows subsequently made sail. At this moment the crew of the *Viper* were below at breakfast, when suddenly they were alarmed by a cannonade from two of the dhows directed at the *Viper*. The Joassamees attempted to board, but the English officers leaping on deck sent the crew to quarters, cut the *Viper's* cable and got sail upon her so that she might have the advantage of manœuvring. A regular engagement now followed between the *Viper* and four dhows, all being armed with guns and full of men. The commanding officer of the *Viper* was wounded, but after tying round a handkerchief still kept the deck, till he fell with a ball entering his forehead. The command then devolved on a midshipman, who continued the fight with great bravery, and the result was that the dhows were beaten off and chased out to sea.

Reverting now to the Company's purely mercantile ships it is well to see how they were armed to withstand the attacks of their enemies. On another page the reader will find the lines of one of the finest East Indiamen of the early nineteenth century. This was one of the Company's ships which carried freight and passengers between England and India and was not one of their cruisers belonging to the Bombay Marine. We may take this vessel as typical of the biggest and most formidable type of their ships at the time of which we are speaking. She measured 165 feet 6½ inches long. Her length of keel (measured for tonnage) was 134 feet. Her extreme breadth was 42 feet, and the depth of her hold 17 feet, her burthen working out at 1257 tons. Such a ship was armed with twenty-six 18-pounders on her middle deck and ten 18-pounders on her upper deck, with two more guns in the after ports as stern-chasers. One of the greatest authorities on shipbuilding and naval architecture of that time, who himself was a Fellow of the Royal Society, went so far as to state that the biggest East Indiamen were not safe owing to their bad design below water, adding that whenever these vessels got ashore in bad weather they usually broke their floors and then filled with water—so weakly constructed were they below.

With respect to the armament of these ships, James, the famous naval historian, in commenting on that incident in which Commodore Dance beat off the French Admiral Linois (already related in another chapter), says that each of the Indiamen under Dance carried from thirty to thirty-six guns apiece, but the strongest of them was not a match for the smallest 36-gun French frigate, and some of these East Indiamen would have found it difficult to avoid yielding to the 22-gun corvette. Speaking of these East Indiamen, he says: "Some of the ships carried upon the main deck 26 medium 18-pounders, or 'carronades,' weighing about 28 cwt. and of very little use: guns of this description, indeed, have long since been exploded. Ten 18-pounder carronades on the quarter-deck made up the 36 guns. Others of the ships, and those among the largest, mounted long 12 and 6 pounders. No one of the crews, we believe, exceeded 140 men, and that number included Chinese, Lascars, etc. Moreover in fitting the ships, so much more attention had been paid to stowage than to the means of attack and defence, that one and sometimes two butts of water were lashed between the guns, and the decks in general greatly lumbered."

The fact was that the old East Indiamen had to go about their work under very trying conditions. They could not be built of more than a certain tonnage for the reason that shipbuilders were not equal to the task. Within their limited size of about 140 feet on the keel a very great deal had to be got in. First and most important of all, the ship must be able to carry a large amount of cargo. Without this she would not be of service to the East India Company. Secondly, she carried passengers and a large crew. This meant that the designer's ingenuity was further taxed to find accommodation for all. Then, although she had to be strong enough to carry all her armament, yet she had to make as fast a passage as she could with safety and caution. In short, like all other ships she was a compromise, but the real difficulty was to combine space, speed and fighting strength without one item ousting the other. To-day the designer of our merchant ships has a difficult problem; but he has not to consider so much how his ship would fare in an engagement, but how he can get out of her the greatest speed combined with the maximum amount of room for passengers and cargo. He has to work on all sorts of data obtained from actual experience of years and experiments made in tanks with wax models. But the designers and builders of the old East Indiamen were tied down to the frigate type and bound by convention. There was very little science in shipbuilding, and practically all that they could do was to modify very slightly the models which had been in vogue for so many generations. If they had been in possession of greater theoretical knowledge, if they could have been allowed to eliminate all thought of the ship being a fighting unit, we should have seen, no doubt, the clipper era appearing some years before it actually did. It is easy enough to find fault with the old East Indiamen for their clumsiness, but it is much more just to remember the conditions which were handicapping the designers and builders of those times.

CHAPTER XXI

THE "WARREN HASTINGS" AND THE "PIÉMONTAISE"

ONE of the most gallant duels which was ever fought between a merchant ship and a man-of-war is that which occurred in the year 1805: and though eventually the former was at last captured, yet the engagement none the less remains to her credit, since the fight lasted for four hours and the enemy was compelled to haul off several times during the action. The incident, in fact, affords an excellent example of the readiness for hostilities which was so marked a feature of the old East Indiamen. James has happily preserved to posterity a full account of this, although in some instances he has not always done full credit to the gallantry and determination of these merchant ships. And I shall make no apology for availing myself of his detailed story.

The *Warren Hastings* was a vessel of 1200 tons, was armed with 44 guns, and her crew consisted of 196 men and boys. She was therefore in size, in armament and crew a distinctly formidable ship, her commander being Captain Thomas Larkins. On the 17th of February 1805 she left Portsmouth bound for China. This was one of the most historic years in the whole history of the sea, and a few months later the Battle of Trafalgar brought matters to a crisis. It was obvious that in consequence of the eventful times no ship, not even an East Indiaman, could dare to begin a voyage unless special precautions had been taken to render her as fully equipped against a French frigate as both money and the ship's own limitations would permit.

In the case of so valuable a ship as the *Warren Hastings* extraordinary precautions had been taken to make her as powerful as possible. Her forty-four guns were composed as follows. She carried on her main or lower deck twenty-six medium 18-pounders, fourteen carronades (18-pounders) on her upper deck, and four carronades (12-pounders) on her poop. The medium gun was six feet in length, and weighed about 26¾ cwt. It will be seen that this was a smaller weapon than that used in the Royal Navy, for the common 18-pounder of the latter measured nine feet long, and weighed 42 cwt. The East Indiaman's medium 18-pounder when run out did not reach out more than a foot from the ship's side. The 18-pounder carronade was five feet long, and weighed about 15½ cwt. The 12-pounder was 3¼ feet long and weighed about 8½ cwt. The *Warren Hastings'* carronades were mounted, says James, "upon a carriage resembling Gover's in every particular but the only essential one, the having of rollers adapted to a groove in the slide. The consequence of this silly evasion of an ingenious man's patent was, that the whole of the ship's quarter-deck and poop guns became utterly useless, after only a few rounds had been fired from them. The first discovery of any imperfection in the new carriage occurred at exercise: but a plentiful supply of blacklead upon the upper surface of the slide lessened the friction, and, with the aid of an additional hand, enabled the gun to be run out. On account, however, of the rain, and the salt water in washing the deck, the application of blacklead was obliged to be repeated every time of exercise."

The *Warren Hastings*, after leaving Portsmouth on the day mentioned, made a safe and uneventful passage to China and duly began her return journey. But this time she was armed not quite so strongly. Four of her main-deck ports had been caulked up so as to afford additional space for a storeroom, and the four guns had been put away in the hold. Nor had she so good a crew, for forty Chinamen had decided to remain at Canton, and there was the usual impressment from the British navy, a warship relieving the *Warren Hastings* of eighteen English seamen: and you can be sure they were some of the best men in the ship. In addition to the four guns already mentioned, four of the 18-pounder carronades were also transferred to the hold. The net result was that when she put to sea for her homeward voyage she mounted 36 guns only and carried a crew of 138 men and boys.

It was on the 21st of June at 7.30 in the morning that, while this ship was foaming along under a smart press of canvas before a strong breeze, she descried a strange ship under treble-reefed topsails and courses. This turned out to be the French frigate *Piémontaise* of 40 guns, commanded by Captain Jacques Epron. This ship was armed rather differently from the rest of French frigates which were so famous at this period, and as we are about to watch the contest between her and the Indiaman it will be well to notice these details. The *Piémontaise* had the usual twenty-eight long 18-pounders on her main-deck. On her quarter-deck and forecastle she mounted ten iron and two brass 36-pounder carronades, two long French 8-pounders, and four long English 9-pounders, these having belonged to the British frigate *Jason*, which had been compelled to throw them overboard when she grounded off Pointe de la Trenche at the capture of the Seine in 1798.

In addition to her forty-six carriage guns, the Frenchmen also carried swivel guns and musketoons in her tops and along her gunwales. On each fore and main yard-arm there was fixed a tripod to contain a shell weighing a quarter of a ton, the idea being that when in combat she got alongside another ship, the shell was to have its fuse lighted by a man lying out on the yard. It would then be thrown from the tripod, fall on the enemy's deck, pass through to the deck below, and then exploding would cause wholesale destruction. Meanwhile, the French crew would rush on board, profiting by this confusion, and the capture of the Frenchman's enemy would be an easier matter. The French crew would also be armed each with a dagger in the buttonholes of his jacket in addition to the boarding-pike which he would hold in his hand. These tactics were, even at the beginning of the nineteenth century, a curious survival of the mediæval methods of fighting. Gunnery was not the chief reliance, but was looked upon merely as a means for quelling the enemy so that she might be boarded and a hand-to-hand fight begun. It seems strange in this twentieth century, when a battleship would open fire at six miles and be pretty sure to keep a good distance from its opponent, that the older fashion should have survived so long. If the French frigates of yesterday were the German light cruisers of to-day, and the old East Indiamen were the crack ships of the Cunard Line of the P. & O., the latter could, if desired, be attacked and sunk without the vessels ever getting within several miles of each other, let alone any thought of boarding, unless the German was determined to spare human life, keep within the limits of international law and take the merchant ship captive. Thus have the conditions changed in the course of time.

But to return to the incident before us. An hour and a half after sighting the Frenchman, the *Warren Hastings* noticed that the frigate was shaking out her reefs from her topsails and was approaching the English ship, the latter still keeping on her course. At half-past nine that morning the frigate was fast gaining on the Indiaman, and nevertheless set her topgallant-sails as well as her fore and maintopmast stuns'ls. Her next act was to hoist an English blue ensign and pennant. However, the skipper of the *Warren Hastings* was far too experienced in the ways of the sea to be taken in by this piece of bluff, and still kept his ship on her way. He replied to the signals by hoisting his English colours and making the private signal, of which we have spoken elsewhere in this volume. The Frenchman, however, made no reply to this private signal, so it was pretty certain that there was treachery.

On came the frigate, tearing through the water with the smart breeze, doing good work all the time. Meanwhile, the East Indiaman's commander was seeing that everything was in readiness for obvious impending trouble. At eleven o'clock he shortened sail, hauled up a point and cleared his ship for action. One hour later the frigate also took in her "fancy" canvas—her stuns'ls and her staysails, but also her mainsail too. And having approached to within one mile hauled down her English colours and sent up her French flag. She had intentionally chosen the leeward position, because of the high wind, and opened fire at the Indiaman's port quarter within musket-shot distance—that is to say, about four hundred yards away; and so soon as the Indiaman could bring her guns to bear this fire was returned. This firing went on for about a quarter of an hour, when the frigate bore away, let her sails fill, and went on ahead. The only damage that had been done to the Indiaman was to carry away part of the rigging.

After the frigate had got about a mile and a half ahead the latter tacked, passed close to leeward of the *Warren Hastings* again, and once more a smart fire was exchanged. This time several of the *Warren Hastings'* crew were killed and wounded, and in addition the whole of the port fore shrouds, the foretopsail tie, her chief running gear, her stays and her ensign were cut away and her foremast seriously injured. The ensign, however, was quickly rehoisted at the maintopgallant-masthead. Quickly the Indiaman repaired her damage, but then the frigate having put about astern of the Indiaman began the action a third time, though this did little more damage than crippling the merchant ship's foremast altogether. Owing to this fact and the heavy sea and high wind the *Warren Hastings* could carry sail only on her main and mizen masts. The result was that the Frenchman could run round her even more easily than before.

The "Sibella," East Indiaman, 721 tons.

(By courtesy of Messrs. T. H. Parker Brothers)

This time she went ahead again, tacked, and was about to make a further onslaught when the *Warren Hastings* opened a hot fire. The Frenchman replied, but it was seen that the Englishman was being injured still more and more. She was now injured not merely at her foremast, but at her main too. Her standing and running rigging had also been considerably damaged, two quarter-deck guns were disabled, five men had been killed and others were wounded. However, in this crippled state she had to sustain a fifth attack. For the frigate, coming on the Indiaman's port quarter, poured in a heavy and destructive fire which smashed the driver-boom to splinters, and soon the mizen-mast went. And as it fell it succeeded in disabling every effective gun on the upper deck. Troubles seldom come singly, and in addition to these misfortunes the lower deck was on fire from the shot which had entered the counter, and as the nail of the tiller rope on the barrel of the steering wheel had drawn, the rudder became useless.

The surgeon was in the act of amputating and dressing the wounded when a shot entered and destroyed the whole of his instruments. Altogether it was a bad business, and the poor, crippled Indiaman, after having done her best to fight against a superior foe, was reluctantly compelled to lower her colours just before five o'clock that evening. She had been rendered almost a mere hulk, she had lost her purser and six men all killed. Thirteen more, including her chief, third and sixth officers and her surgeon's mate had been wounded, whereas the Frenchman out of her enormous crew of 385 men and boys had lost only seven men killed and five badly wounded. Her hull was practically undamaged and her rigging and sails were only partially injured. But this, of course, was natural enough, for the frigate's weight of broadside was 533 lb. as against the Indiaman's 312 lb. The Indiaman carried only 138 men and boys, as against the Frenchman's 385.

But it is necessary also to bear in mind that a warship exists solely for the purpose of being an efficient fighting unit. This frigate had to think of nothing else. Whenever she cruised about, her intention was to find some opportunity of inflicting injury on an English ship. The Indiaman, on the other hand, had to consider primarily how best she could carry the greatest amount of cargo, how she could get this to port in the quickest manner: and then only in a secondary sense had she to contemplate being an able fighter. Necessarily, therefore, the frigate was always better armed and more ready for war. It so happened that the *Warren Hastings* was still further handicapped by the fact that she could make very little use of her upper deck and poop batteries after the second or third round of shot. Owing to lack of men she could man only eight out of her eleven guns on her lower deck, while the frigate was in no way impeded.

"Under these circumstances," says James, "the defence made by the *Warren Hastings*, protracted as it was to four hours and a half, displayed a highly commendable zeal and perseverance on the part of Captain Larkins, his officers, and ship's company, but with all their gallant efforts, the latter could never have succeeded in capturing—although, had the ship's guns been in an effective state, they might, in beating off—an antagonist so well armed, manned, and appointed as the *Piémontaise*."

But we have not yet concluded. The *Warren Hastings* being dismasted, and a heavy sea running, the ship was allowed to fall off. And as the French frigate was lying close to leeward, under three topsails, with the mizen one aback and the main one on the shake, this warship had to bear up to avoid collision with the Indiaman. The former filled her maintopsail, but as there was none left at the helm she luffed up into the wind and fouled the *Warren Hastings* on the latter's port bow. You can readily imagine that with such a sea running there followed a series of sickening thuds as these two heavy ships banged against each other's sides. But the situation was now suitable for boarding tactics, and the Frenchmen, led by the first lieutenant, poured aboard the merchant ship. But they came not as conquerors, but as assassins, with uplifted daggers and threatening the lives of all.

One of these villains dragged the English captain about the ship, accusing him of an attempt to run the frigate down in order to cripple her masts. The first lieutenant also stabbed the captain on the right side. It was a brutal affray, which cannot be said to redound to the credit of any naval officer. Captain Larkins, brave man though he was, soon fainted through loss of blood, and was then ordered on board the frigate. It should be added that the first lieutenant and many of his men were highly intoxicated at the time and so cannot be held fully responsible for their base treatment of their victims. The second officer, the surgeon and the boatswain's mate were also stabbed, and a midshipman was pierced in seven different places by the first lieutenant. The ship was afterwards pillaged by this drunken gang, but after such excesses had been allowed to have their way the French captain did his best to make the survivors comfortable. The *Piémontaise* then steered for the Isle of France, taking her fine prize in tow, one of the handsomest vessels which the Honourable East India Company ever possessed. Captor and captive arrived at the Isle of France on the 4th of July, and a strange sight these two must have made as they proceeded. The reader may have marvelled that the *Piémontaise* had been able to overhaul the *Warren Hastings* so quickly and to manœuvre so easily when she kept returning to make one attack after another. But these French frigates were splendid craft and wonderfully fast, for although the East Indiamen were built on frigate lines more or less, yet they were modified to allow of a large cargo being carried, and this of course could be done only by sacrificing speed possibility. Some idea of the pace which these French frigates could reach may be gathered from the statement that the *Piémontaise,* in a moderate breeze, carrying three single-reefed topsails, foresail and mizen staysail, was able to tow her prize, a deeply laden ship of bigger tonnage than herself, having very small jury-sail set, at the rate of seven and a half knots an hour.

This fight and capture show the kind of adventure that was always imminent during a great portion of the East Indiaman period. It is almost difficult for us who travel with safety and punctuality in modern steamship liners to realise the uncertainty, the danger and anxieties with which the old merchant ships to the East proceeded on their way. There was not a species of disaster peculiar to maritime travel that was not ready to bring the career of such fine ships to a speedy end. Every conceivable kind of enemy seemed to be lying in wait for these craft: and the wonder really is, not that they were so often lost, but that they got to port. Knowing, as we do, something of the characters of the commanders who took these East

Indiamen over the ocean, we need not be altogether surprised that their sagacity, their determination, leadership, seamanship and ability as navigators and tacticians when tested did so much for the honour of their service and for the safety of the ships and cargoes which the Company entrusted to their care. They were men of whom the Company and the country had every right to be proud.

CHAPTER XXII

PIRATES AND FRENCH FRIGATES

Another pirate who was a thorn in the flesh to the East Indiamen was a man named Jean Lafitte, who was born at St Malo. This man was no stranger to the Eastern seas. He had been appointed mate of a French East Indiaman which was bound from Europe to Madras. But on the way out the ship encountered bad weather off the Cape of Good Hope, by which she was so damaged that the captain determined to call at Mauritius: and a quarrel having sprung up between Lafitte and the captain, the former decided to quit the ship at the island. Now there were several privateers or pirates fitting out at this island, and before long Lafitte became captain of one of these vessels.

For a time he cruised about the seas robbing whatsoever ships he could, but was eventually chased by an English frigate as far north as the Equator: and from there he later on came south and proceeded to the Bay of Bengal to obtain provisions. His ship was of 200 tons, with only two guns and twenty-six men. This should be noted, because it shows how much inferior as a fighting unit she was to any Indiaman. Nevertheless whilst off the Bengal coast he fell in with the East Indiaman *Pagoda,* which was armed with twenty-six 12-pounders and had a crew of a hundred and fifty men. With this disparity in strength it was obvious that Lafitte could only hope for victory by employing artifice. So he manœuvred as if he were a pilot for the Ganges ready at his station cruising about. The *Pagoda* came along and was quite taken in by this trickery, and, to cut the story short, when it was all too late to get out of the trap, the East Indiaman found Lafitte's ship alongside, and the pirate, together with his men, suddenly leapt on board the merchant ship, overcame every opposition and very speedily captured the ship. And it was this same pirate who at a later date became skipper of that notorious *Confiance* of which we have had need to speak in this volume.

We pass over the intervening period until we come to the year 1807, when we find Lafitte during the month of October still on the prowl. Off the Sand Heads he fell in with the East Indiaman *Queen,* a vessel of about 800 tons, a crew of nearly four hundred, and carrying forty guns. She was such a fine ship that this Frenchman determined to become her owner. Compared with the pirate the *Queen,* with her tall masts and high freeboard, her guns and crew, seemed absurdly superior to the smaller vessel. But Lafitte was as plucky as he was adventurous, and this apparent inequality only added zest to his plans. As the two ships were getting nearer and nearer, he exhorted his men with that wild, almost fanatical enthusiasm which was usually an electrifying force to a band of desperadoes, and then having manœuvred his ship with no little cleverness, brought her alongside the

Indiaman. Just as he did this the English vessel greeted him with a broadside, but the Frenchman was expecting this, and ordered his men to lie flat on the deck. And when the first fire had been made, the pirates all got up again, and from the yards and tops hurled down bombs and grenades into the Indiaman's forecastle.

These tactics entirely surprised the *Queen's* captain, and great havoc was wrought. Lafitte realising the amount of consternation which had now been caused sent aboard the *Queen* forty of his men with pistols in their hands and daggers between their teeth, and as soon as their feet touched the Indiaman's deck they drove the terrified and astonished crowd into the steerage, where the latter endeavoured to defend themselves as best they could. Lafitte now reinforced his forty men with another division, and himself went as their leader, and the result was that the *Queen's* captain was killed and the rest of the survivors were swept into one terror-stricken crowd. He then caused a gun to be loaded with grape and pointed to the place where the crowd were gathered, and threatened to blow them into eternity. Upon this the English determined that further opposition was useless, and surrendered. Lafitte therefore ceased his bloody slaughter, and became possessor of the ship. The incident, when the news reached India, caused a deep sensation, and the name of this scoundrel was spoken of with horror. But as East Indiamen now began to traverse the Indian Ocean only under powerful convoys, Lafitte found his opportunities very few and rare, so he betook himself to other waters, to end his days with a violent death.

We come now to the year 1810. About this time the French frigates were very actively on the *qui vive* for our East Indiamen and other merchant ships, and the neighbourhood of Madagascar and Mauritius was popular for setting forth to lie in wait for the victims. When any prisoners were brought in here from the Company's ships they were made to form part of the crews of these French frigates. And if any British soldiers were also found on board they were likewise destined to become part of the frigates' complement. Some were made so to do only by vehement threats if they declined: while some others were base enough to desert the English flag.

On the 3rd of July of the year just mentioned, just as the day was dawning, the French frigates, *Bellone* and *Minerve*, and the corvette *Victor*, having stood leisurely up the Mozambique Channel, were about thirty-six miles off the island of Mayotta, when they were sighted by three outward-bound East Indiamen, who were steering to the north before a fresh breeze from the south-south-east. The frigates were about nine miles off to the north-north-east, close-hauled on the port tack. A signal was made by the senior officer or commodore of the British ships half-an-hour later, and the three Indiamen hauled their wind on the port tack under double-reefed topsails, courses, jib and spanker. The names of these vessels were the *Ceylon* (commodore's flagship), *Windham* and *Astell*, the commodore being Captain Henry Meriton. At half-past seven the *Ceylon* made the private signal, as was customary. This was in accordance with the secret code provided by the Admiralty: and if the strange ships had been British naval frigates or fellow East Indiamen they would have answered in accordance with the code. Failure to reply would have indicated that they were hostile.

The "Queen," East Indiaman.

(By courtesy of Messrs. T. H. Parker Brothers)

Inasmuch as there was no reply in this case the East Indiamen's commodore ordered his ships to clear for action. There could be no sort of doubt now, and every minute was valuable, for the enemy was passing on the opposite tack. At half-past nine the *Astell* was carrying rather more sail than she could do with and made a signal to that effect: the *Ceylon* and *Windham* therefore shortened sail to keep her company. Captain Meriton now telegraphed to his two consorts the following message: "As we cannot get away, I think we had better go under easy sail and bring them to action before dark." It was the only thing to be done: otherwise the *Astell* might have been lost. The *Windham,* however, replied thus: "If we make all sail and get into smooth water under the land we can engage to more advantage." But half-an-hour later, as the force of the wind had increased, it became necessary for the East Indiamen to heave-to and take in a third reef in their topsails. But even under this shortened canvas the ships were making heavy weather of it. As a fact, they heeled over so much that the high sea that was running made it quite impossible for the lower-deck ports on the lee side to be kept open.

James, with his characteristic love of detail, has given full particulars of this incident, and we can well watch with him what followed. At 11.30 A.M. the *Minerve* tacked in the wake of the Indiamen and at about six miles away. Soon afterwards the *Bellone* and the *Victor* also went about. When Captain Meriton had watched these tactics and observed the *Minerve* coming up at a great rate astern he made the following signal: "Form line abreast, to bear on ships together, *Ceylon* in the centre." So the *Windham, Ceylon* and *Astell* formed a close line in the order named and awaited the oncoming of the enemy, and the *Victor* and *Minerve* were approaching rapidly on the starboard quarter, which was also the weather side.

Presently the *Minerve* arrived abreast of the British centre, the *Victor* being ahead. Up went French colours, a shot was fired at the *Windham* and then a whole broadside was fired into the *Ceylon,* which was so close astern of her consort as almost to touch her. The *Astell,* however, was a long way to leeward and astern of the *Ceylon*. When the corvette opened fire the action became general between the *Minerve* and *Victor* of the one side and the *Windham, Ceylon* and *Astell* on the other. But inasmuch as the *Ceylon,* by reason of her situation, was just abeam of the frigate, this Indiaman received a pretty hot time. After a little while the corvette found the fire of the British too warm, so bore up and passed to leeward of the *Astell,* and the captain of the latter becoming wounded severely, the chief mate had to take command. It is quite certain that an officer of a modern steamship liner is a much abler navigator than those who served in the old East Indiamen. But it is unquestionable that even if he were a Royal Naval Reserve officer, and had served for a year in his Majesty's fleet, he would not be such a master of tactics as his forefathers who served in the "John" Company. I have not the slightest doubt in asserting that if a European war broke out to-morrow every officer in the British mercantile marine would render an excellent account of himself for resource and bravery. Recent disasters and rescues in mid-ocean have shown that the fine old British stuff still goes to the making of our sailors. But if their ships were attacked by cruisers the merchantman would have no opportunity for displaying fighting tactics, since there is to-day a far greater difference between the fighting qualities of a liner and a navy's cruiser than there existed between an armed East Indiaman and a French frigate. And this even if we include the recently built *Aquitania* of the Cunard line, which happens to be the most heavily armed British liner which ever put to sea.

In these sea-fights, then, between the Indiamen and their foreign enemies we have a condition that is not comparable with anything to-day. It belongs to the past absolutely, and therefore the difference between the captains of yesterday and to-day is also different, and that not merely owing to the fact that one commanded a ship propelled by sails, whereas his successor handles a steamship. We cannot help admiring the many-sided ability of the East Indiamen captains. Taking them by and large, with all their defects in respect of smuggling and other delinquencies which need not be enlarged upon, they were extraordinarily successful in most complicated circumstances. It is characteristic of any kind of seaman, in whatever service he is enrolled, that he is adaptable, but could you find a greater strain imposed on any man than that which had to be borne by the commanders of the vessels whose history we are considering? As exponents of the art of pure seamanship they were never beaten, unless by their immediate successors, who made such wonderful passages during the clipper-ship era. And certainly as tacticians and fighting men they had few superiors even in the Royal Navy of that time. I feel that it is only just to emphasise these points, for with the transition from one period of the ship to another the ability of our mercantile officers has changed not in degree but in kind: and very shortly the last link—in the person of a steamship captain who formerly commanded a sailing ship—connecting the ships of yesterday with to-day will have been broken for ever. No one can fail to admire the consummate cleverness with which a modern mercantile captain brings a gigantic liner through a narrow, twisting channel in a strong tideway and berths his ship so quietly as not to break the proverbial eggshell. No one can help being struck with the scientific and practical ability by which perfect land-falls are made and punctual voyages are carried through even in thick weather. The captains of the Indiamen of yesterday were never called upon to bear the kind of responsibility which attaches to a man who has a 40,000-ton ship and 5000 lives under his care. But at the same time our modern commanders in the merchant service have never yet been called upon to think out battle tactics and manœuvre so as to fight a superior enemy without losing one's ship or cargo.

This was always the anxiety which an East Indiaman's skipper had to think of. Was he justified in remaining to fight: or was his chief duty to run away? His command was not primarily a fighting ship, but a means of trade. And even if he got his ship safe in port would he incur the displeasure of the Honourable East India Company's directors? His job was too valuable to be thrown away by an error of judgment. It would be a fine feather in his cap if he could follow the example of Commodore Dance, and he was sure to be well rewarded by his Company. To deal a smashing blow at the nation's enemy would ensure fame for this captain to the end of his days and after. But—*if* he should forget that his first duty was to get the valuable cargo home he might find himself a broken man and not a hero.

Such, then, was the position of Captain Meriton in the incident we are discussing. He had to take in the situation at a glance and form a quick but not hasty judgment, and then act accordingly, flinging out his signals and disposing his squadron. At four o'clock the *Minerve* went ahead and then bore down as if intending to get alongside the *Windham*. Now this was a mode of attack which the Indiamen in the present instance had reason to fear least of all, for they chanced to have plenty of soldiery on board. The *Windham* therefore made sail so as to strike the French frigate on the port side at the quarter, whilst the *Ceylon* and *Astell* closed on their consort so as to assist in this manœuvre. However, the *Windham* had been greatly damaged in regard to her sails and rigging, so did not possess enough way to act as she had hoped. The result was that the *Minerve* was able to cross her bows only a few yards away. All this time the three Indiamen had kept up an incessant and well-aimed musketry fire from their troops on board.

Just as the *Minerve* got out of gun-shot—that is to say, about a mile away—the *Astell* passed astern of the *Windham* and became the headmost and weathermost ship. The *Windham* was now the sternmost and leewardmost vessel of the three, and the *Minerve*, true to the best tradition of tactics employed by Nelson and other great admirals, endeavoured to cut the *Windham* off from the other two: but the best laid schemes of clever tacticians sometimes do not fructify: for the *Minerve* now lost her main and mizen topmasts, and there came a lull in the contest, though not for long. It was now six in the evening, and the *Bellone*, followed by the *Victor*, began a most destructive fire on the *Windham*. Taking up her position presently a little farther on, the *Bellone* began to attack the commodore's ship, whilst with her foremost guns she attacked the *Astell*. The *Victor* was some distance away, and so her fire at the *Windham* was not so effective. Captain Meriton now endeavoured to close with the French frigate in order that he might be able to give full opportunity to the troops' musketry, but had the misfortune to receive a severe wound in the neck from grape-shot. The command therefore fell to the chief mate, Mr T. W. Oldham. But the latter, being himself wounded not many seconds later, was obliged to yield the command to the second mate, Mr T. Fenning. By seven o'clock the poor *Ceylon*, which had endured much, was in a sorry plight. Her two principal officers had been wounded, her masts, rigging and sails were all damaged badly, all the guns on her upper deck had been disabled and five on the lower deck. Her hull, too, had been so badly holed that she was leaking to such an extent that she made three feet an hour. In addition, many of her people had been killed and wounded.

She therefore came out of the firing-line and passed astern of the *Bellone*, which was engaging the *Windham* all the time. And then there appears to have been some misunderstanding. The *Windham* hailed the *Astell* time after time, asking her to join in making an attempt to board the *Bellone*: but the *Astell* put out her lights, crowded on sail, and went off, receiving a heavy parting fire from the frigate. As for the *Ceylon*, there was nothing left for her to do but to haul down her colours, and she then had the humiliation of being taken possession of by a prize crew sent off in a boat from the *Minerve*. As the *Ceylon* passed the *Windham*, the former hailed the latter that she had struck. The *Windham* was therefore now left alone: and since she, too, was considerably damaged as to her masts and rigging, so that it was impossible to set sail, she doggedly continued the action, so that the *Astell* might be able to make good her escape. Nine of the *Windham's* guns had been put out of action, many of her crew had been killed or wounded, so finally she too had to haul down her colours, and was taken possession of by the *Bellone*. Meanwhile the *Victor* had gone in pursuit of the *Astell*, but the latter was able to get right away owing to the extreme darkness of the night and the length of time which had been taken in securing the two prizes.

The result of this fight, which had lasted almost from dawn till after dark, was melancholy: but the Indiamen had fought very gallantly, and it is not always that success comes to those who seem assuredly most to deserve it. Each of these merchant ships was of 800 tons, and their armament was quite unequal to that of the French frigates, which had no cargo to carry and could mount more numerous guns. There were about two hundred and fifty troops on board each of these Indiamen, in addition to a hundred lascars, but there were only about twelve or a score of British seamen. So in respect of numbers the merchant ships were quite inferior to the trained men-of-war's-men of the French. The *Ceylon* lost four seamen, one lascar and two soldiers killed. Her captain, chief mate, seven of her seamen, one lascar, one lieutenant-colonel and ten soldiers had been wounded—a pretty heavy toll to pay. The *Windham* had a seaman, three soldiers and two lascars killed: and seven soldiers, two lascars and three of her officers and half-a-dozen others wounded. The *Astell* had four seamen and the same number of soldiers killed: whilst her captain, her fifth mate, nine seamen, a lascar, five cadets and twenty soldiers were all wounded.

Everyone in these Indiamen had fought splendidly against heavy odds. The commodore had fulfilled his part as well as the difficulty of the situation allowed him. Soldier and sailor alike had done their level best. How did the East India Company eventually consider this forlorn fight? It may be said at once that, in spite of the result, the directors showed their appreciation of their servants by presenting each of these three captains with the sum of £500, whilst the rest of the officers and men were also handsomely rewarded. The captain of the *Astell* received a pension of £460 a year from the East India Company, whilst the officers and crew were presented with the sum of £2000 between them. It is said that one of the *Astell's* seamen, a man named Andrew Peters, nailed the pennant to the maintopmast-head and was killed as he was on his way down: and the *Astell's* colours were shot away no fewer than three times.

To show their appreciation of the *Astell's* fine defence the Admiralty granted the ship's company protection from impressment for three years. But even all this exhibition of approbation must have been unable to wipe out from officers and men the miserable recollection of having been compelled to yield to the nation's deadly enemy.

CHAPTER XXIII

THE LAST OF THE OLD EAST INDIAMEN

It must not be thought that even after that momentous change of 1834, when the "free traders," as they were called, began to send their ships to India, the Company were freer of anxiety. It has already been shown that they were being badly defeated in the new competition. But this was not all. In the year 1816 the owners of thirty-four ships which had been engaged by the Company under the Act of 1799 for six voyages on a settled peace freight now complained that these rates were inadequate to meet the increased charge of outfit and repairs. For since the Treaty of Paris the cost and equipment of ships had gone up, and to an extent that could not have been expected. The long duration of the war, and the extraordinary price of articles of a ship's inventory continued long after the cessation of hostilities: and therefore it was but natural that an improved rate should be granted for the remainder of the voyages.

And with the much larger number of men required for the bigger ships it was frequently found when lying in an Indian port that with "dead, run, or discharged" men a vessel had not the required number of crew in her that she ought to have. So now these East Indiamen were allowed to sail with less than their full complement. Great Britain had won her fights chiefly on the sea, yet for all that she was not abundantly blessed with seamen.

And then came the final change, which had really been foreshadowed by that event of 1814. True the East India Company had been bereft of their Indian monopoly, but China had been reserved to them. However, in 1832 the subject had to be faced again in Parliament. The mind of the public was distinctly adverse to the Company and its monopoly: too long it had been permitted to enjoy these privileges and keep back the stream of trade. Discontent increased both in vehemence and volume, and so at length the Company were powerless to hold on to their China monopoly. Private shipowners desired to trade with all parts of the Orient, and this desire had to be met. From the year 1833, then, the East India Company lost their exclusive trading privilege. And inasmuch as the free traders had done so much, and were determined to do more, it were useless for the Company to continue in commerce at all. Instead they became entirely a political body and permitted British subjects to settle in India. Actually the Company's commercial charter came to an end in April 1834, and thereafter it proceeded to close its business as soon as possible.

The East Indiaman "Malabar", built of wood in 1860.

Built of wood in 1860 at Sunderland for Mr. Richard Green. Her tonnage was 1,350, her length 207.2 feet, beam 36.6 feet, depth 22.5 feet. She was copper fastened and her bottom sheathed.

For a Company that had always relied for its success on protection from competition, paying high prices for its ships, and being squeezed very tightly by many of its servants, it could not be expected that when the free traders introduced their voyages to China and a strong, sensible spirit of competition that this ancient but decaying Company could hold its own. The new blood would be too vigorous, the enterprise would be irresistible, and in any case the Company would be doomed to further humility. No other course, therefore, was possible than to submit to what had come as the result of the advance of time. In a word, that East India Company which had ruled the Eastern seas for so long now resolved to get rid of the whole of their fleet. Some of these were condemned and some were bought up by those new aspirants to Eastern wealth. Some of these old "tea-waggons," as they were nicknamed, were broken up for their valuable copper fastenings, and the rest were sold, not at once, but after they had completed their voyages to India and China.

One of the very last of the Company's ships to make the voyage to China in the employ of this ancient corporation was the *Elizabeth,* which sailed from the Thames in the spring of 1833, arrived in China in January 1834 and left there in March. From there she proceeded to St Helena, where she arrived in June, and then crossed the Atlantic, arriving in Halifax the following August. Probably this was the very last of the Company's ships to leave China. I have examined her log-book and have been able to verify the dates, but what happened after she reached Halifax I cannot find out. Probably she was sold there. But, at any rate, there is a sentimental interest attached to her voyage, and the following few abstracts from her log may form a connecting link with the last voyages of a fleet whose inception dates back to the time when Elizabeth was on the throne.

The log opens on 23rd May 1833 with the usual details of getting the ship ready for sea and taking aboard cargo in the Thames. It ends on 3rd September 1834, when the last of the cargo had been landed at Halifax. Her master was John Craigie, and, as was the custom at this time, the manuscript log-book is prefaced with a page of black-faced print which read as follows:—

"The Honourable Court of Directors of the United Company of Merchants of England trading to the East Indies have ordered me to send you this log book, in which pursuant to your Charter-party, you are to take care that a full, true, and exact account of the ship's run and course, with the winds, weather and her draught of water at the time of leaving every port, and all occurrences, accidents and observations, that shall happen or be made during the voyage, from the time of the ship's first taking in goods, until the time of her return, be duly entered every day at noon, in a fair and legible manner. And that the officer commanding the watch from eight o'clock till noon, do, before he dines, sign his name at length to every day's log so entered...."

This vessel drew 17 feet 6 inches forward and 17 feet 4 inches aft when she left Gravesend, and after bringing up in nine fathoms off Margate rode to forty-eight fathoms of cable until she received the Company's dispatches which she was taking out to the East. As she proceeded down Channel she was handicapped by light easterly breezes and calms, so that although she passed Beachy Head on 28th July, it was not till 2 P.M. of the following day that she was off Brighton, where she dropped her pilot. Six hours later she had passed the Owers Lightship (off Selsey Bill), and so after leaving the Wight made her way past Portland Bill and out into the Bay of Biscay. We need not follow her throughout her passage, but on Sunday, 6th October 1833, she was caught in very bad weather, as the following extracts show:—

"3 A.M. Hard squalls attended with most tremendous gales. In fore and mizen topsails. Reef'd fore sail and close reefed main topsail.

"5 A.M. Heavy sea running, ship labouring much. Hove to under close reefed ... topsail, reefed foresail ... staysail and fore-topmast staysail. Housed fore and mizzen topgallantmasts.

"Noon. Hard gales and a tremendous sea running. Ship labouring much."

Two days later there is this entry:

"During the late severe gale I find from the heavy labouring of the ship many seams in the upper and lower decks much opened and the caulking worked out, and from the great quantity of water ship'd over all and the ship requiring constant pumping during the above period, I apprehend considerable damage is done to the cargo."

However, she got safely across the ocean to China, and brought up on 28th January 1834 at her port with small bower anchor in seven fathoms, giving her thirty-five fathoms of cable to ride to. As the ship approaches her port we see interesting little details entered in the log, such as these: "Bent larboard bower cable and unstowed the anchor"; then a little later on, "bent starboard chain"; and again, "bent the sheet cable." On the 13th of March she weighed anchor, proceeded south, crossed the Indian Ocean, as so many of the Company's ships had done for over two centuries, rounded the Cape of Good Hope and dropped anchor off St Helena on 19th June 1834, eventually arriving in Halifax harbour on 18th August 1834, where she proceeded to Mr Cunard's wharf—Mr Cunard was the East India Company's agent, as we have mentioned—and thus brought her voyage to an end. By 3rd September the whole of her cargo was taken out of her.

But already, long before the East India Company had decided to sell their fleet, the death-knell of the steamship had been sounded in the Orient, though actually the decease was to be preceded by a wonderful rally in the famous China clippers. In the year 1822 a public meeting had been called together in London to discuss the practicability of running steamships to the East, and as a result a steam navigation company was formed. Lieutenant (afterwards Captain) J. Johnson was sent out to Calcutta to see what could be done in this respect, and the outcome was that a steamship called the *Enterprize* was built at Deptford and proceeded to India under the command of this Captain Johnson. She was of only 470 tons and 120 nominal horse-power. She started on 16th August 1825, and after a voyage of 113 days reached Calcutta, though ten of these days were spent in taking on board fuel. Her average speed was only a little under nine knots: but here was a precedent. She had come all the way under steam, and some day soon this speed would be improved upon. Already in that same year the *Falcon*, of 176 tons, had also voyaged round the Cape to Calcutta. But this vessel was an auxiliary steamship, using partly steam and partly sails; so the *Enterprize* was really the first Anglo-Indian steamship. It was not till the year 1842 that the P. & O. Company started sending their steamers to India via the Cape of Good Hope. This was another nail in the coffin of the sailing ships which had been trading to the East for so long a time. The name of the first ship was the *Hindostan*. She was a three-master with a long bowsprit, setting yards on her foremast for foresail, topsail and top-gallant sails, while her main and mizen were fore-and-aft-rigged: and before long other steamers followed her.

But before the Government built its transports specially for trooping the modern sailing Indiamen—that is to say, the successors of the East India Company's ships—carried all the military to the East. Even when, in the days before the opening of the Suez Canal, the P. & O. were the only steamships voyaging to India, most of the passengers still travelled to the Orient in the East Indiamen, with the exception of the wealthy and the principal officials. Therefore, though the East India Company was dead as a commercial concern, those private firms who had bought up the Company's ships or built new ones were doing a good business both in freights and passengers.

Before the Suez Canal was opened there were three ways of reaching India. You could go by a sailing East Indiaman round the Cape of Good Hope or in a P. & O. steamship by the same route, or you could go by P. & O. steamship to Alexandria, then overland by camels, and then by boat on the Mahmoudieh Canal to the Nile, whence passengers proceeded to Cairo by steamer. From there they went across the desert to Suez. Three thousand camels had to be employed for transporting a single steamer's loading, and every package had to be subjected to no fewer than three separate transfers. The opening of the Suez Canal, therefore, in the year 1870, made all the difference in the world, and by the end of the next year scarcely any passengers went round the Cape in sailing ships, but journeyed to the East in steamships via the canal. Troops were also taken through the latter, and so the old and the new East Indiaman sailing ships passed out of existence.

After April 1834 the directors of the East India Company were not traders, but rather a council advising and assisting in the control of the political India. In 1857 occurred the Indian Mutiny. The martial races began suddenly to move, the native army of Bengal revolted, and the northern predatory races rebelled. As everyone knows, the Mutiny was eventually quelled, but for our present consideration the most important result was that it was to bring to an end the great career of the East India Company. It was deemed best that Queen Victoria should assume the direct government and rule through a Viceroy, the first of whom was Canning. On 1st November 1858 proclamation was made throughout India that the government had been transferred from the East India Company to the British Sovereign. The Board of Control was abolished and a Council of State for India instituted. Thus, having ceased to be either traders or a political power, this unique corporation came to an end. It had lost its prestige, lost its privileges and strength in India and China, sold its fleet, and at length, on 15th May 1873, came the resolution to dissolve the Company altogether, as from 1st June 1874. East India House, which had been built in the year 1726, enlarged in 1799, was sold with its furniture in the year 1861 and pulled down in the following year. Of course there had been a much earlier East India House in Leadenhall Street also, and the accompanying reproduction of an old print shows the house which stood from 1648 to 1726. The reader will notice on the building a picture of a seventeenth-century ship.

By many of the Indian natives the East India Company had been known as the "Honourable John Company." The origin of this designation is not quite clear, but it was in effect a personification of the corporation taken quite seriously by the natives. John he knew as a man's name, for was not his English master called John? Naturally enough, therefore, the Company might also be called the "John" or "Honourable John." The idea imprinted in the native's mind was that the Company was one mighty prince, who had to be respected.

But before we close this chapter we want to know what became of the ships and men. If the Company had come to an end the East Indiamen and those who used to work her across the ocean were not *ipso facto* wiped out of existence. Some of the ships fetched quite good prices, considering that the sale was virtually compulsory. The *Earl of Balcarres*, for instance, that big ship of which we spoke on a previous page, fetched the sum of £10,700, and she sailed the seas for fifty-two years before being turned into a hulk. The *Lady Melville* also was sold for £10,000; that fine, handsome ship, the *Thames*, of which we have given an illustration, obtaining £10,700 as her price. The *Buckinghamshire* fetched £10,550; the *General Kyd*, £9100; the *Asia*, £6500, whilst other ships fetched sums from about £4500 upwards. Of those sold for breaking up were the *Waterloo*, which fetched about £7200; the *Atlas*, £4100; the *Canning*, £5750; the *Princess Charlotte*, £3000; the *London*, £5900; *General Harris*, £6600; *Farquharson*, £6000. Of course, not all these were sold at the same time. In some cases, the Company having foreseen the inevitable, began to sell as far back as 1830, and they went on selling until the end of 1834. Those shipowners who were out looking for bargains knew that these vessels would not fetch the highest prices, yet they were known to be soundly put together of first-class material. The best prices were obtained by the Company, not in auction, but privately. Among the buyers one finds such well-known shipping names as Joseph Somes, Wigram & Green. The former was one of the founders of Lloyd's Register. Robert Wigram and Richard Green built and owned some of the finest sailing ships which ever floated in the Thames, and these men, together with the Smiths of Newcastle and other shipowners, began to construct more modern frigate type of ships for the China and India trade now that all privileges had been thrown on one side. These ships used to snug down at night like their predecessors when crossing the sea. But they were run commercially on more sensible lines, and the extravagant privileges to the captains were largely curtailed.

And inasmuch as many of the captains, officers and crew who had served in the East India Company's craft were now employed in the ships of the new firms there was not such a vast change in the conditions as might have been imagined. Gone was the stately dignity, gone the semi-naval character of the East Indiamen, but in most other respects matters were much the same. Gradually as the newer types of ships began to be built, improved models were effected with finer lines, and the old kettle-bottom type of the Company's ships gave place to that which was to become historic as the China tea-clippers of 1850 to 1870. With these, however, our present story has no concern. But it was a long time before the main traditions of the East India Company died entirely. Frigate-fashion had been the motto of the shipbuilder for too long for this to be thrown over at once. The *Blenheim* and the *Marlborough,* for instance, which came out in 1848, were constructed exactly like the contemporary naval frigates: in design and scantlings they were identical with a 40-gun ship of that class, the Government surveying them and reporting them as fit to carry armaments. These two ships had been built by Messrs T. & W. Smith of Newcastle-on-Tyne. They carried enormous jibbooms "steeved" very high. With their overhanging stern, figurehead, row of square ports, stuns'ls, and dolphin-striker they were very picturesque craft. As regards speed these were an improvement on the ships possessed by the East India Company, and represent the intermediate stage between the latter and the famous China clippers which were to come in a few years' time. The new type of East Indiaman, frigate-built and copper fastened, cost about £40 a ton to build, so that a 1000-ton ship cost about £40,000. The ships of Messrs Wigram & Green were not pierced for guns, the square windows in these vessels at the poop being used for lighting the passengers' cabins. These were ships of finer lines than the old East Indiamen or even the vessels which Smith built. Duncan Dunbar also owned a number of fine East Indiamen; in fact, he became at one time the largest shipowner in Great Britain, and many of his vessels were constructed in India, as, for instance, the *Marion,* of 684 tons, which was launched at Calcutta in 1834, and from that date sailed the seas until she was wrecked off Newfoundland nearly fifty years later. But even before the East India Company lost their China monopoly they possessed a very few ships whose speed was just about as good as any of the more modern successors until the coming of the first tea-clippers of about 1840 onwards. The East Indiaman *Thames*, of which we give an illustration, was certainly one of the fastest.

At the time when the East India Company lost their China charter and sold off their fleet, the commanders and officers considered themselves very much aggrieved. It is quite true, as we have stated, that a good many of them afterwards shipped on board the modern East Indiamen, who, of course, did not fly the naval pennant which the Company's ships had been allowed to wear. But these officers, in July 1834, banded together and sent a letter to the directors of the East India Company, in which it was pointed out that the Company's ships and seamen—otherwise known as the Maritime Service in contrast with the Bombay Marine or East India Company's navy—had been employed for over two hundred years. These ships and men had been instrumental to a great degree in securing the vast territory of British India. These commanders and officers of the present day had entered the Company's service in the confident expectation that it was a provision for life. But now they found themselves deprived of their profession owing to the sudden ceasing of the Company's trade. Although the commanders and officers were in the first instance recommended by the shipowners to the Company, yet the latter examined and approved them, and into the latter's service they were sworn. They were paid, fined, suspended or dismissed by the Company—and not by the owners. They wore the Company's uniform, enjoyed rank and command under the latter, and became eligible to offices of high honour and emolument. And the extraordinary fact was that they even took precedence of the Company's Bombay Marine. These maritime commanders ranked with the field officers in India, were saluted with guns, and were eligible for important offices of profit in India.

The "Blenheim," East Indiaman, 1,400 tons.

(By courtesy of Messrs. T. H. Parker Brothers)

The position now was therefore not one which seemed to have a bright outlook. They had served in capacities of great trust, and many of them had devoted the whole of their lives to service in the Company's ships. But when the "free traders" now came on to the scene the latter did not care to employ captains and officers who had been accustomed to navigate only vessels of the size and expensive equipment of those of the East India Company. Only one-fifth of these men were therefore at once taken over by the shipowners, who were now buying up the Company's ships or building new ones. As for the rest of these officers they had enjoyed the dignity and privileges of the Company for so long a period that they did not care to be employed in "free trade," considering it derogatory. In any case they could not obtain, from the new owners, the same amount of remuneration as they had been accustomed to receive from the Company. For the latter's extravagant methods were to give place to a more business-like method. In plain language, the rest of the merchant service rather fought shy of employing these former East Indiamen skippers, and the latter were not anxious to degrade themselves by signing on in these interlopers.

So the captains and officers appealed to the East India Company for compensation in the shape of pensions. The petition was received with little enthusiasm, but the directors could not deny that there was a good deal of truth in what was set forth by these men, and ultimately decided to grant compensation to all commanders and officers who had been actually employed in the Maritime Service for five years on 22nd April 1834. Thus a commander received a monetary payment of £1500, with lesser sums for the other officers. In addition to this, each commander received £4000 for three unexpired voyages, £3000 for two voyages and £2000 for one voyage which they would have made had they continued in the service. Besides these sums, commanders who had served for ten years were granted a pension for life of £250 a year, the chief mate receiving a pension of £160, and so on down to the carpenter and gunner. The condition being that these men assured the Company of their inability to obtain further employment, and that any income which they possessed was to be in abatement of these pensions.

Thus, at last, the historic East India Company came to an end, its ships and men scattered or employed by other owners. No company in the world, no fleet of mercantile vessels can boast of such a long and adventurous story as this: no ships of commerce were so closely and continuously concerned in establishing political power in the East. For this reason the old East Indiamen sailing ships, whether of the seventeenth, eighteenth or nineteenth centuries, must always possess a unique interest for Britons generally, for Anglo-Indians in particular, and for all who take an interest in the world's development. People ordinarily do not realise the full extent of their indebtedness to the ships and sailors of the past in respect of discovery, empire, power and wealth. Such men as worked the vessels which we have been considering in this volume were very far from perfect in respect of many virtues. But they are deserving of our great respect and admiration for their pluck, their endurance and their enterprise: for without them India would have been the possession of some other European nation.

Printed by Libri Plureos GmbH in Hamburg,
Germany